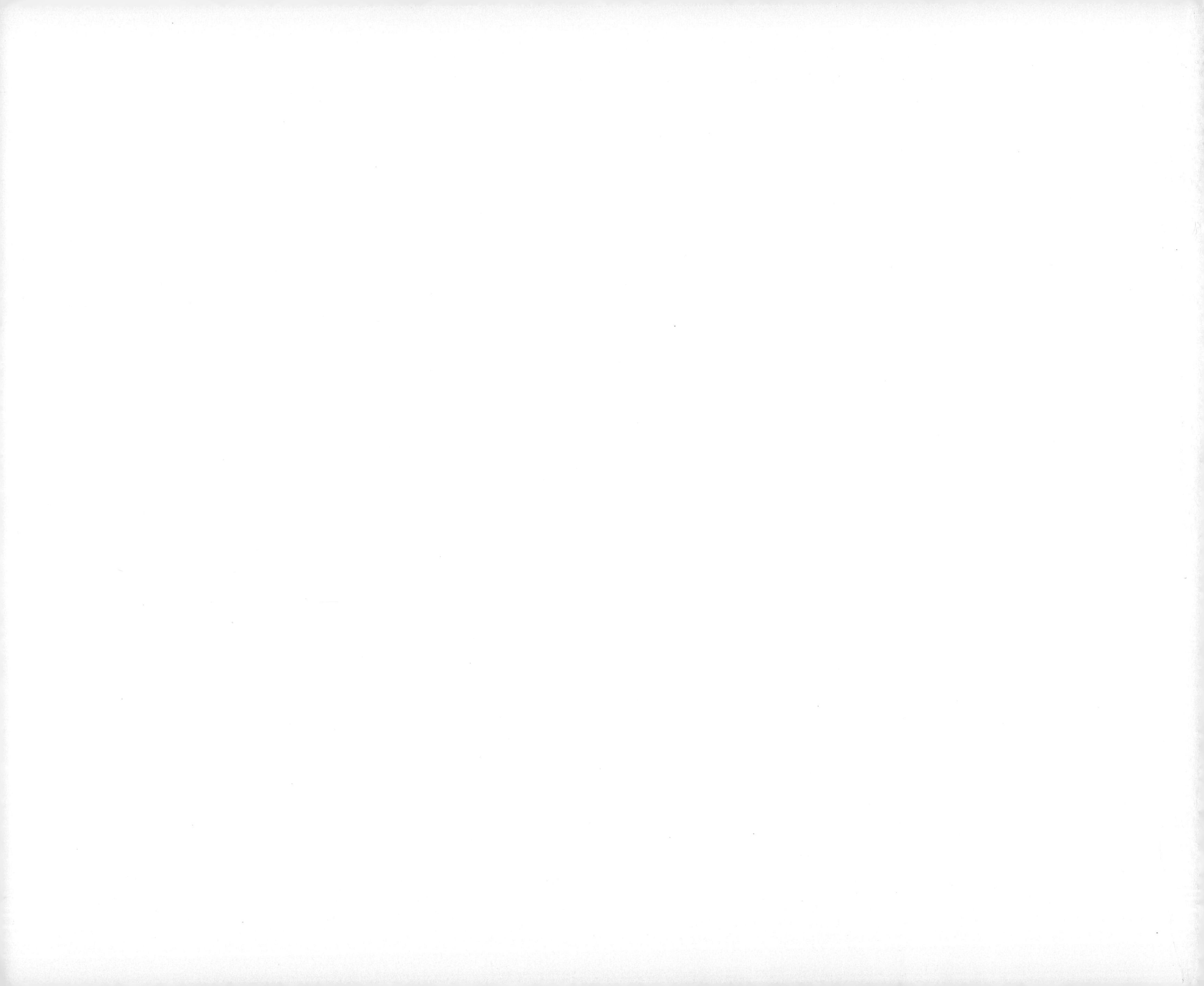

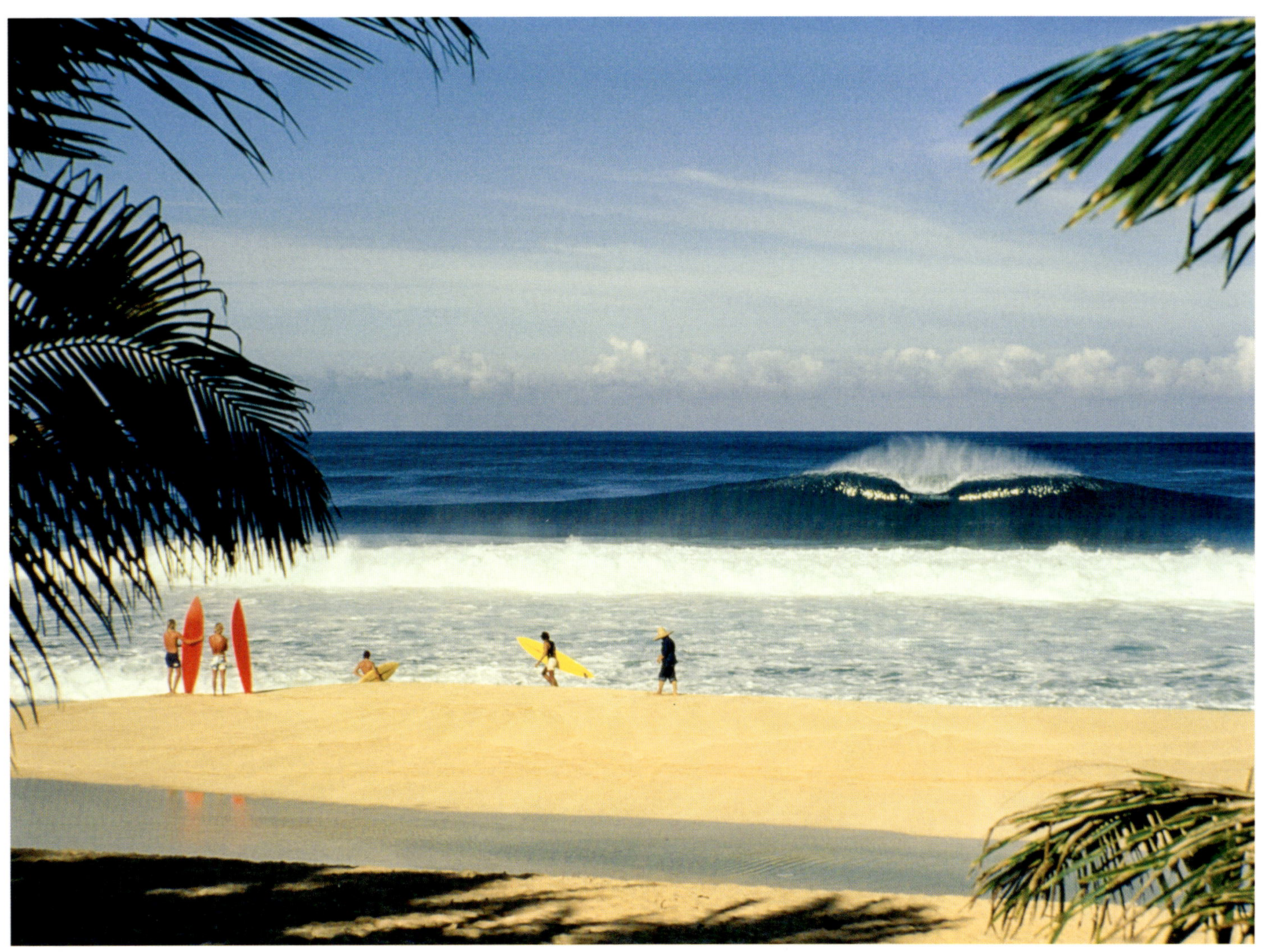

Pipeline, Oahu, HI 1975

JEFF DIVINE

SEVENTIES SURF PHOTOGRAPHS

INTRODUCTION BY WILLIAM FINNEGAN

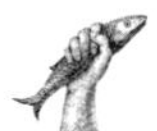

T. ADLER BOOKS, SANTA BARBARA

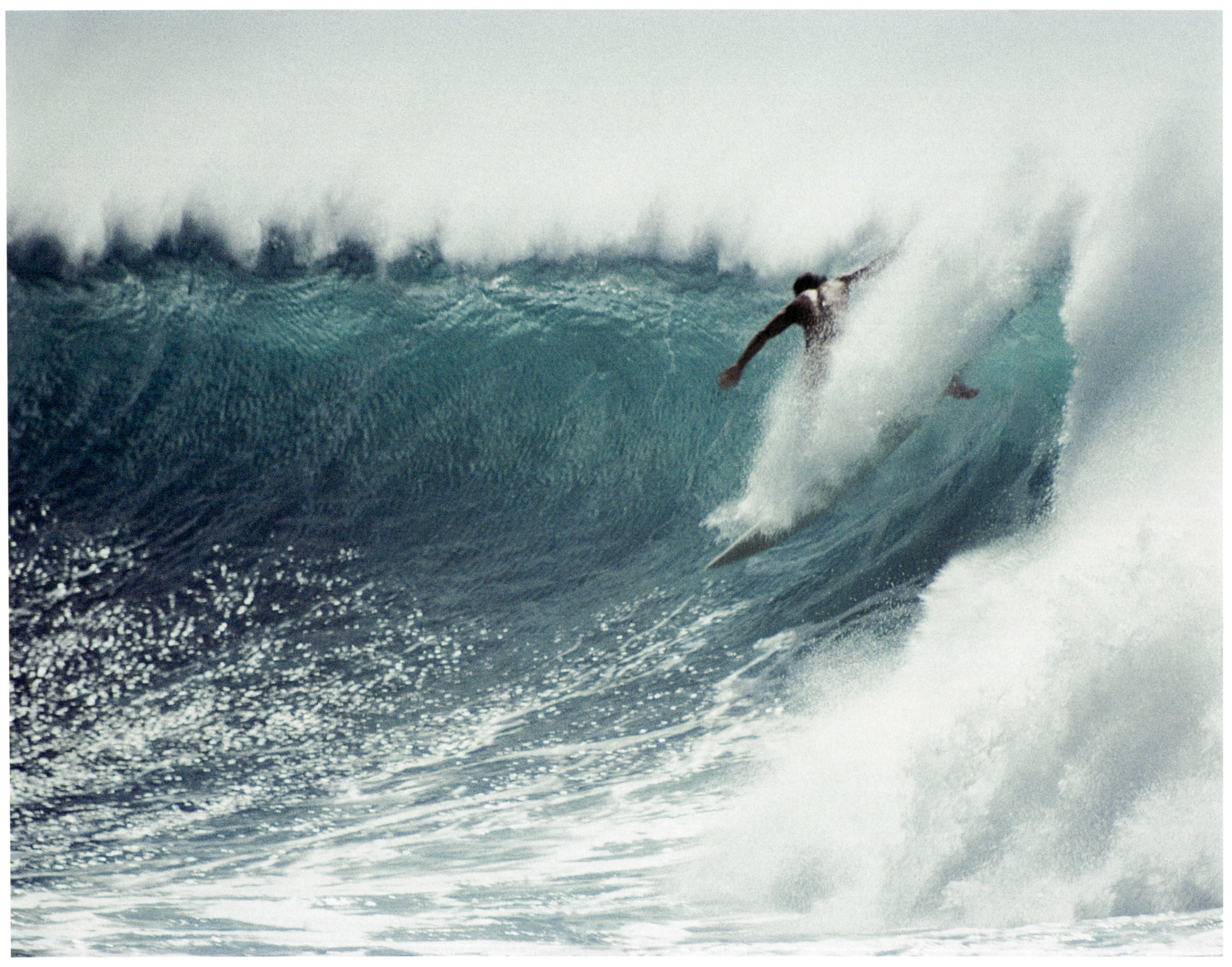

Barry Kanaiaupuni, Makaha, Oahu, HI 1976

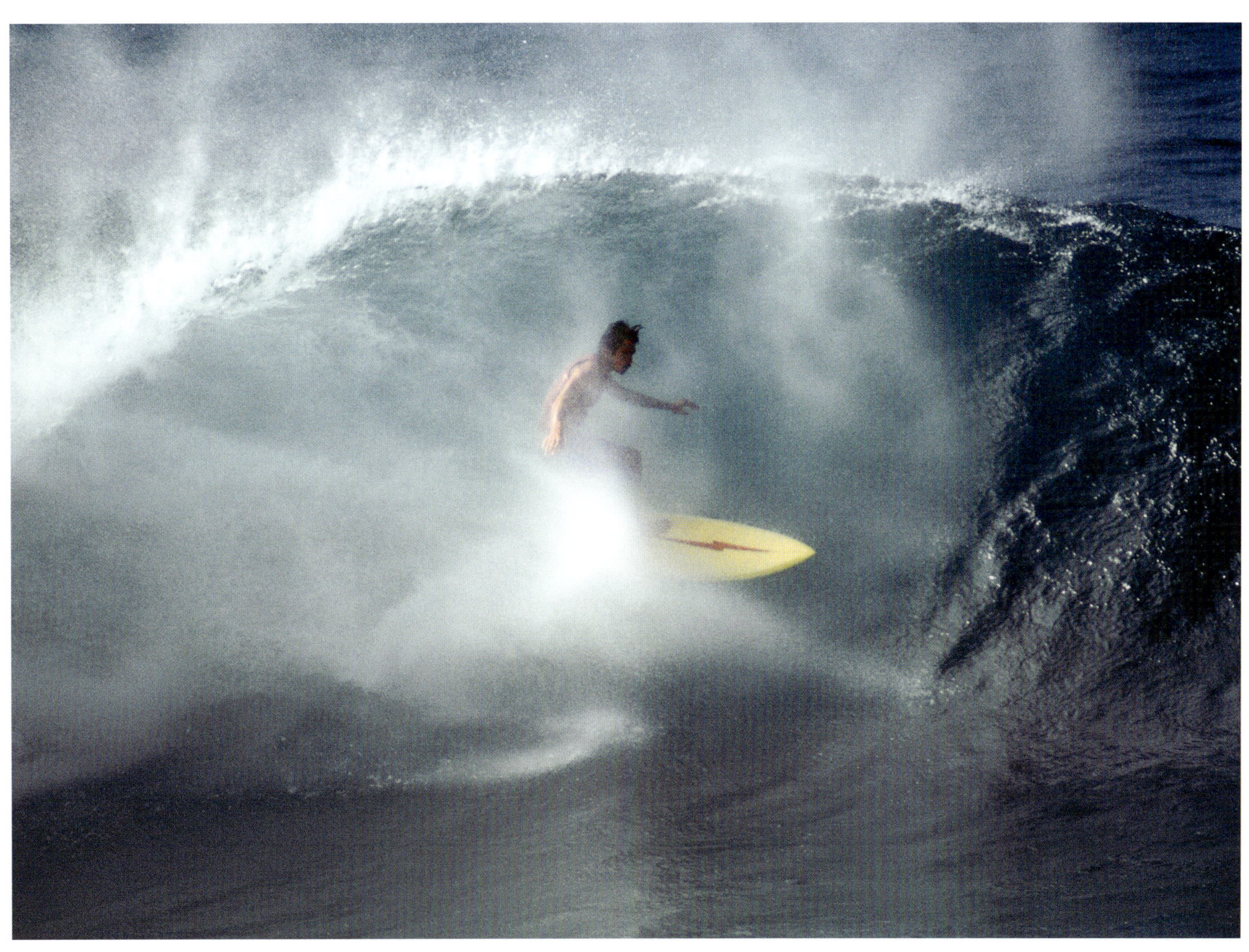

Gerry Lopez, Pipeline, Oahu, HI 1979

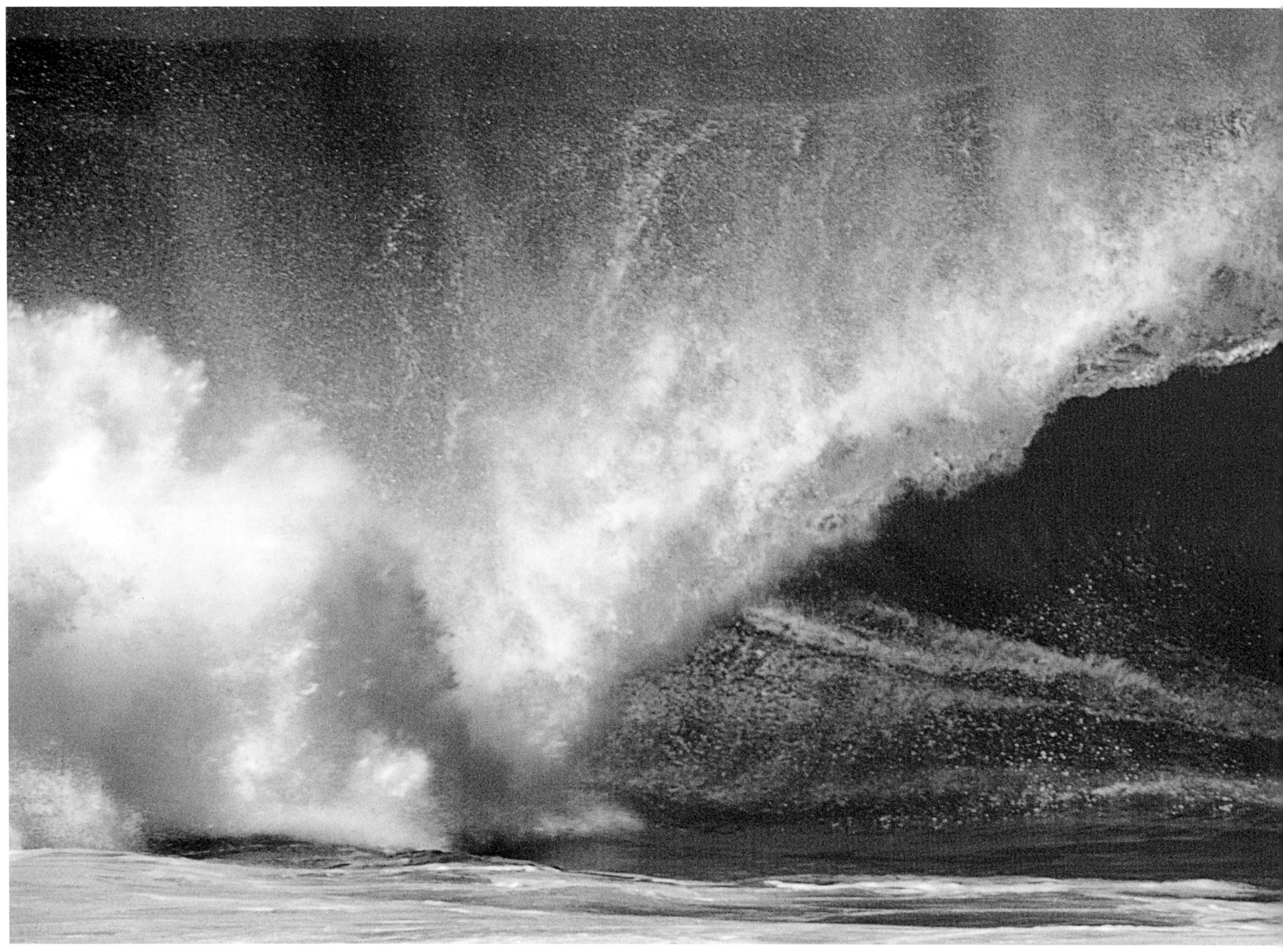

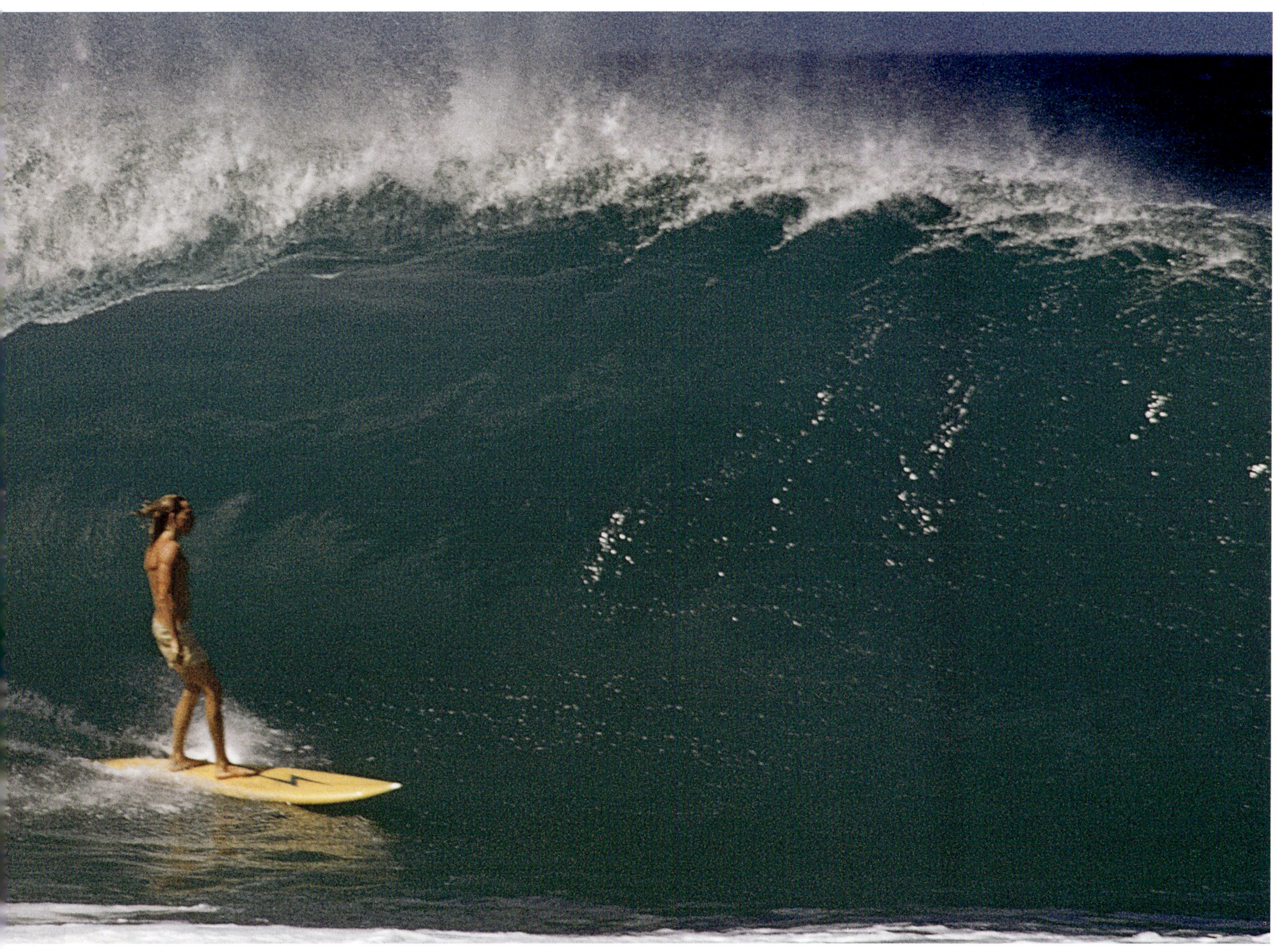

Rory Russell, Pipeline, Oahu, HI 1973

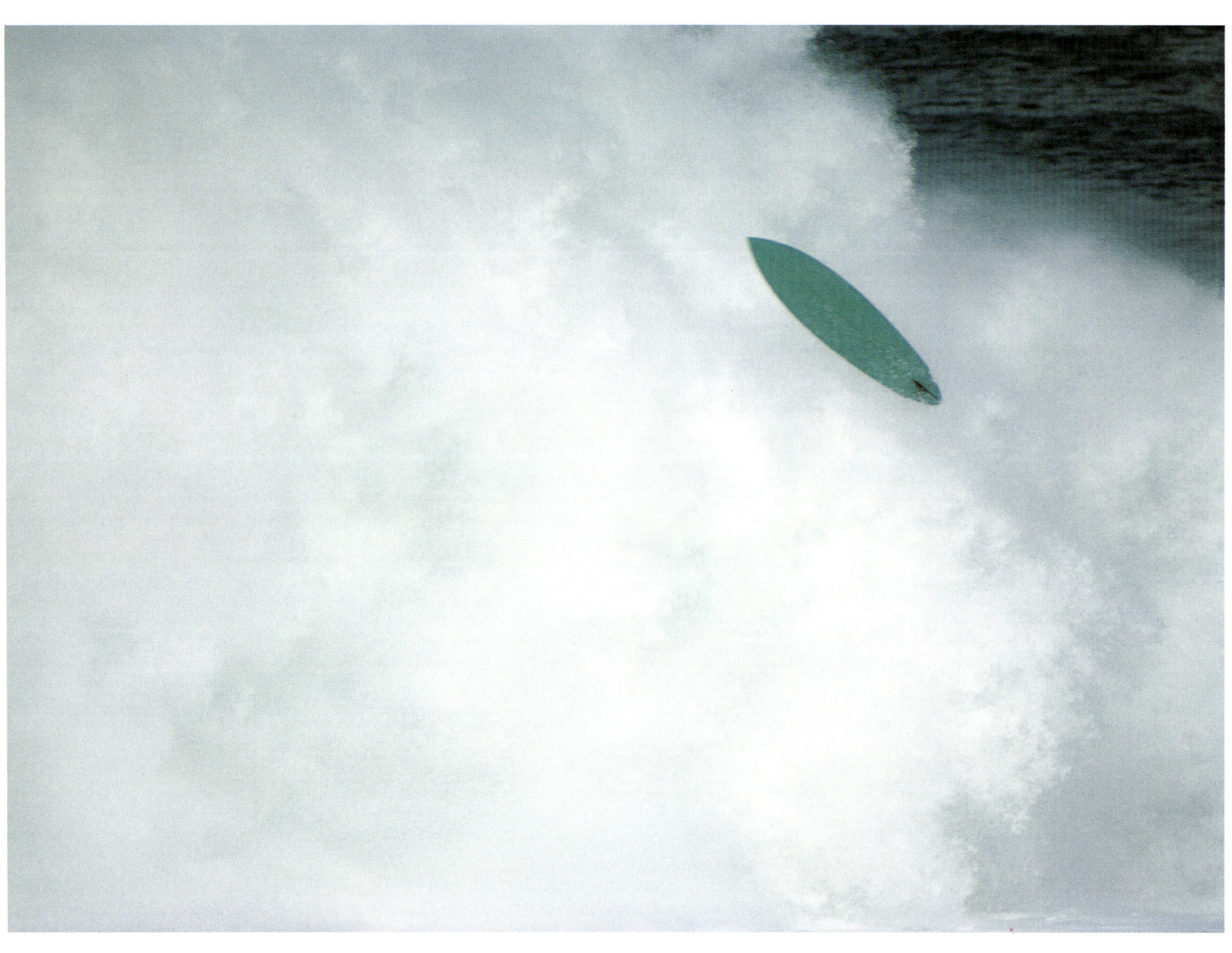

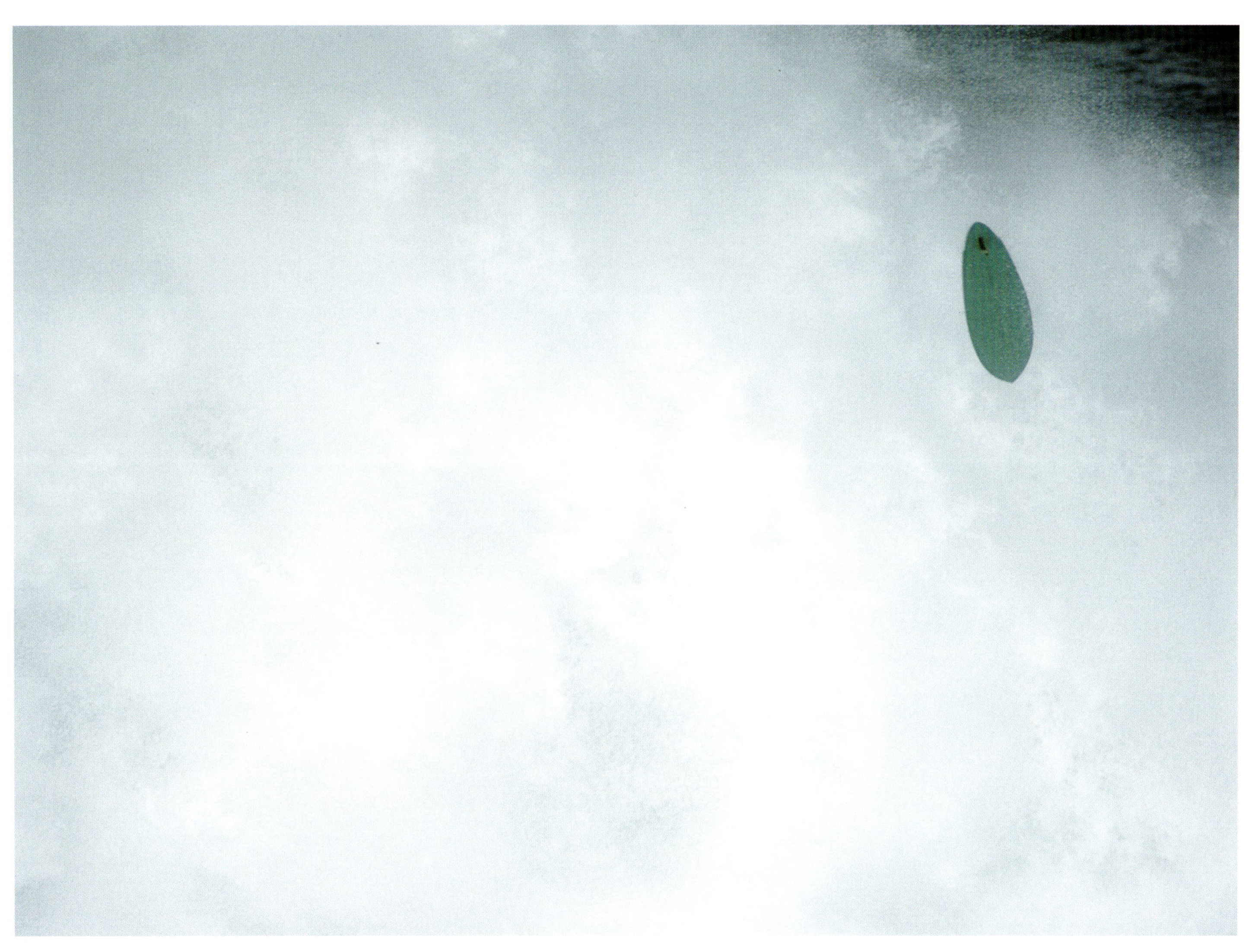

Flight Pattern, Pipeline, Oahu, HI 1974

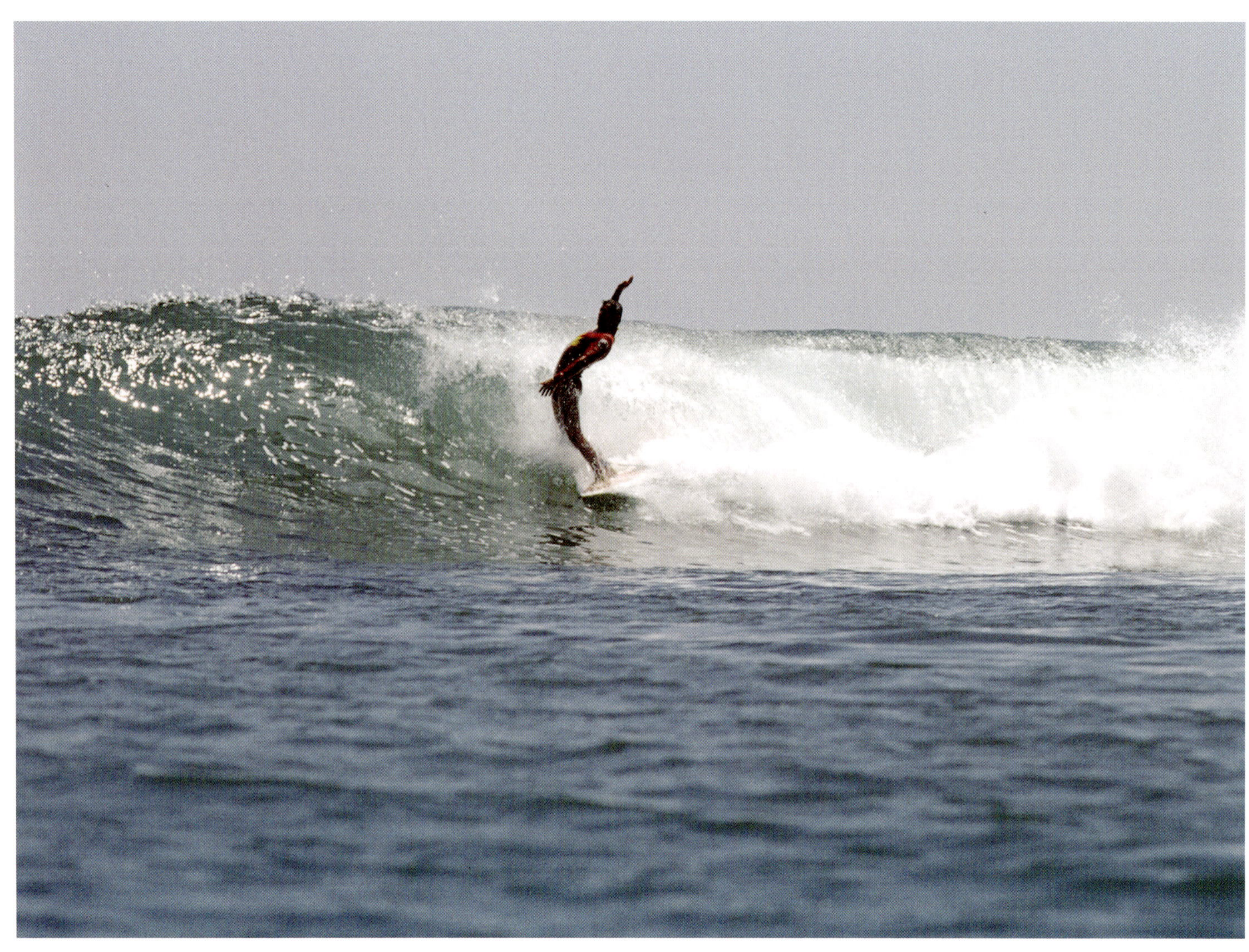

Herbie Fletcher, Malibu, CA 1979

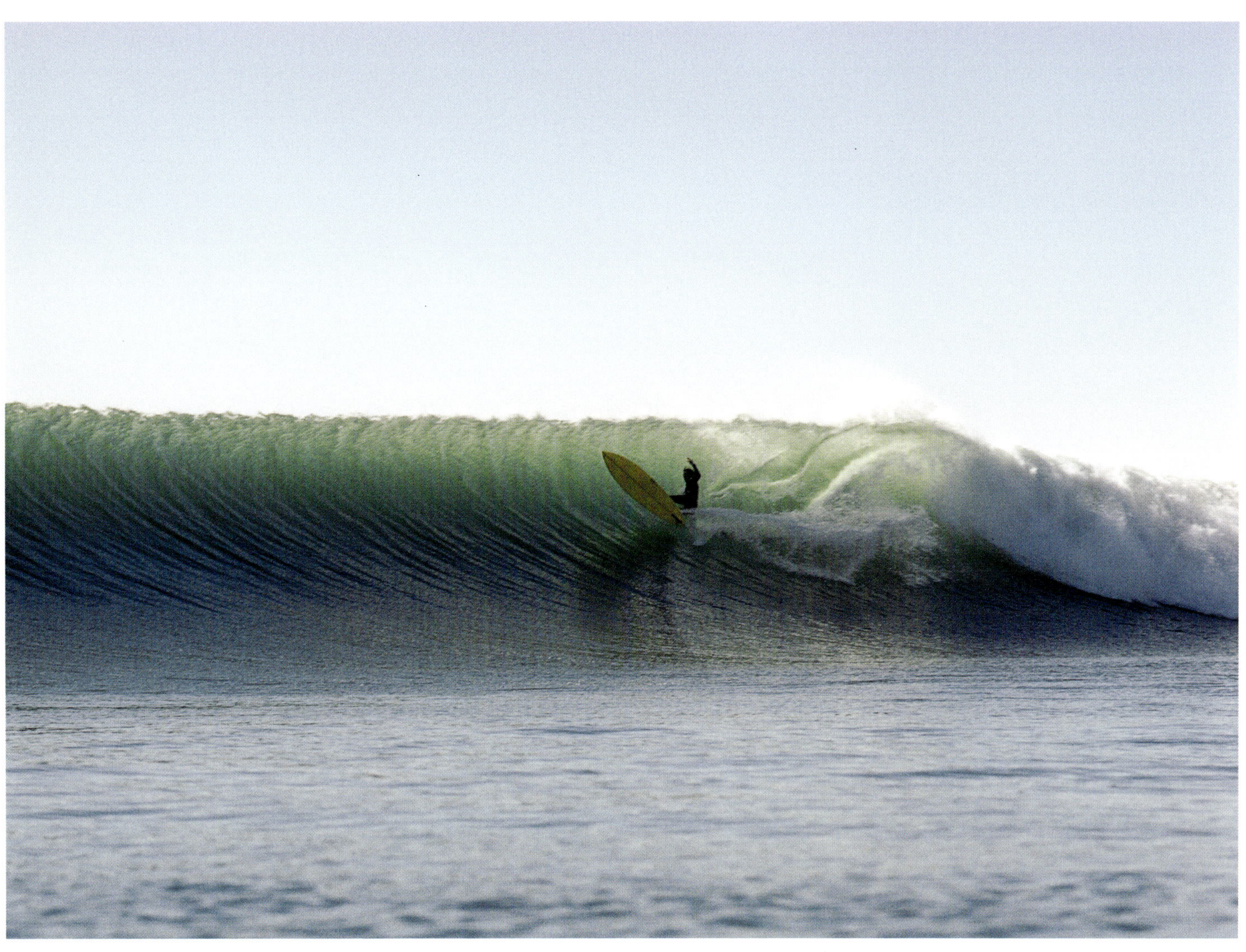

Greg Lee, Big Drakes, Hollister Ranch, Santa Barbara, CA 1972

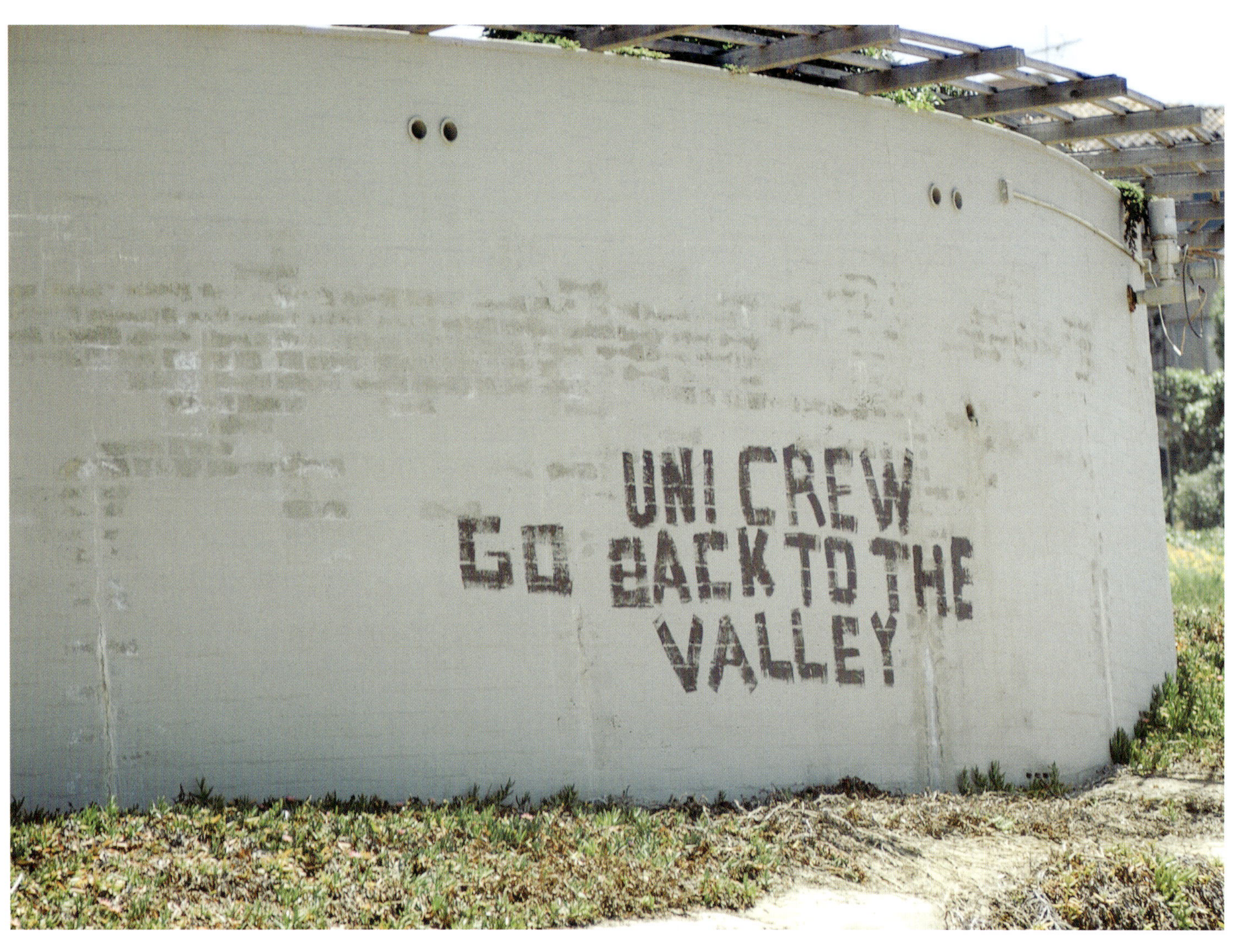

Big Rock, La Jolla, CA 1972

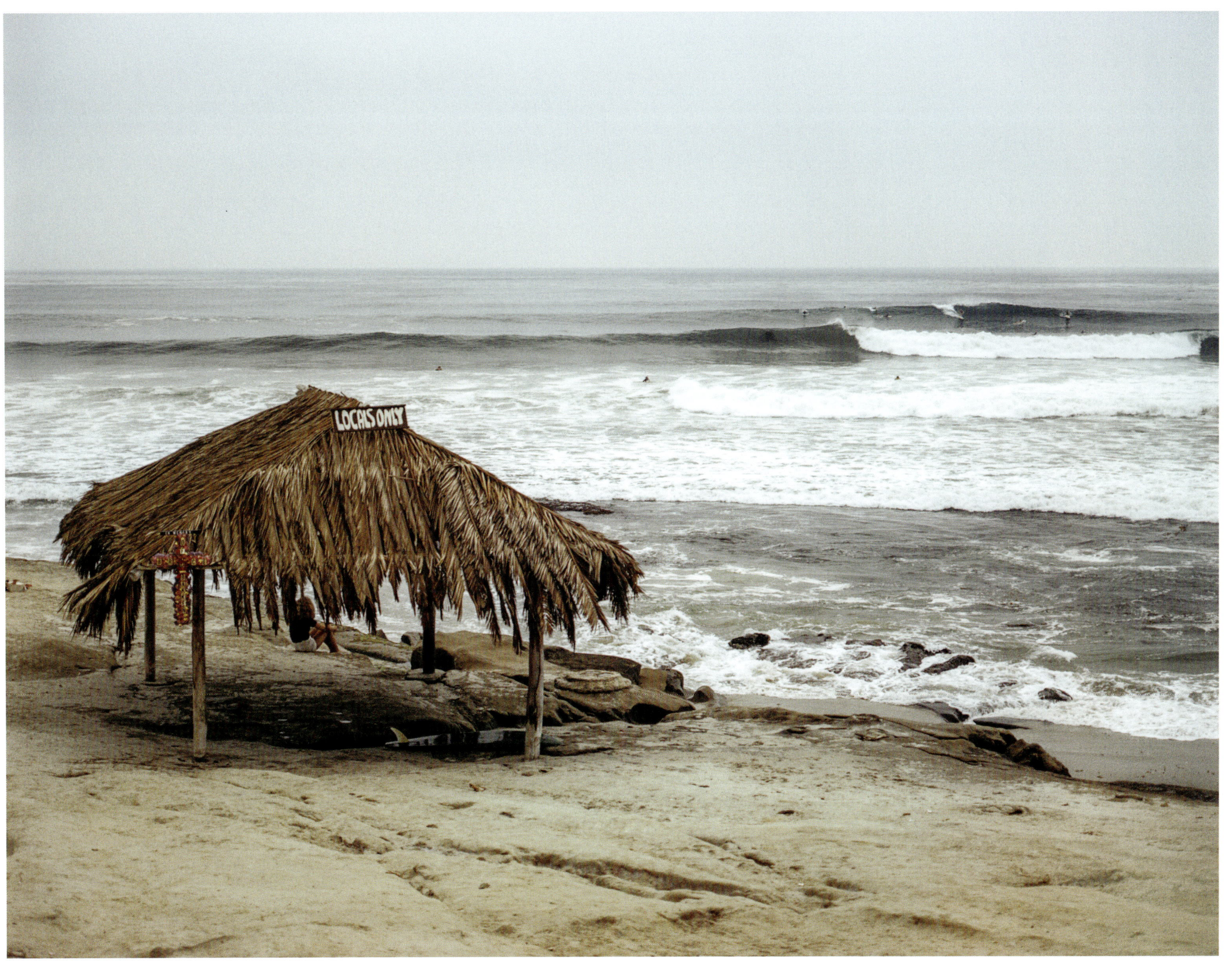

Windansea, La Jolla, CA 1973

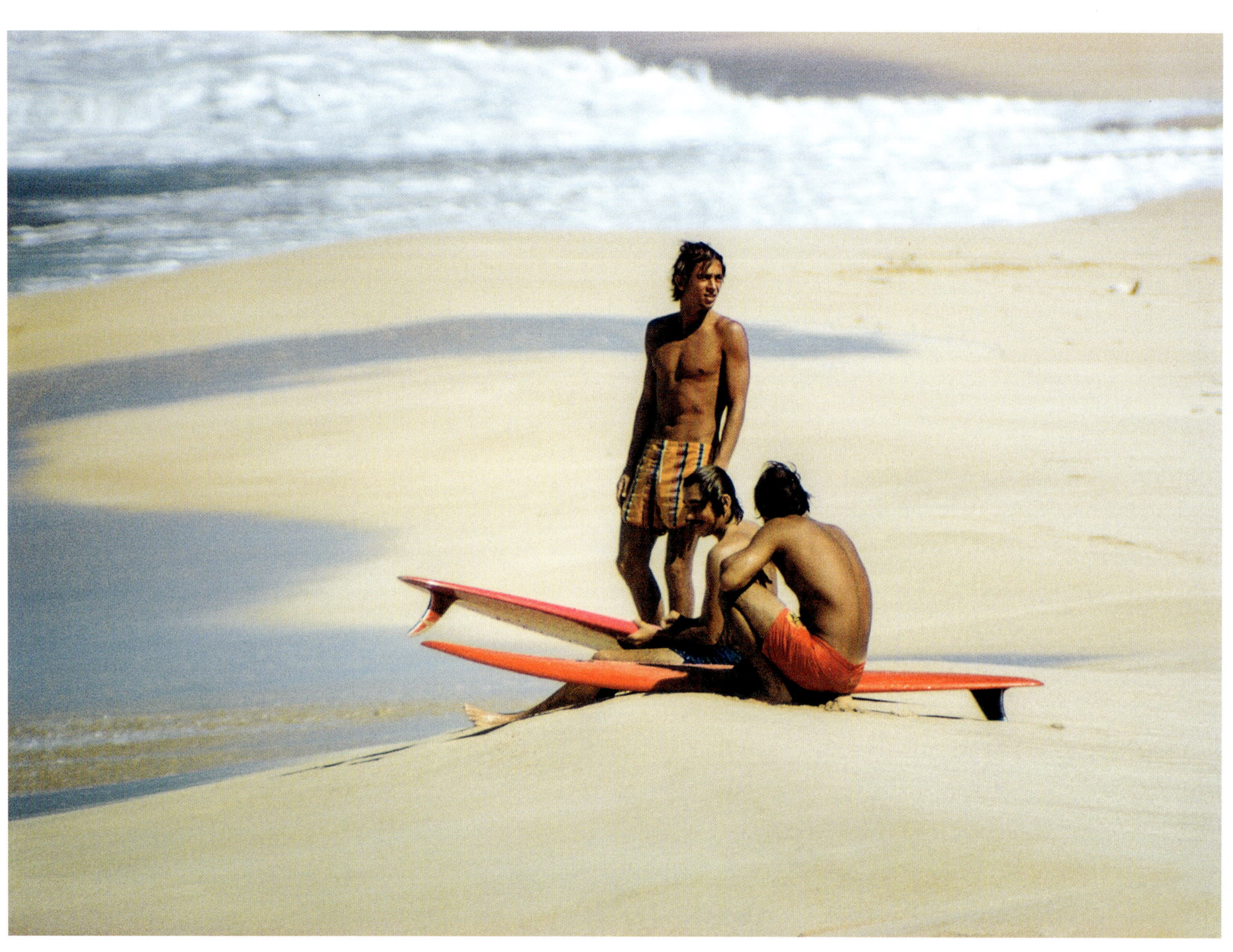

Herbie Fletcher, Gerry Lopez, Barry Kanaiaupuni, Sunset Beach, Oahu, HI 1971

INTRODUCTION

WILLIAM FINNEGAN

If you were there, even just for some of it—Hawaii, California, surfing, the seventies—the memories and stories will come pouring off these photographs. Jeff Divine was there for all of it, of course, and these images have been culled from an enormous personal archive. Divine was shooting for *Surfer*, the monthly magazine that was our Scripture in those days. It was required reading, mandatory gawking, for the devout, which meant basically everybody in surfing. I was working in a bookstore on Maui in 1971 and our shipments of *Surfer* went out the door nearly as fast as we could open the boxes, with some copies actually paid for.

But anyone can see, I'm guessing, that something extraordinary was going on. It was a moment when everything in our little world felt up for grabs. Surfing had boomed in popularity in the beach-blanket sixties, failed its audition as a mainstream televised sport, and then blown itself up in a late-sixties design revolution that reduced boards, seemingly overnight, from nine feet six inches to six feet six, from twenty-five pounds to less than ten. Suddenly, people were turning twice as hard, going twice as fast, and, most transformingly, pulling into heaving barrels that had been unridable, off-limits, the stuff of idle fantasy until yesterday. These changes have all been lasting. The social upheavals of the period touched surfing, but only glancingly—in music, fashion, a wavelet of Eastern mysticism, more than a wavelet of recreational drugs, and a few muddy shining pockets of back-to-the-landism in places where the land happened to abut pumping waves.

Speaking of country living, have a look at the house on Bummer Hill (great name!) on page 54. Divine lived there, with friends, till drugs rendered that untenable. The waves on the North Shore of Oahu are, among other things, intensely glamorous, but the living there is not. When Divine, who grew up in California, first started visiting, an evening's entertainment was cockfights and gambling. There was no TV reception, and no cars on the road at night. The area has endured many upgrades since those years, and today it has traffic and much higher rents, but it's still pretty down-home, at least to my frequent visitor's eye.

But look at the empty morning lineup at flawless Pipeline on this book's first page. That was definitely then. Today it would be mobbed. Not that crowds weren't a problem in 1975, they were. The charming "Locals Only" signs seen here all happen to be in California, but population pressure on good waves was already a problem in Hawaii, too. It's just worse now everywhere.

Divine's purpose is not to idealize this period, obviously, but to record what he saw, which includes bits of skeezy social history and some character portraits that I actually find piercing, even painful. Michael Peterson's expression in 1976 has a grim agitation that foretells the mental illness that would soon consume him. Glenn Kaulukukui's expression on the facing page is also all wrong. I knew Glenn well, and admired him desperately, when we were kids. He later lost his way and, though it may just be hindsight, I think I see it coming in this shot. The double-portrait of Mike Purpus, a leading California pro, with his airbrushed love board, has a goofy poignancy and pitiless accuracy. Even the multiple portraits of the great David Nuuhiwa are sad. He was past his peak in the seventies, and here he looks like a deposed king, wandering the wilderness of the Pacific Coast Highway with a pink blanket pulled around him, conferring with dubious courtiers.

Away from the beach, the unnamed drug dealer's mugging while he fans out his bricks of hash is a perfect, joyless moment of self-awareness, or at least that's how it reads today. In reality, he was probably delighted to be holding so much valuable product, and yet the shot Divine chose to include has an ominous, the-landslide-starts-near-here quality.

The landslide of commercialism, branding, ubiquitous media, professionalized surfing—the world we live in now—yes, that corporate future shimmers in the margins of these images, too, and sometimes inside the margins. Margo Oberg has her little yellow World Surfing Champion car courtesy of a local business. It's quaint and must have been embarrassing to drive. A subtler, infinitely cooler, and more effective form of advertising is the lightning bolt logo you see on most of the boards in this book. The Lightning Bolt Company was started in 1970 by Jack Shipley, a surf-contest judge, and Gerry Lopez, the consensus top surfer at Pipeline. (Pipe, which Lopez rode peerlessly for years, has long been considered the most beautiful, and most dangerous, wave in the world.) They sold high-quality boards made by a consortium of Oahu shapers, and actually gave boards free to the best surfers who came to ride the North Shore each winter. The result was that virtually every ripper in the mags was on a Bolt, which made everybody else want one.

Some of those visiting rippers, from Australia and South Africa, helped create the modern pro tour on the backs of their dazzling mid-seventies North Shore performances. Shaun Tomson, Peter Townend, Wayne "Rabbit" Bartholomew, Mark Richards—they are all here, their brilliance carefully documented by Divine. Their direct successors, I should mention, today's world champs, don't need print mags, ironically. They have their own filmers, provided by their sponsors, and they're up on Instagram within hours of any noteworthy moment in the water. They're also expected to drop video "edits" periodically online.

But the beating heart of this book is not, although they are certainly in the mix, surf journalism or mordant observation, any more than it is front-lit nostalgia. It is rather, to my mind, a celebration. Of Sam Hawk's bottom turn under crushing pressure at Pipe. Of Barry Kanaiaupuni's balls-out air drop at Makaha. And of looking good, always, while doing the extremely difficult.

Check out the hands. On Eddie Aikau's high trim at small Sunset, he has both hands thrown behind him and wide open. I've never seen this particular dance move before, but it looks superfine and its purpose is clear in the immaculate, neutral, seemingly weightless track he's found. See Ben Aipa's torqued back arm, also at small Sunset, also in service of a high line on a feathering wall. Jericho Poppler's full-stretch puppeteer's finger waggle at Haleiwa, lifting her own weight somehow into the air so that she can put five toes precisely over the nose at speed. Jeff Hakman's reach for the sky on a drop behind the boil at steel-gray Waimea. Mark Richards, the wounded gull, in full flight at Pipe, then off the top at Off the Wall, his wrists bent at angles that have never been seen again in surfing since he retired with four world titles. Buttons Kaluhiokalani, who was way ahead of his time, cutting back so hard that his hands are planted in the water behind him. This was on a single fin with a lot of bulk and virtually no rocker. All of these surfers are on clunky single-fin darts of some kind, and Divine knows just how hard it was to push back the performance frontier on such boards. I think he's celebrating that, too.

And then there are Rory Russell's hands, when he stands in the pit at dredging Pipe, his knees hardly bent, his back straight. His hands are down at his sides, so relaxed that he might be about to put them in his pockets. It's the most modern shot in the book, except that Russell has trusted his life to the worst-looking board in the book. It might as well be an old ironing board with a Lightning Bolt logo.

While these wonders unfolded on surfing's main stage, I took another road. I chased waves through the South Pacific, Australia, Indonesia, and beyond. It was a quintessentially seventies thing to do, and I did not see *Surfer* for years on end. But the deep surf news, as reported and recorded by Divine and his colleagues, found me eventually, wherever I was, just as it found most surfers. Our world was small. We needed to hear from one another, needed to see what the best surfers were up to now, and where. Also, what the hell it was they were doing with their hands.

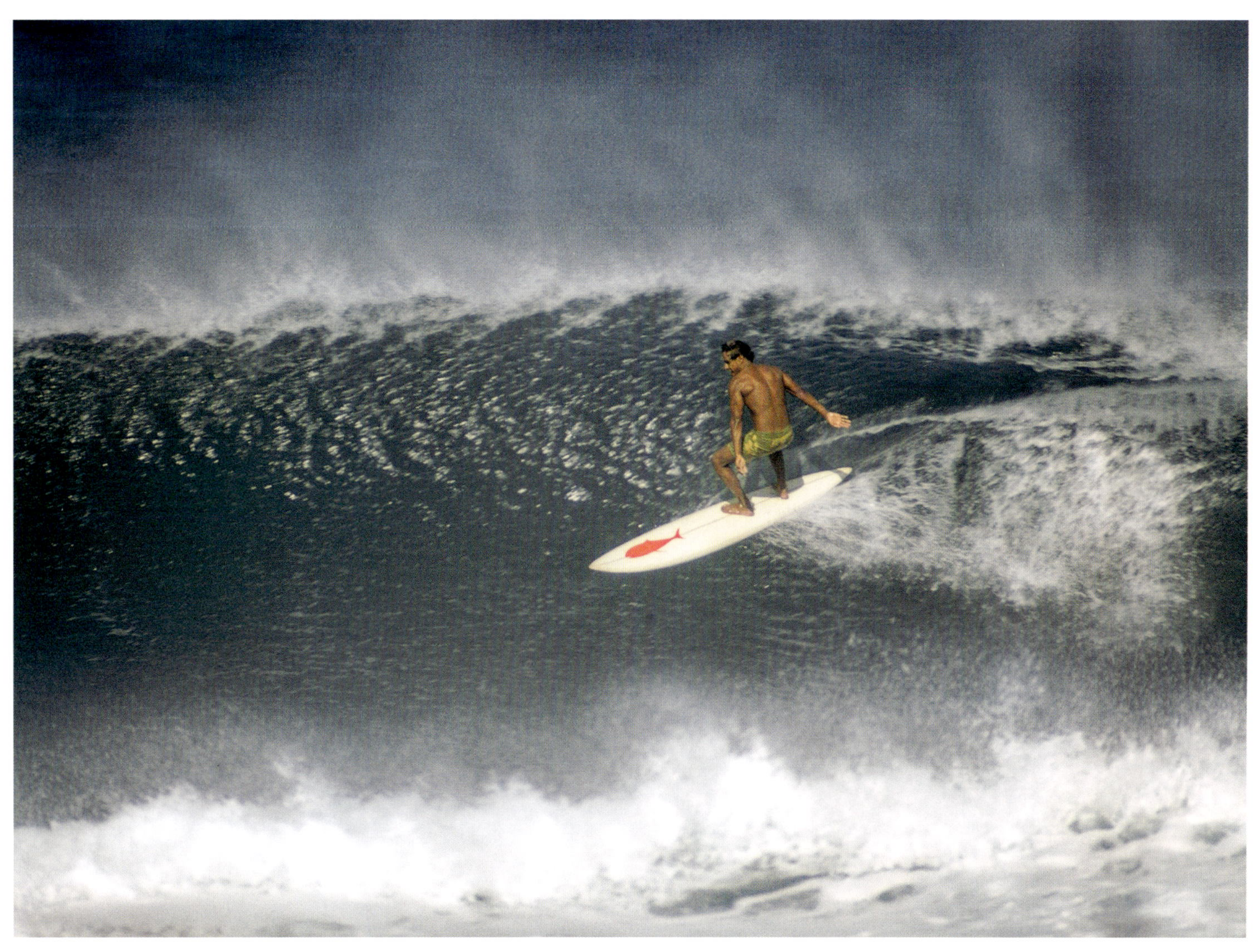

Eddie Aikau, Sunset Beach, Oahu, HI 1971

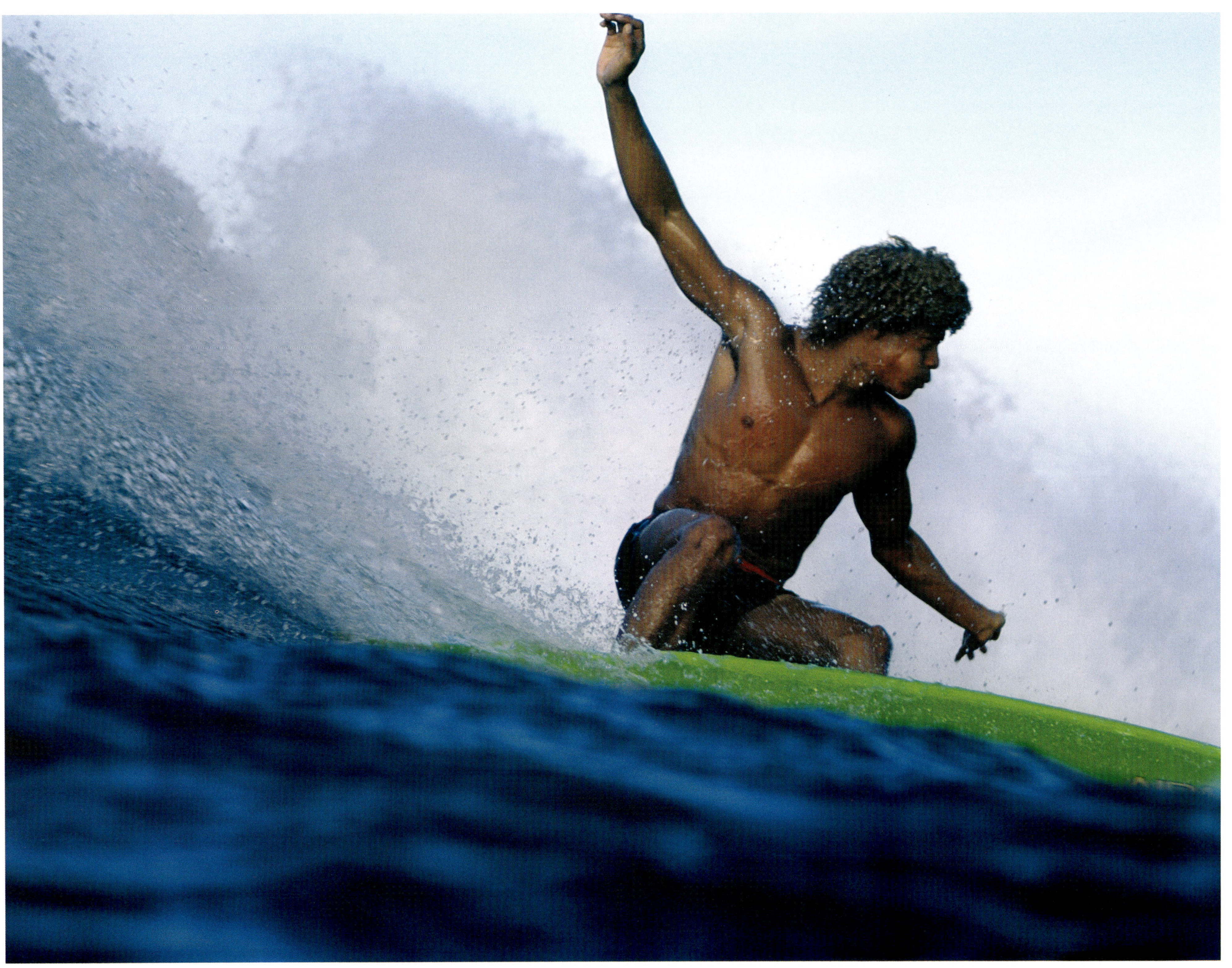

Buttons Kaluhiokalani, Velzyland, Oahu, HI 1974

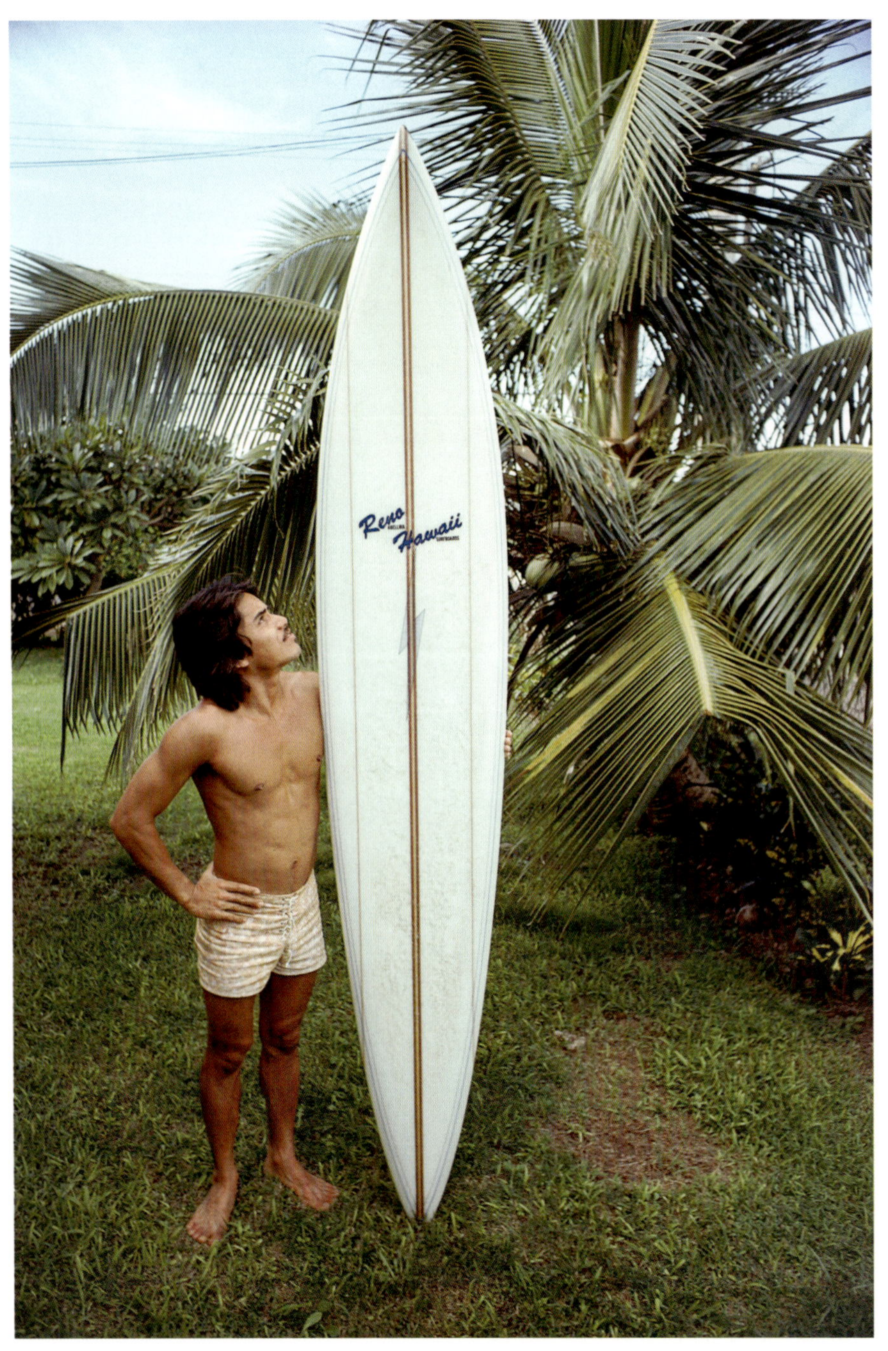

Reno Abellira, Sunset Beach, Oahu, HI 1974

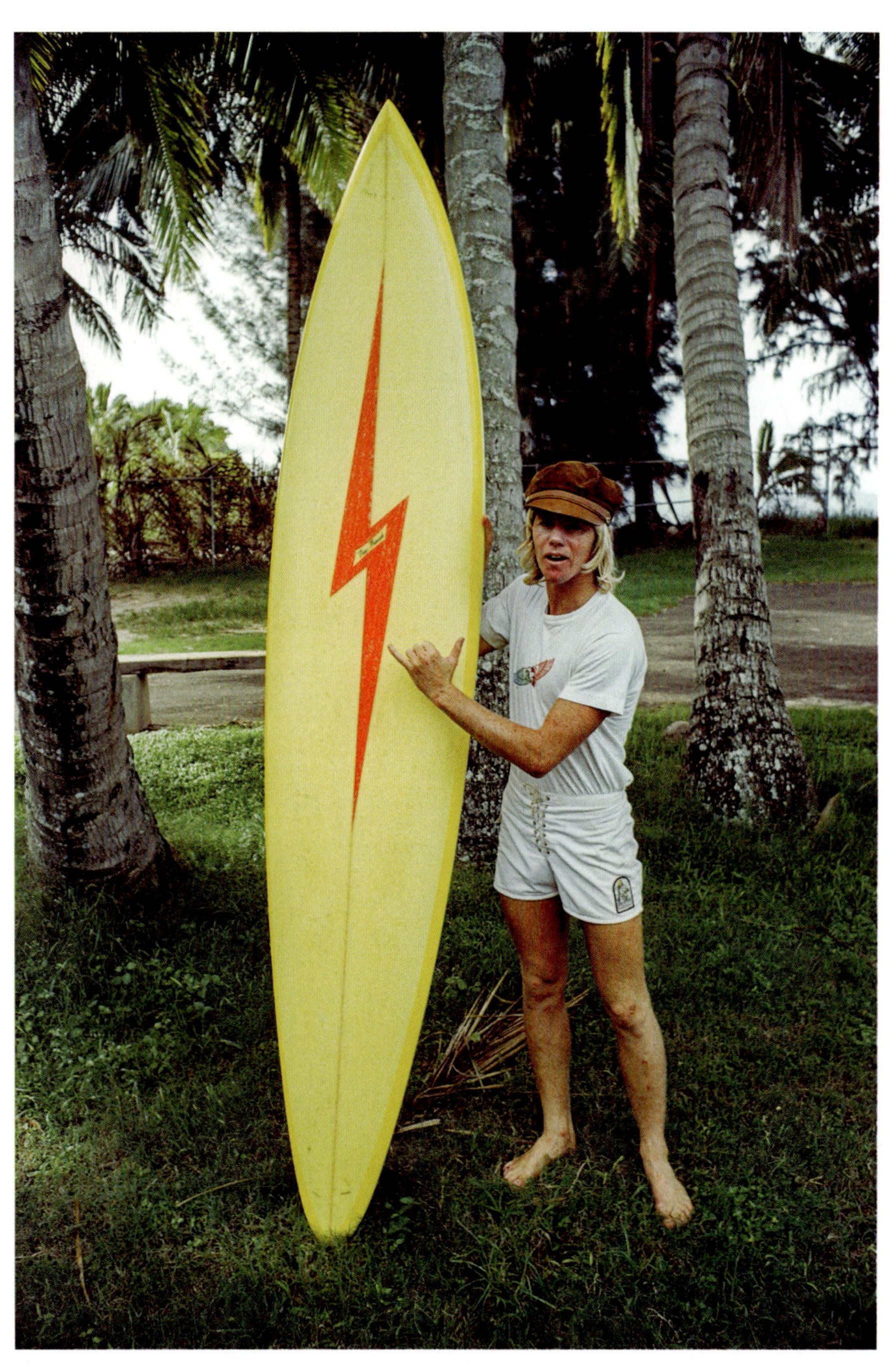

Wayne "Rabbit" Bartholomew, Ke Iki Road, Oahu, HI 1976

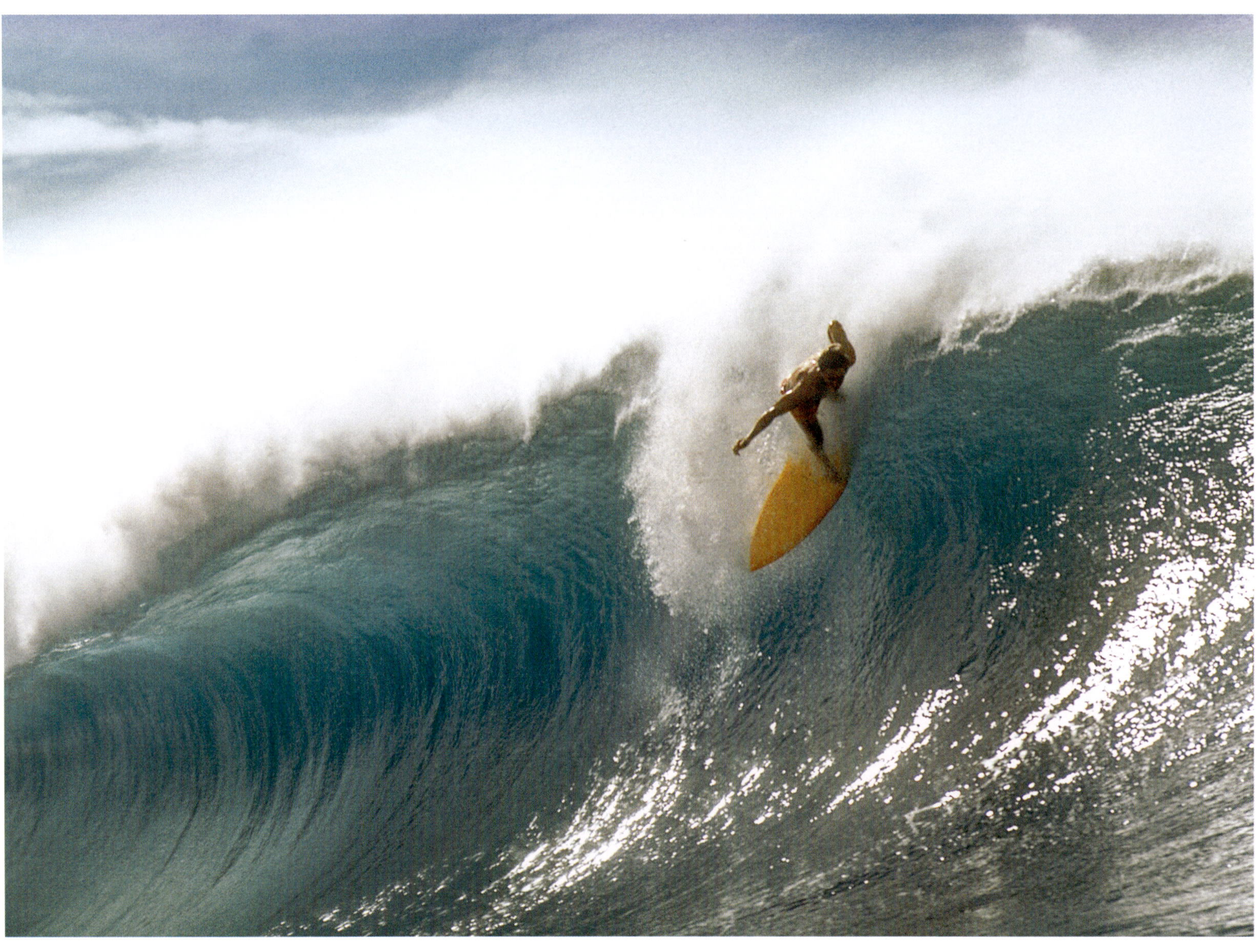

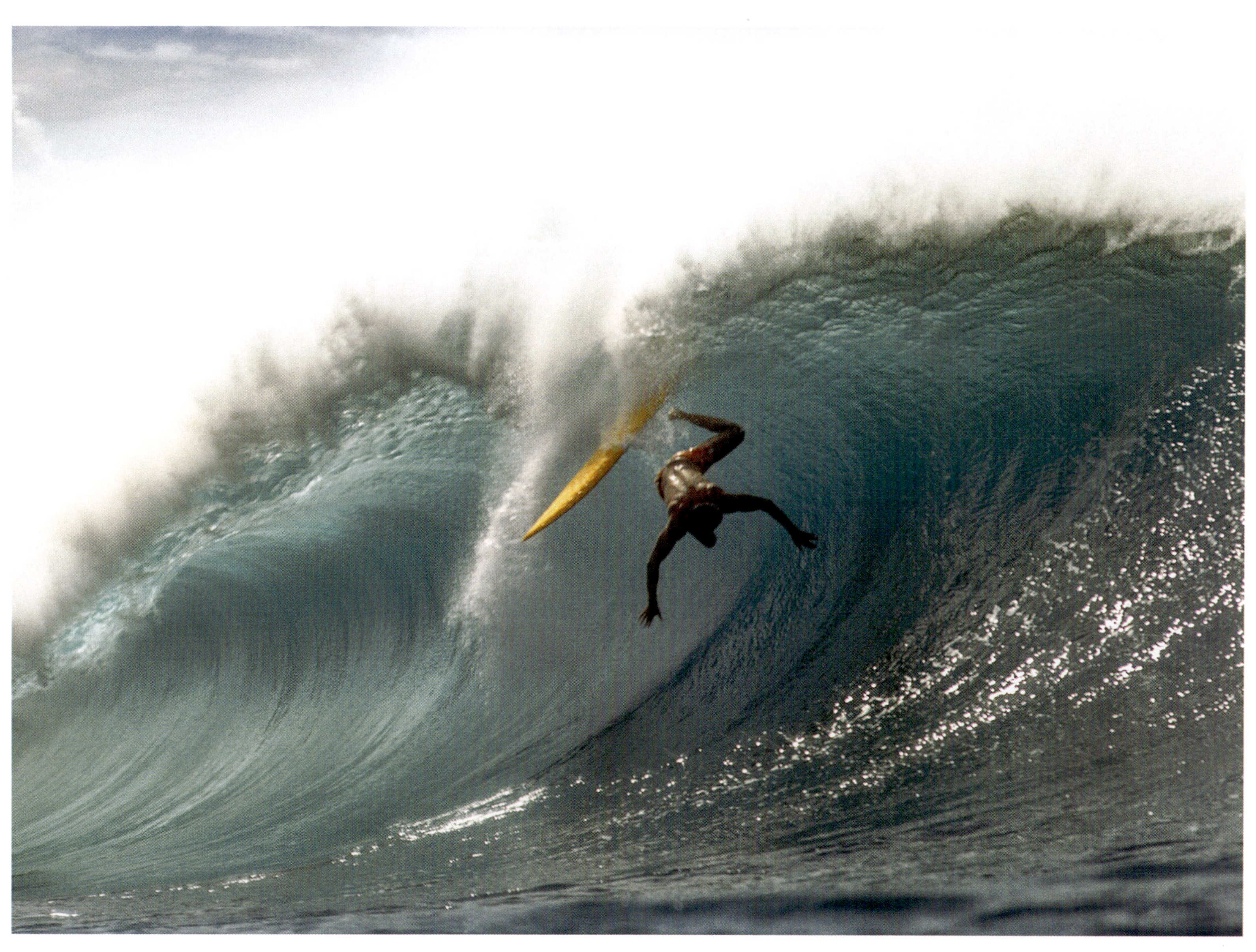

Launched, Pipeline, Oahu, HI 1976

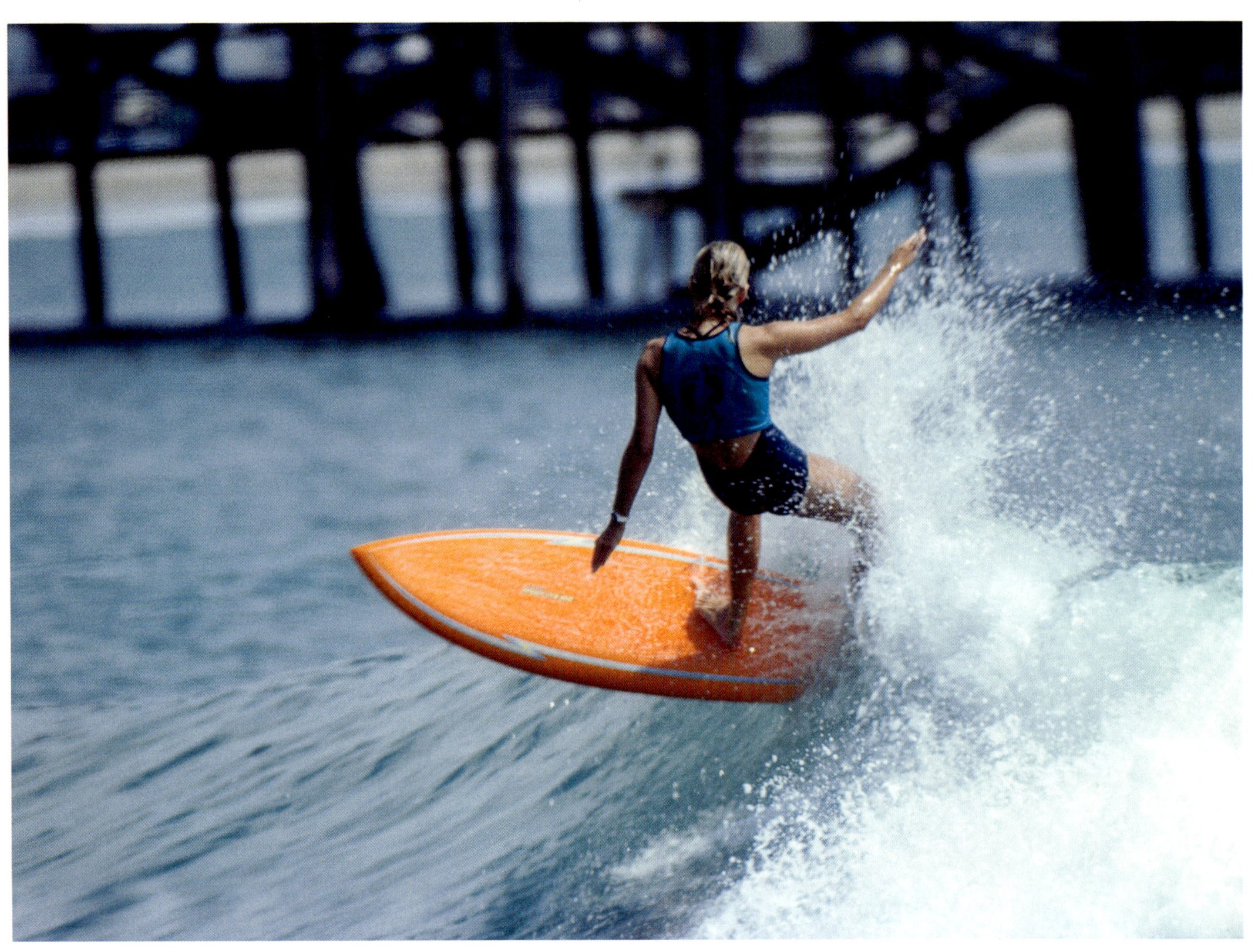

Margo Godfrey Oberg, Malibu, CA 1978

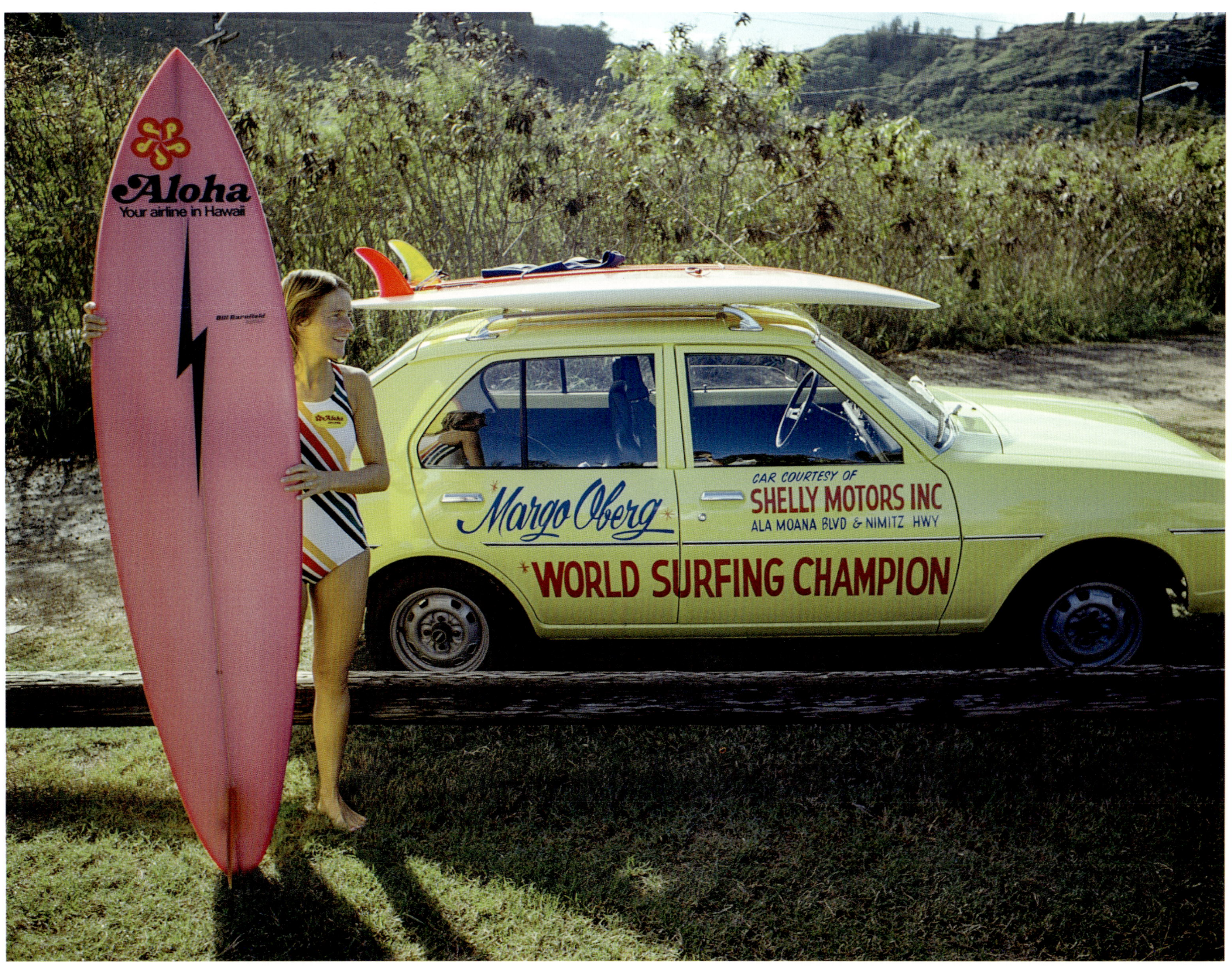

Margo Godfrey Oberg, Sunset Beach, Oahu, HI 1977

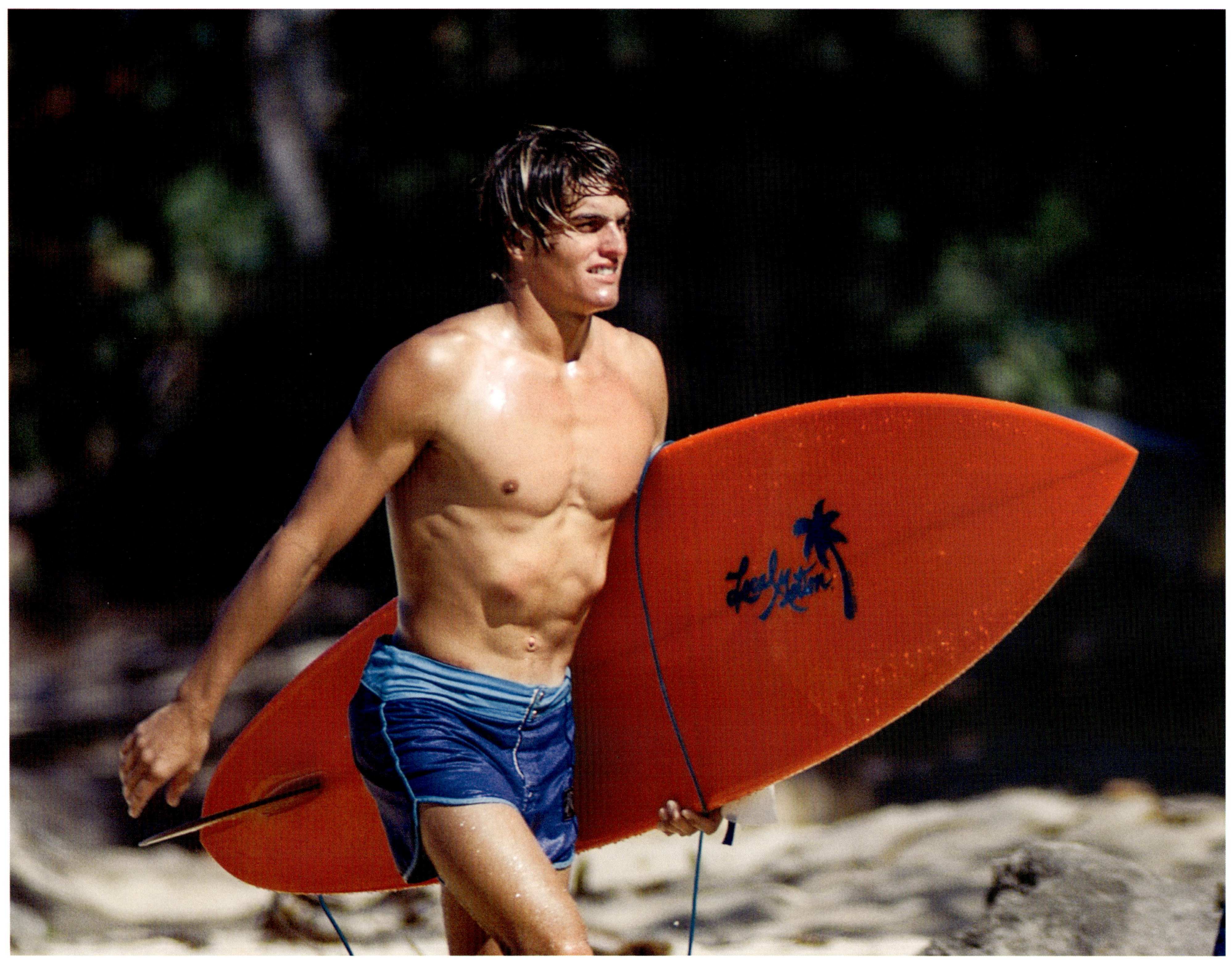

Buzzy Kerbox, Pupukea, Oahu, HI 1978

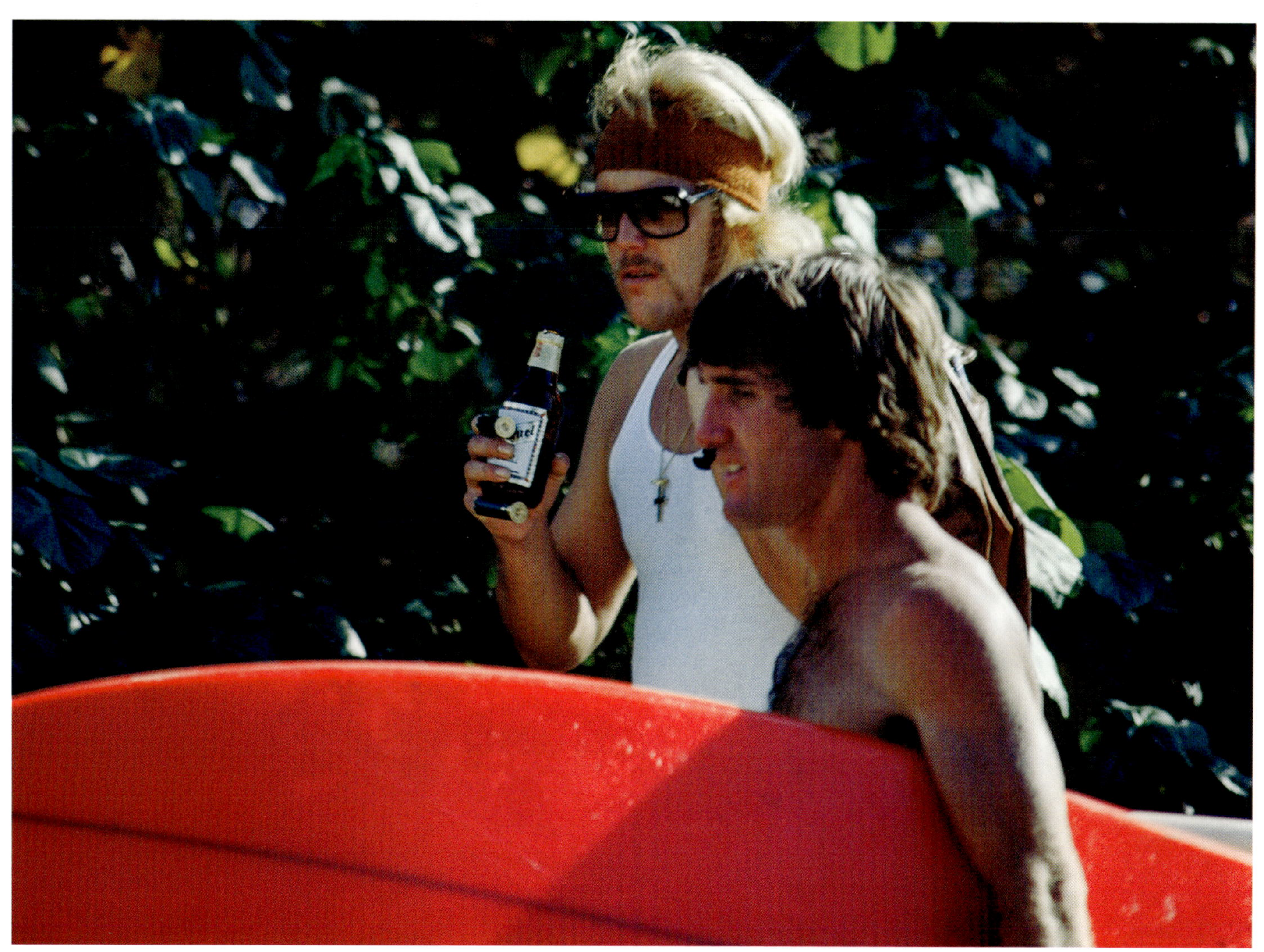

Bunker Spreckels, Jeff Hakman, Sunset Beach, Oahu, HI 1976

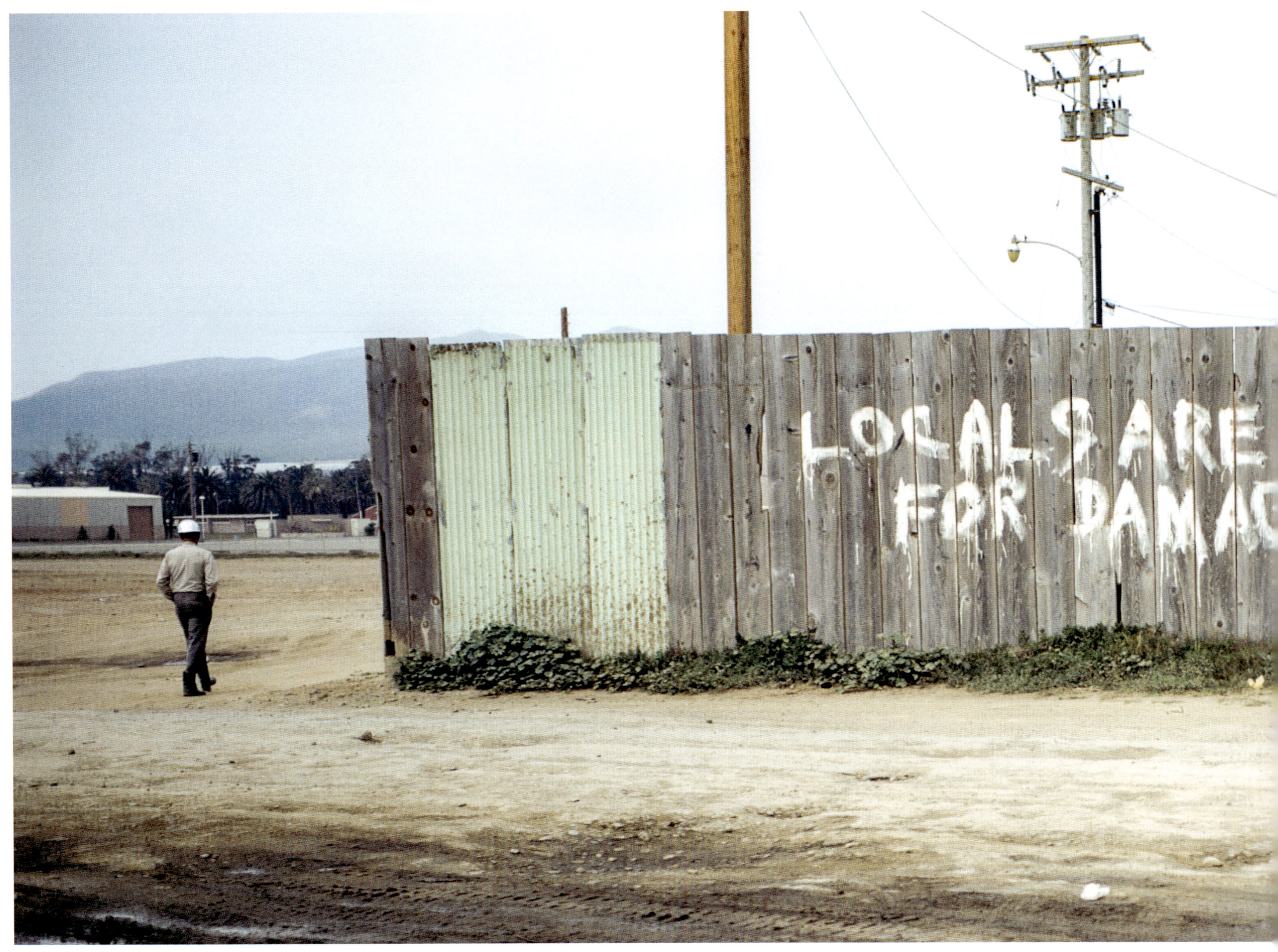
LOCALS ARE
FOR DAMA

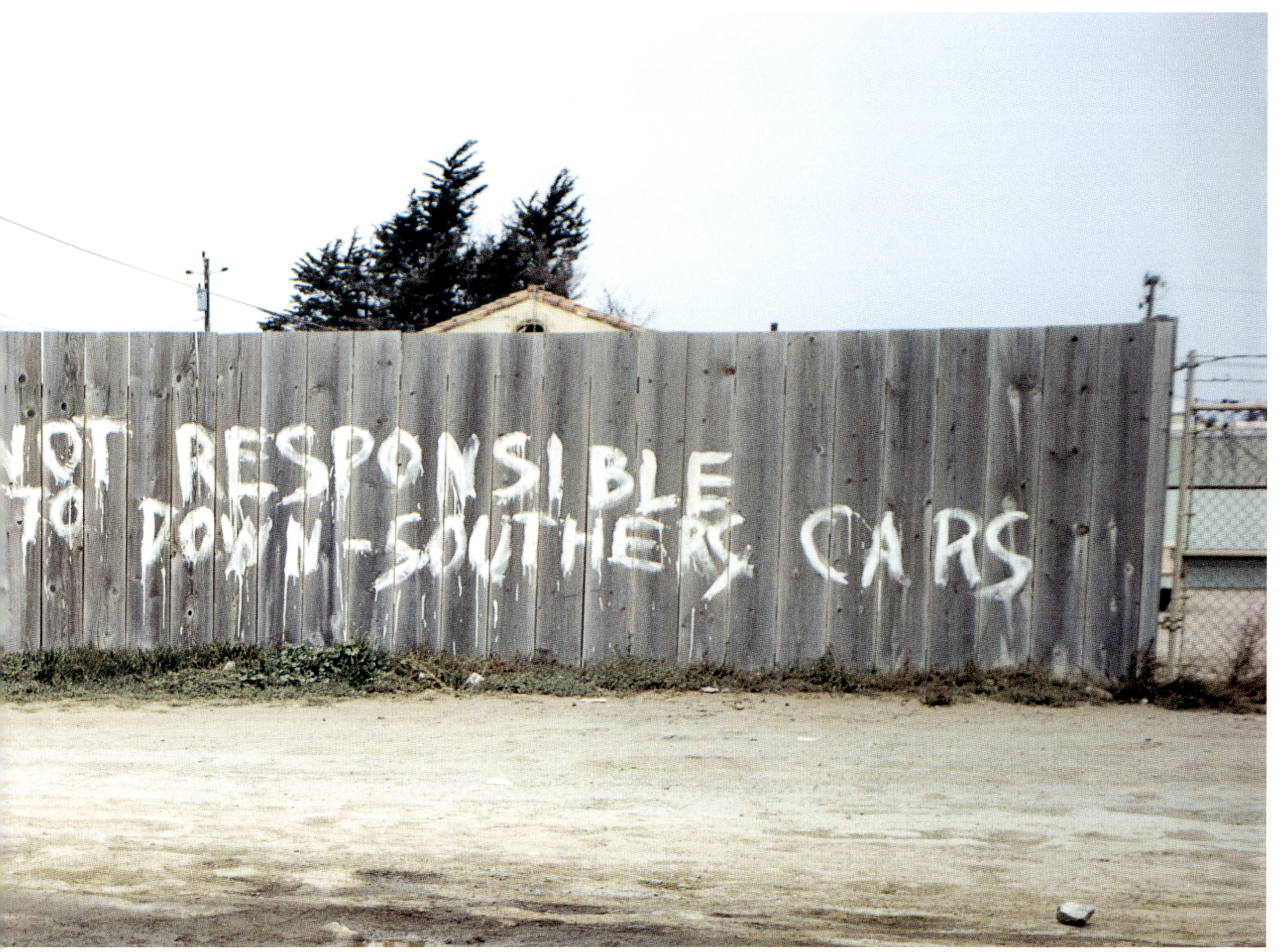

California Street, Ventura, CA 1972

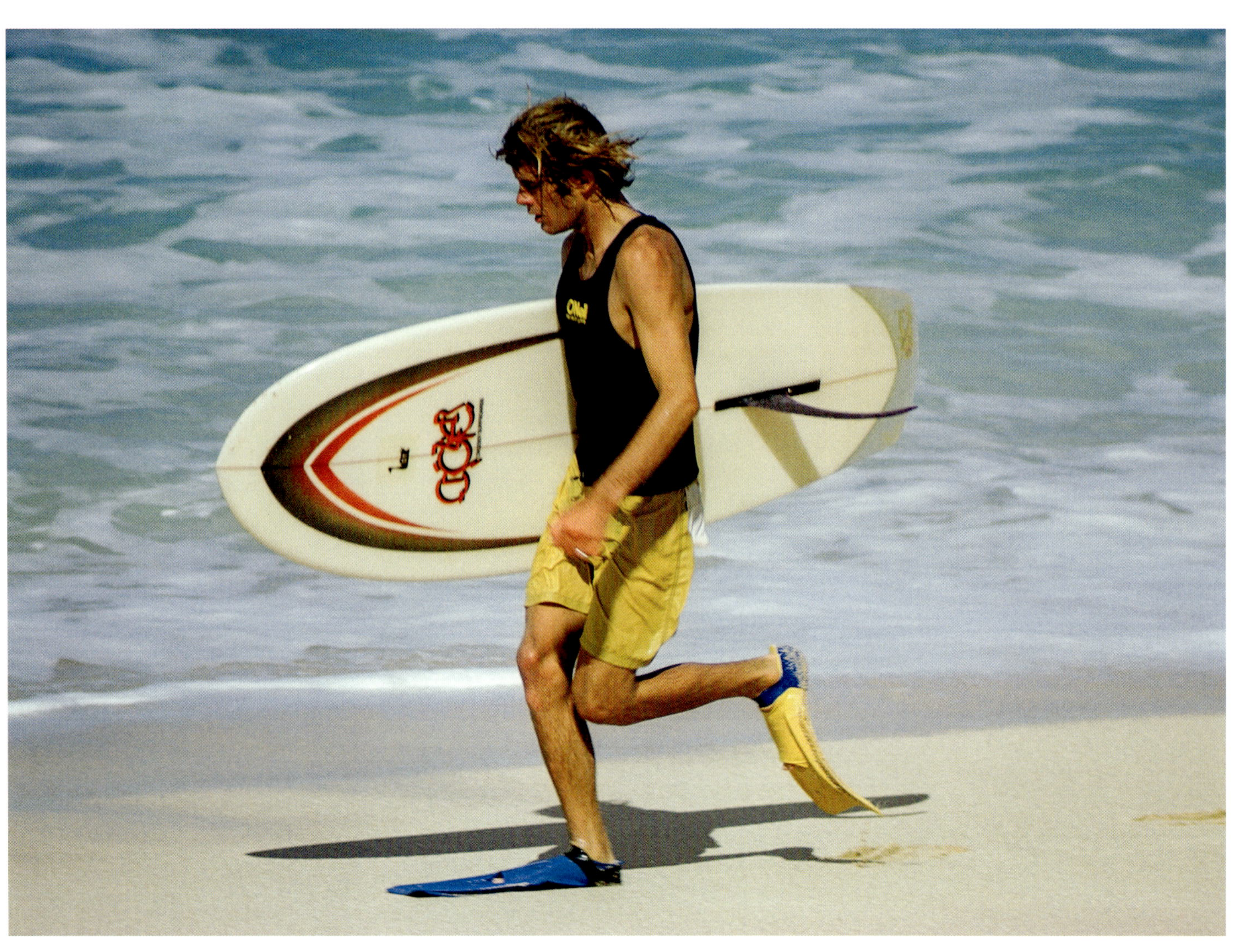

Peter Crawford, Rocky Point, Oahu, HI 1976

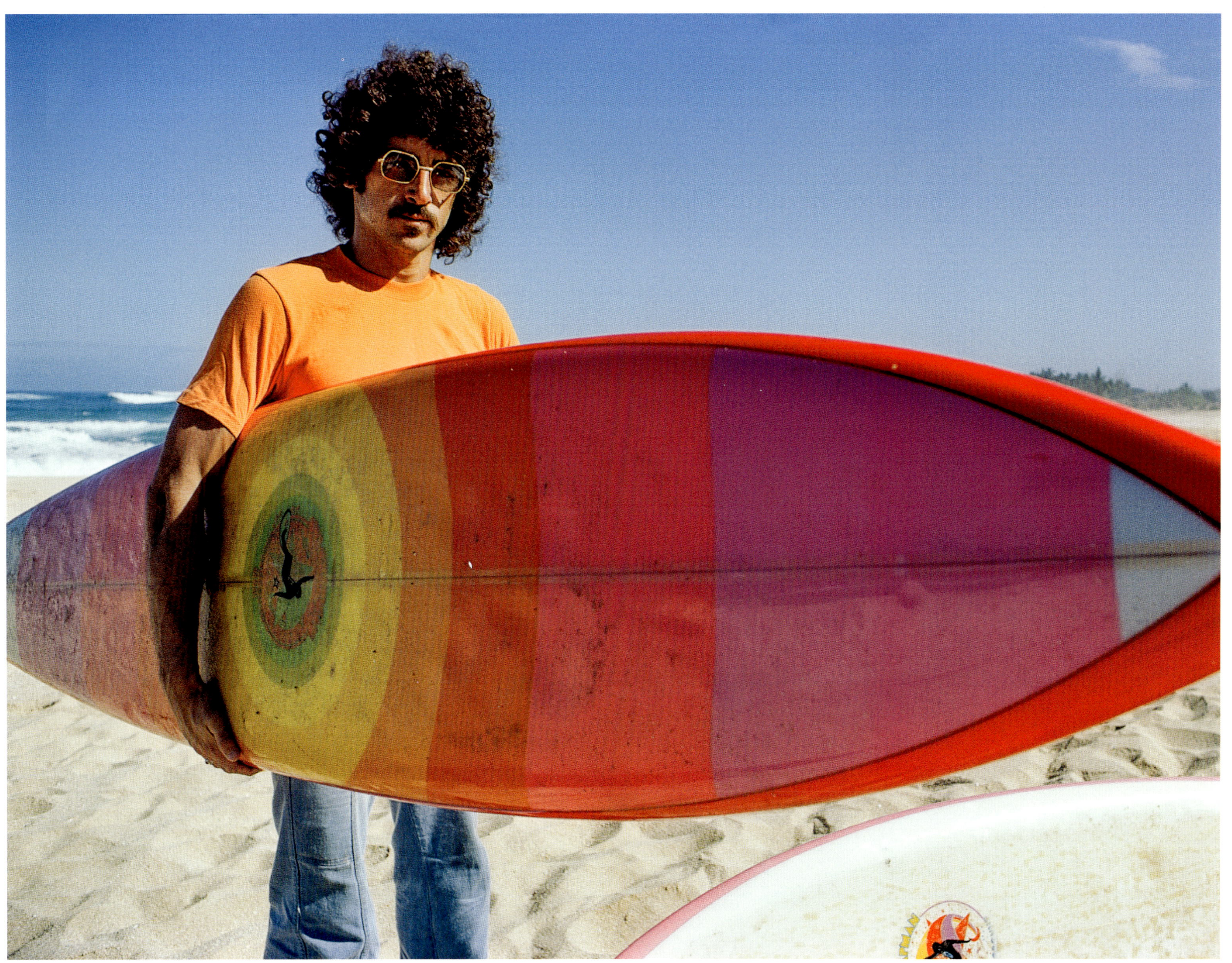

Craig "Owl" Chapman, Sunset Beach, Oahu, HI 1977

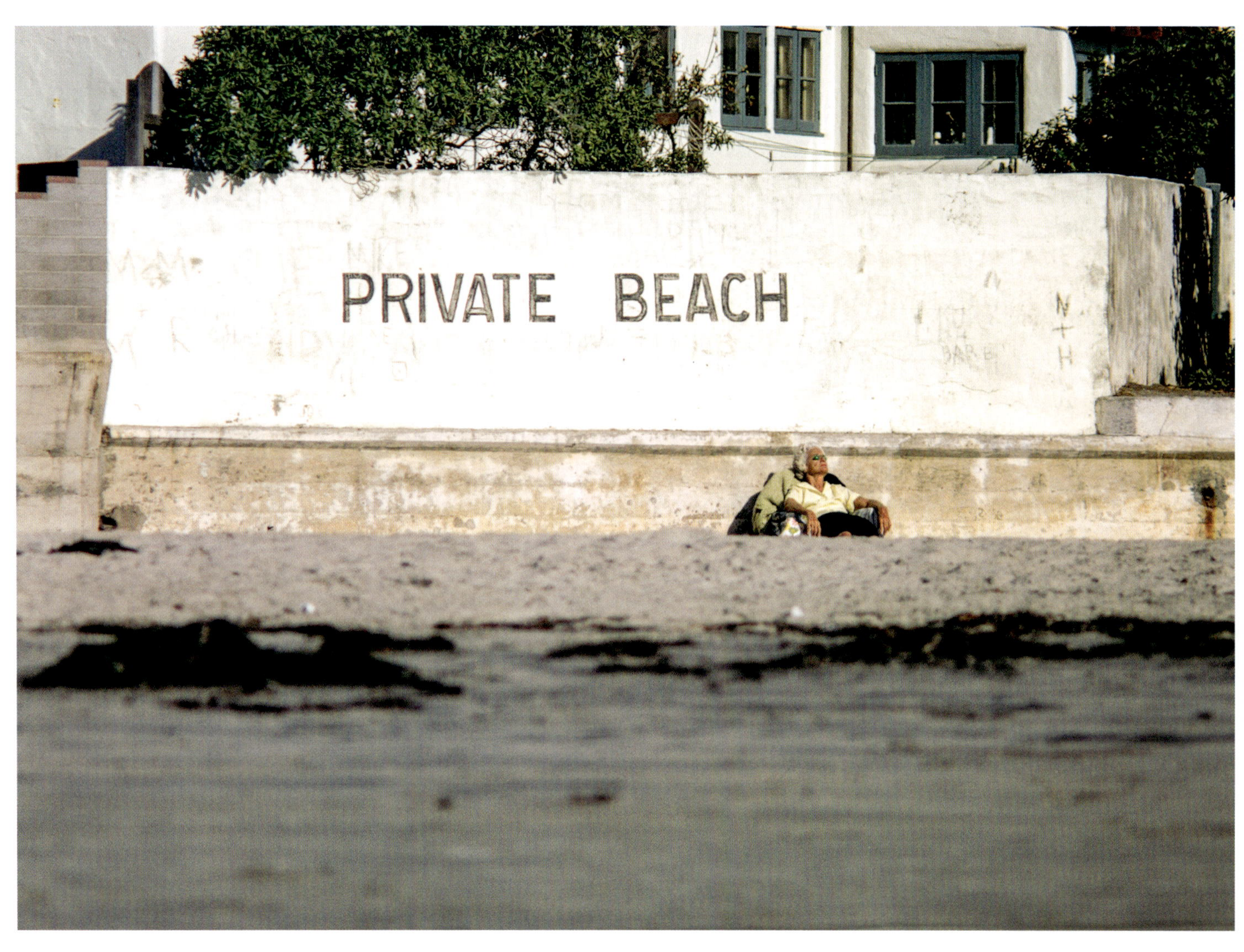

La Jolla Shores, CA 1971

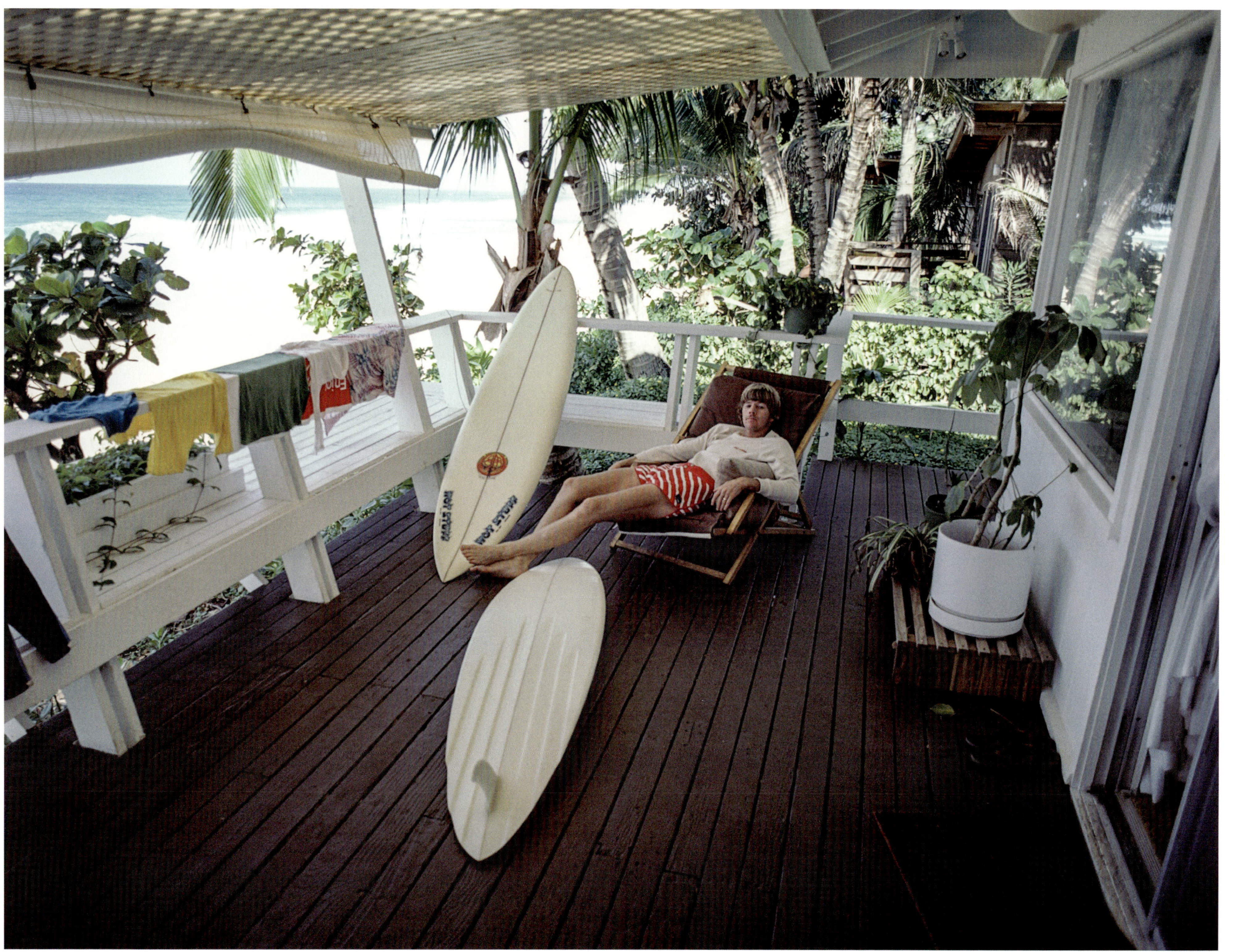

Wayne "Rabbit" Bartholomew, Off The Wall, Oahu, HI 1979

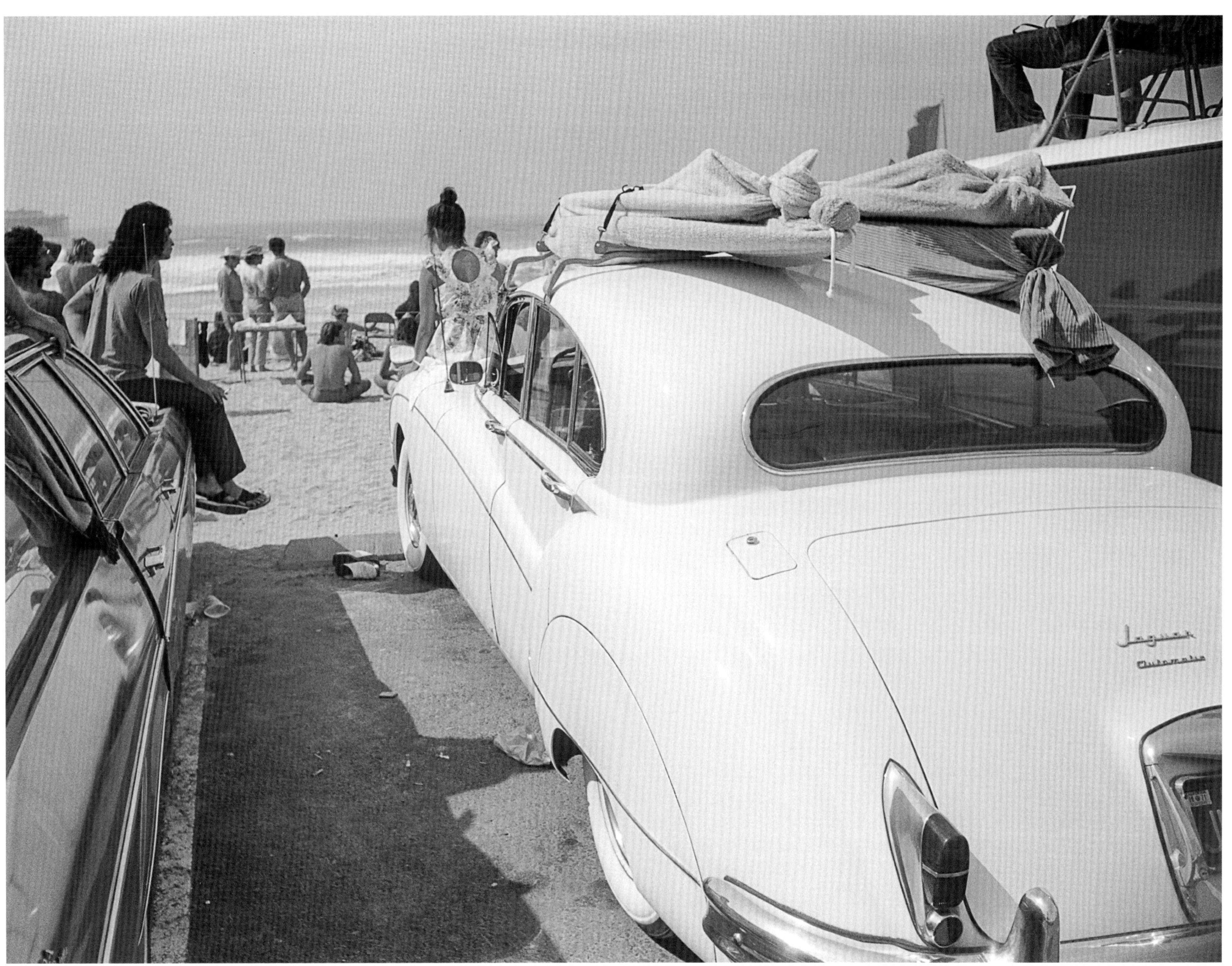

David Nuuhiwa, Oceanside, CA 1972

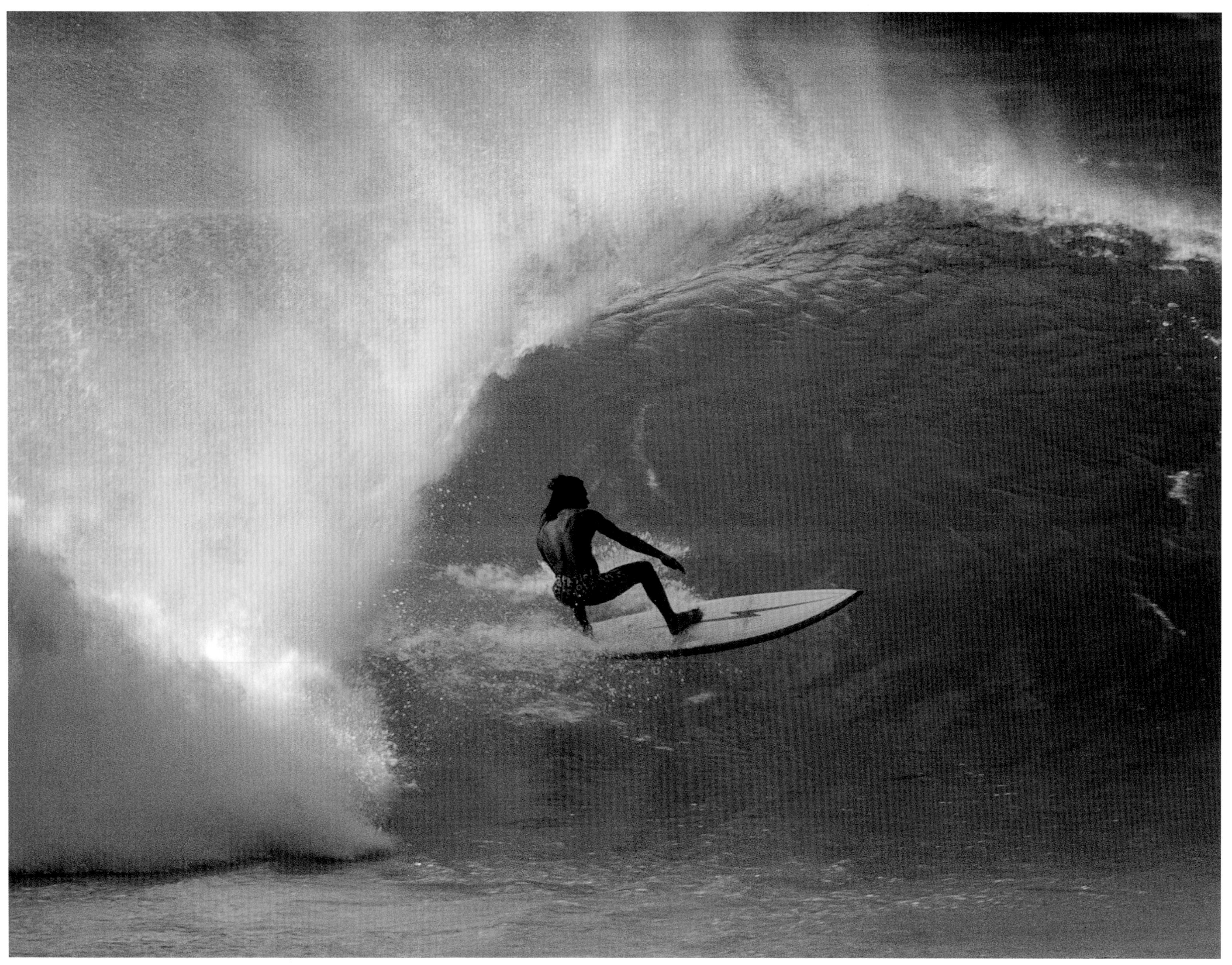

Brian Hamilton, Pipeline, Oahu HI 1974

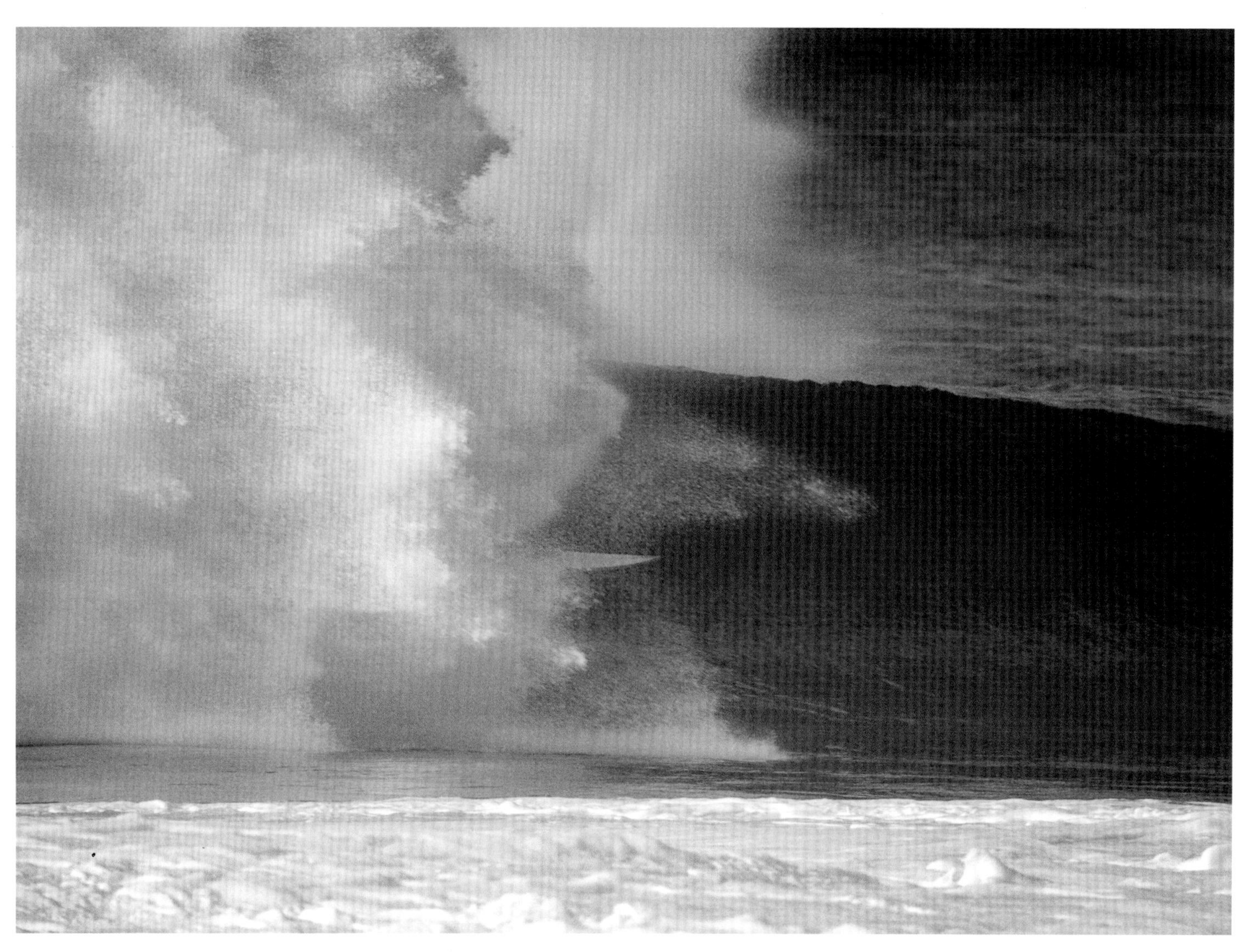

Rory Russell, Pipeline, Oahu, HI 1975

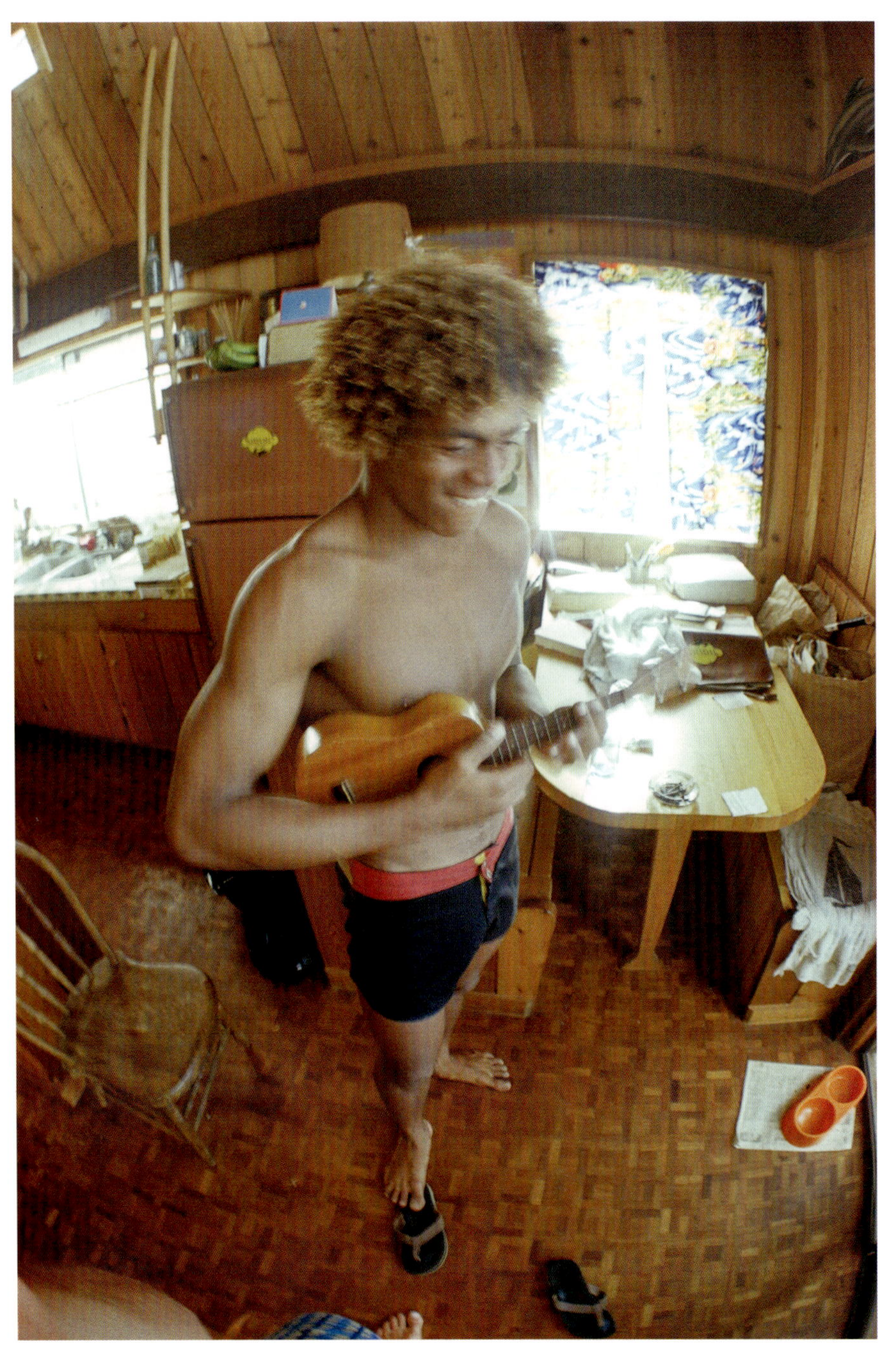

Buttons Kaluhiokalani, Off The Wall, Oahu, HI 1975

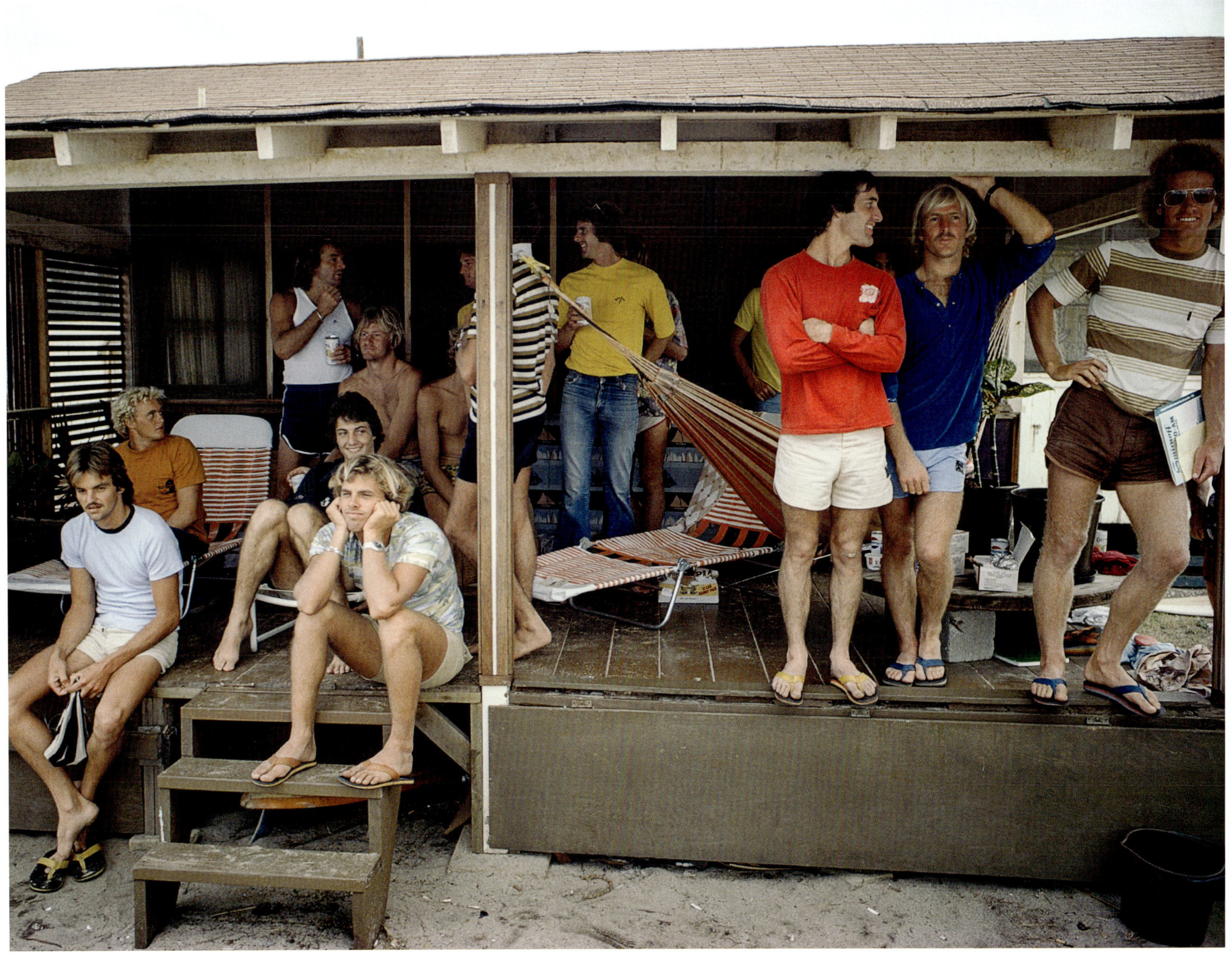

(L TO R) Paul Naude, Larry Blair, Peter Droyun, Simon Anderson, Shaun Tomson, Chris Fullston, Harry Hodge, Jeff Hakman, Phil Byrne, Terry Fitzgerald, Sunset Beach, Oahu, HI 1976

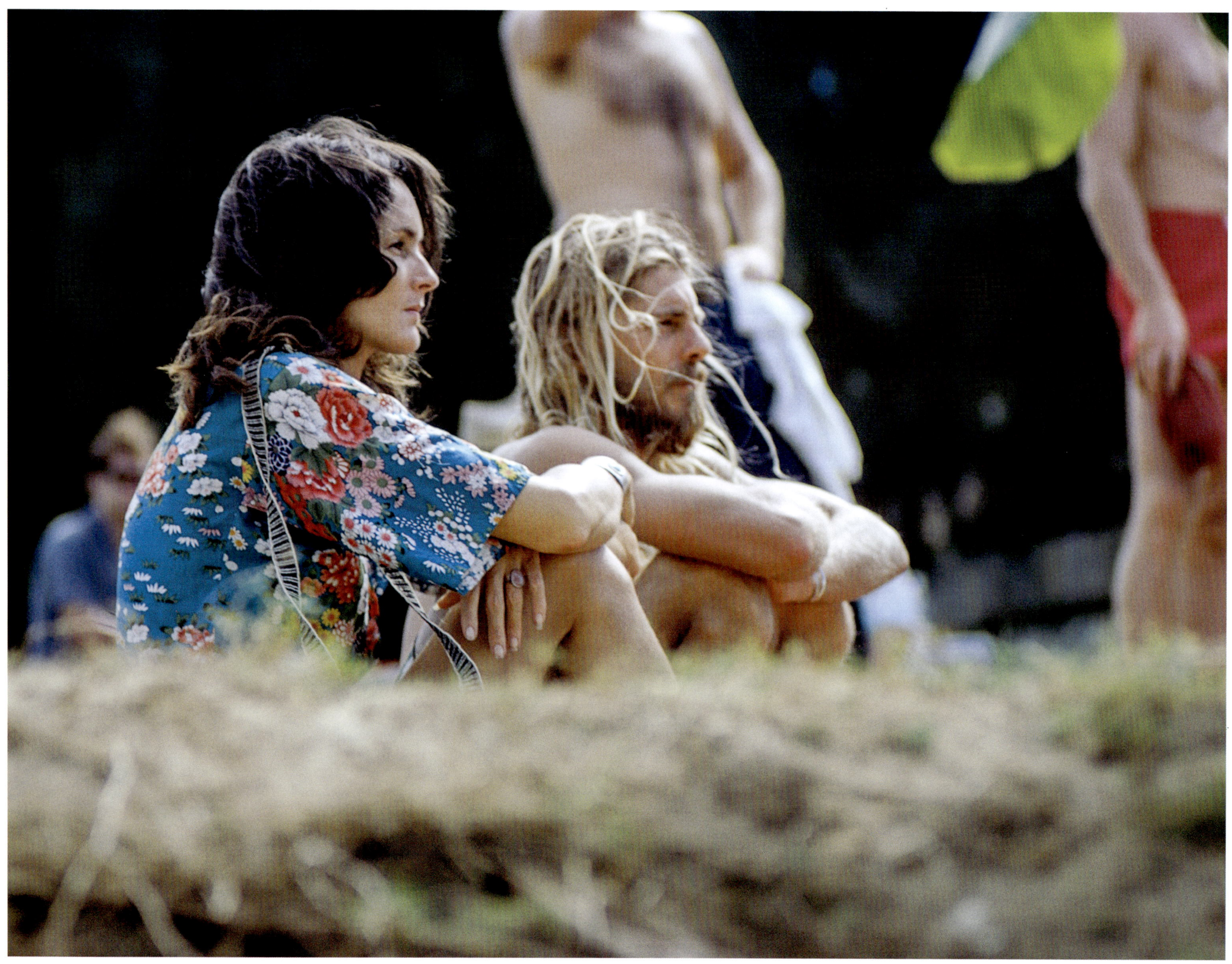

Melinda Merryweather, Mike Hynson, Pipeline, Oahu, HI 1971

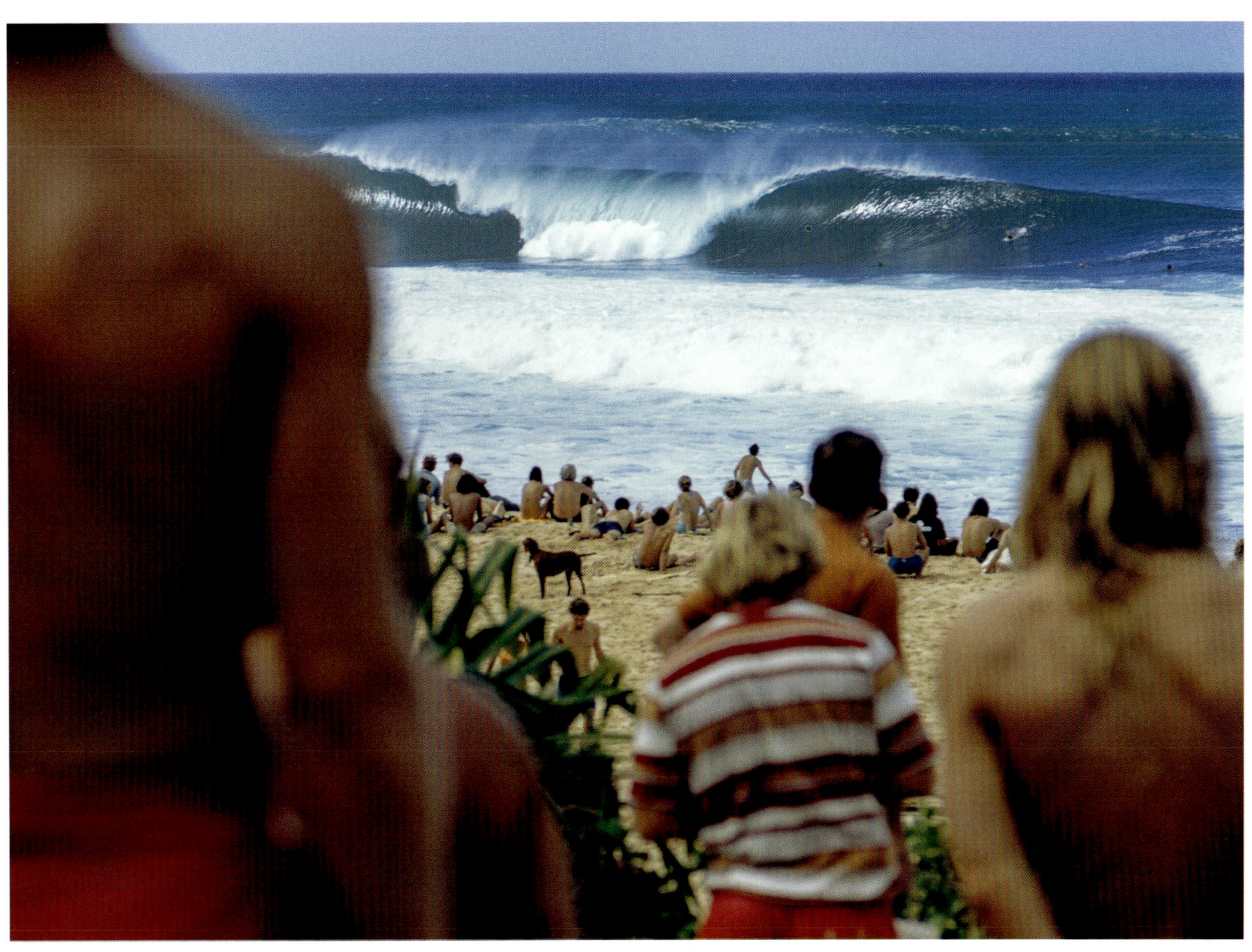

“Expression Session” morning, Pipeline, Oahu, HI 1971

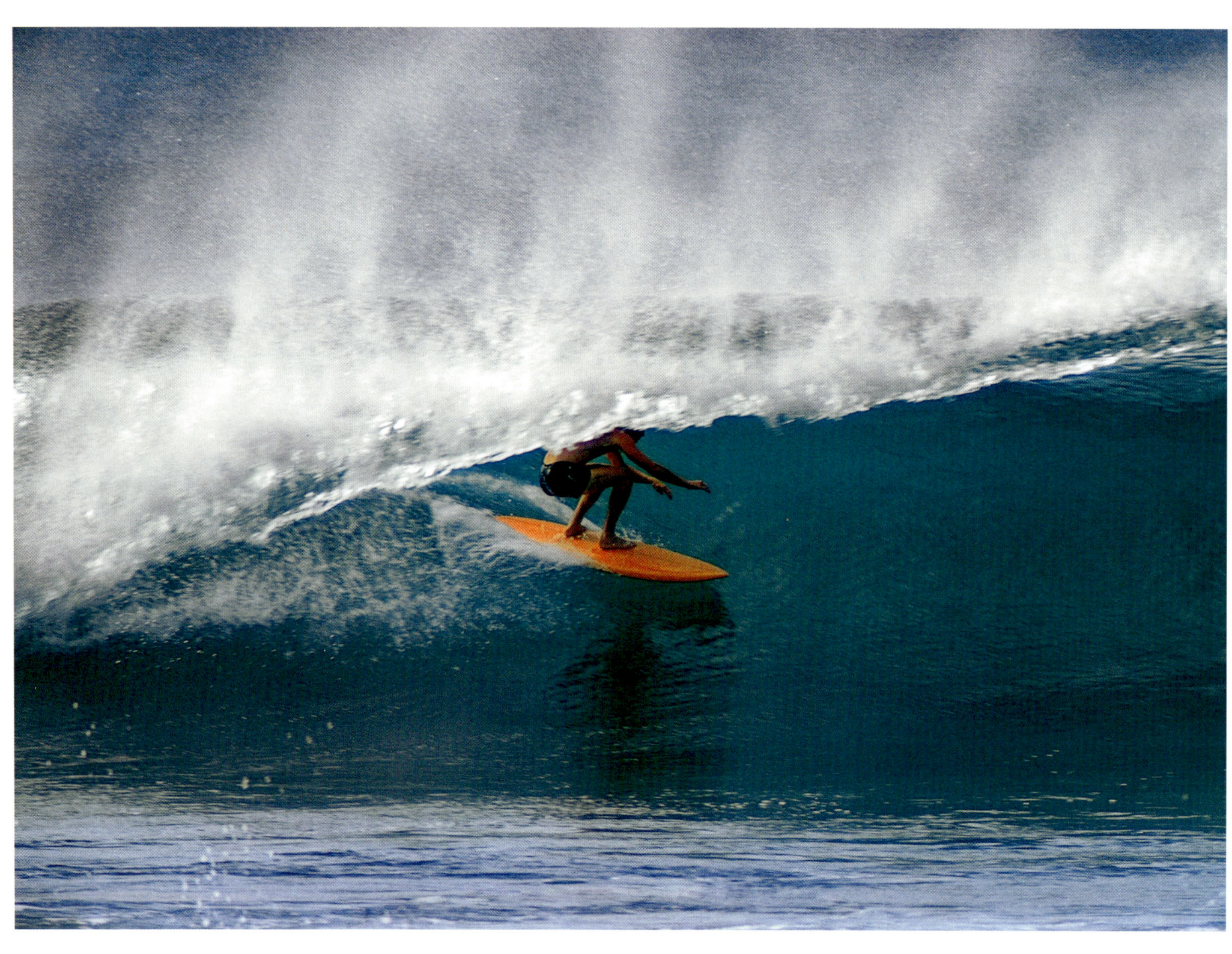

Ed Farwell, Gas Chamber, Oahu, HI 1974

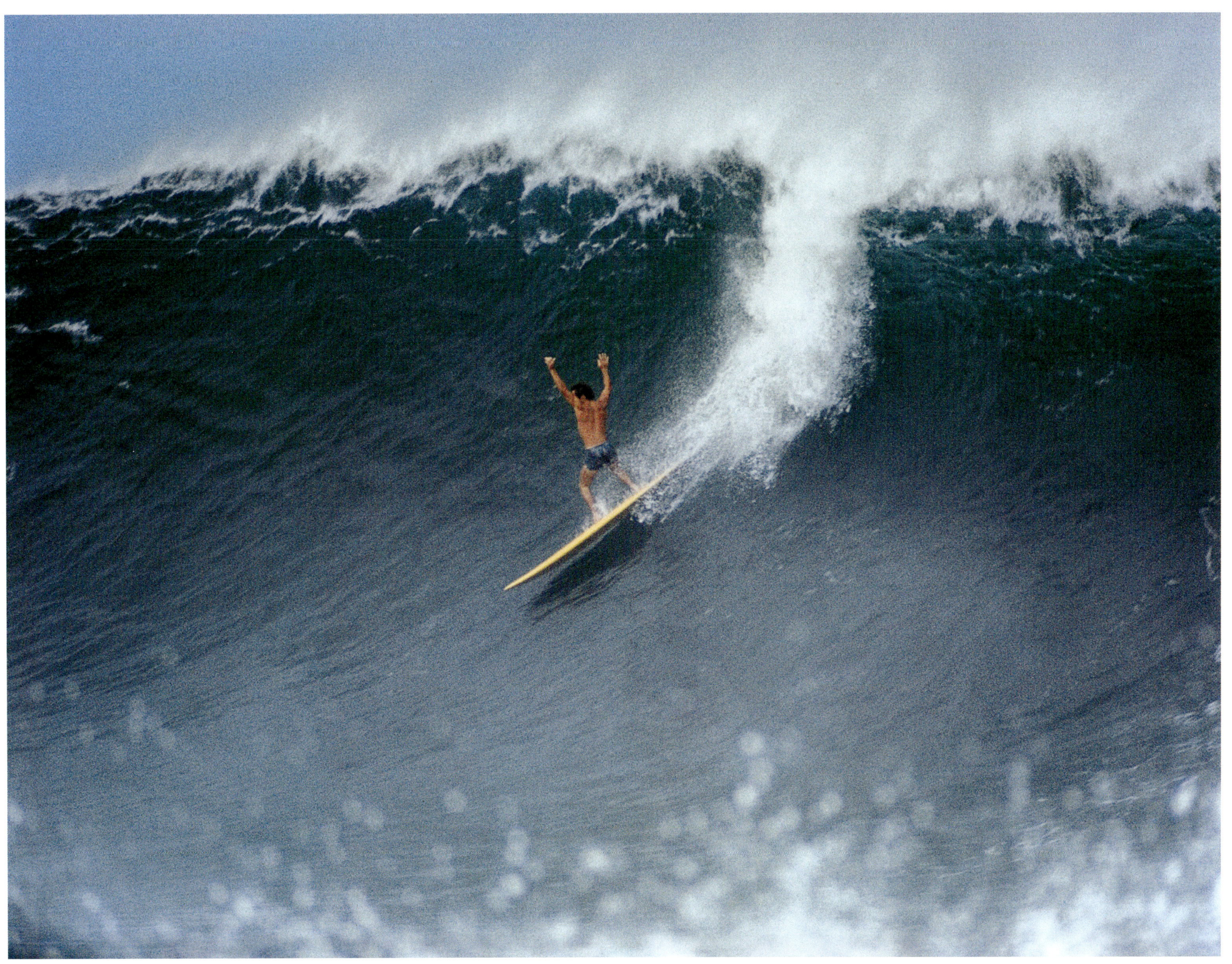

Jeff Hakman, Waimea Bay, Oahu, HI 1974

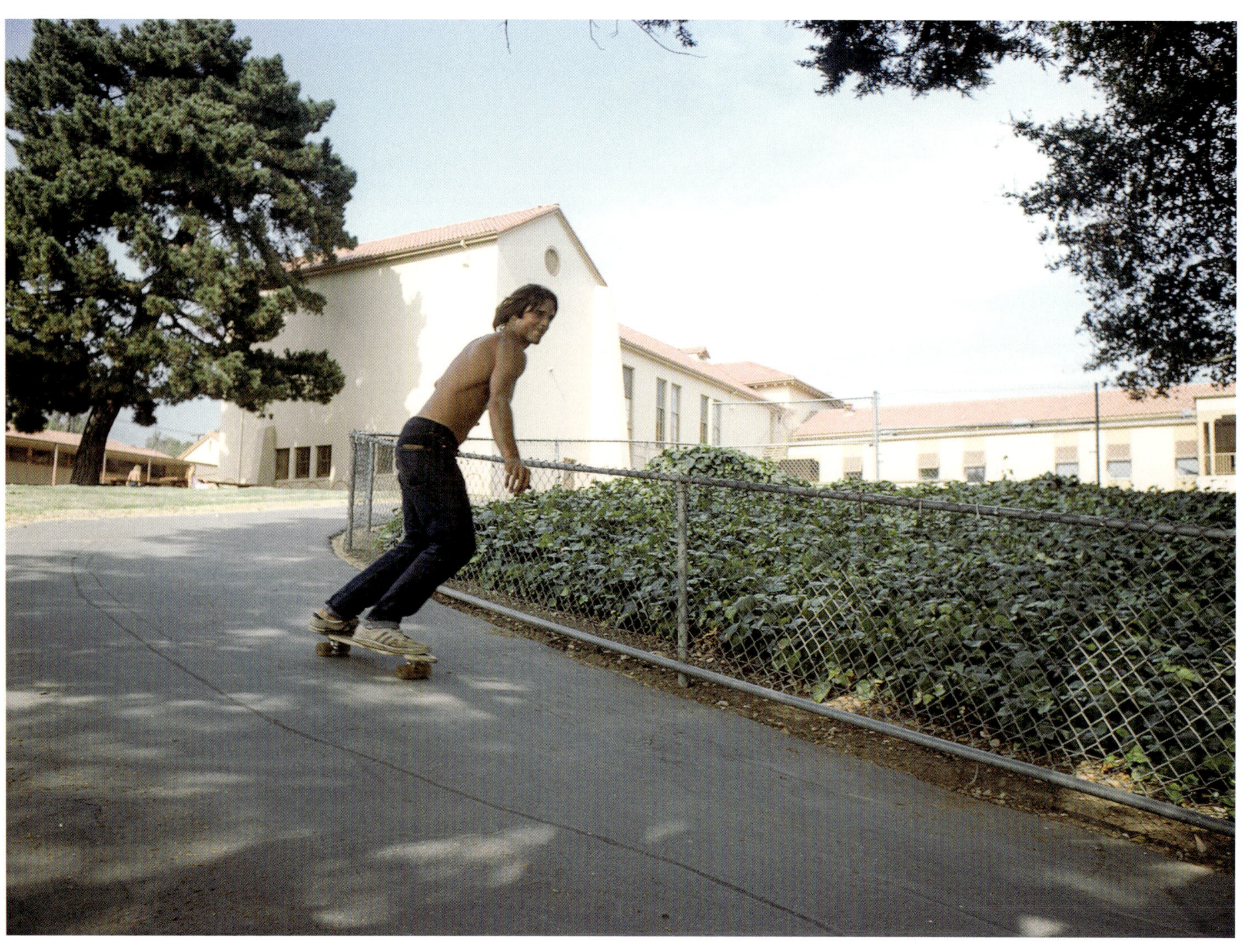

Matt Moore, Montecito Union School. Santa Barbara, CA 1975

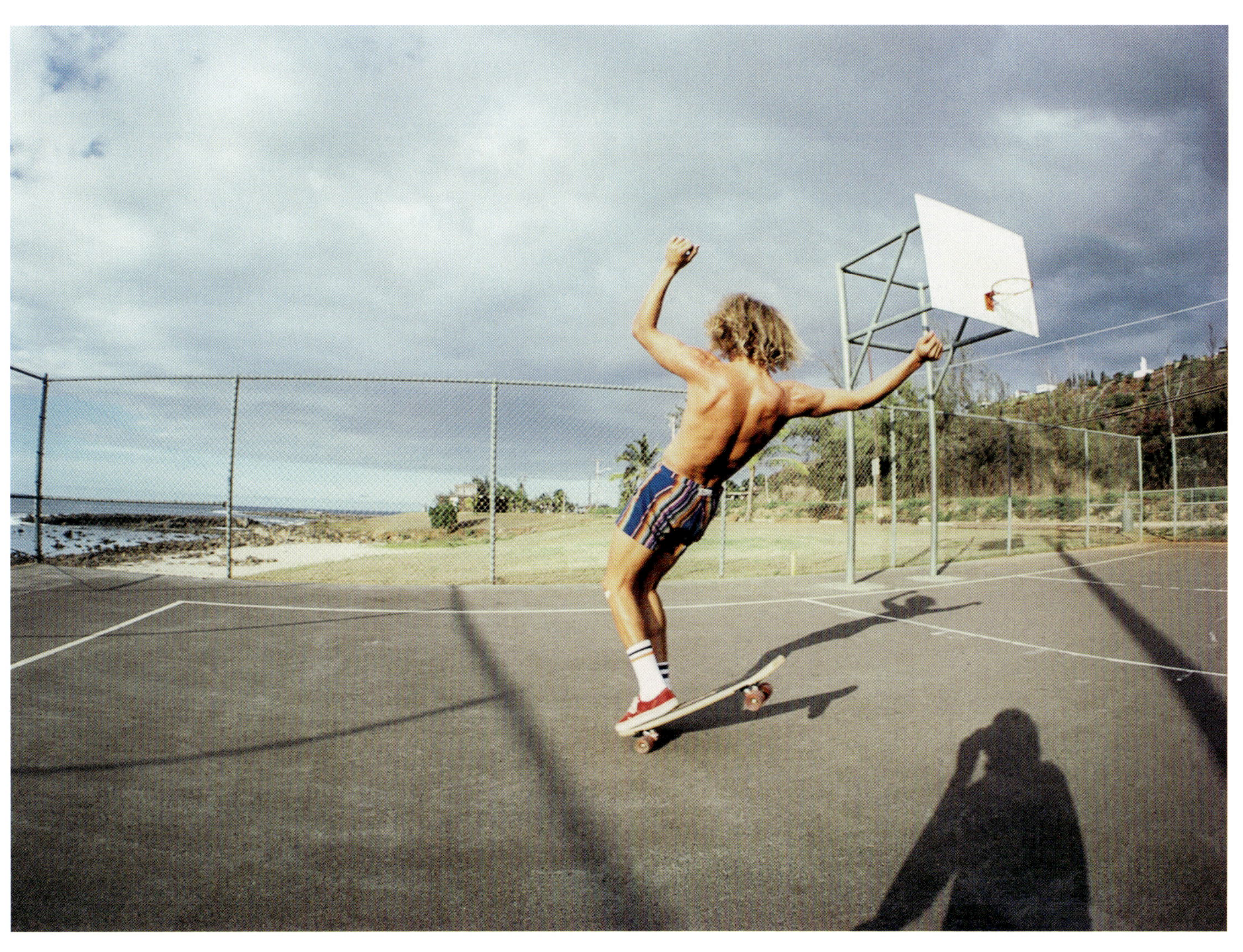

Tony Alva, Pupukea, Oahu, HI 1976

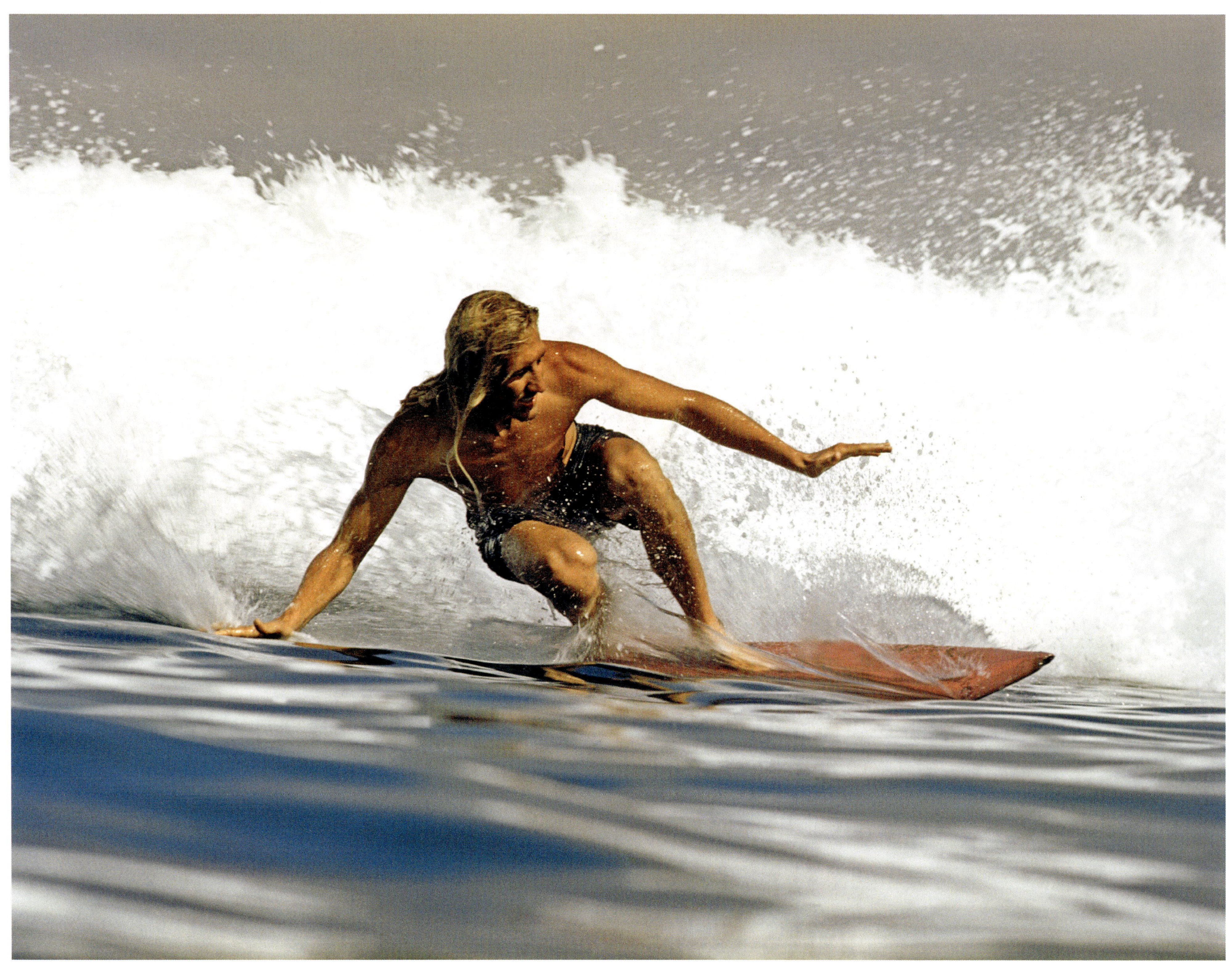

Tom Ortner, Windansea, La Jolla, CA 1971

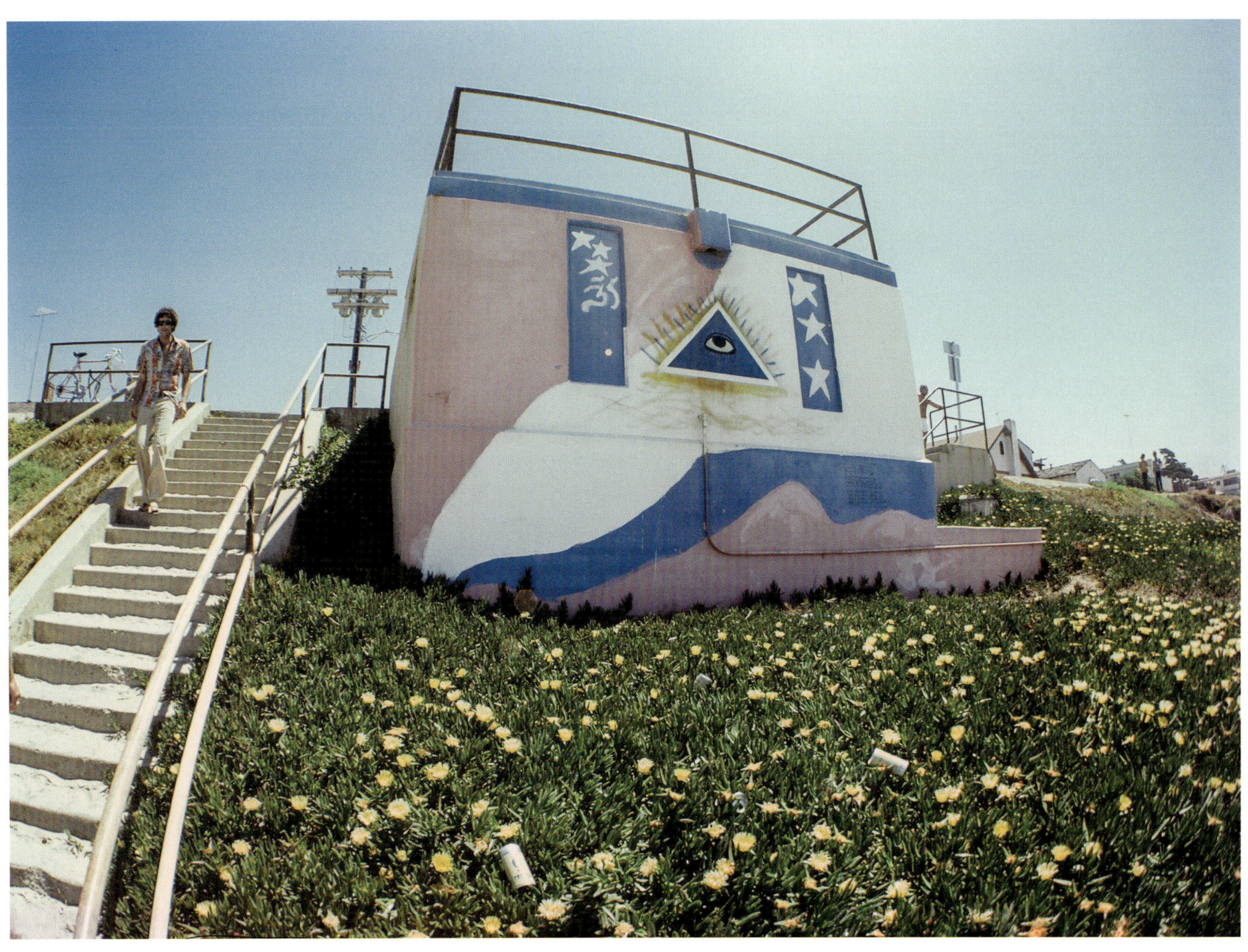

Windansea Pumphouse, La Jolla, CA 1977

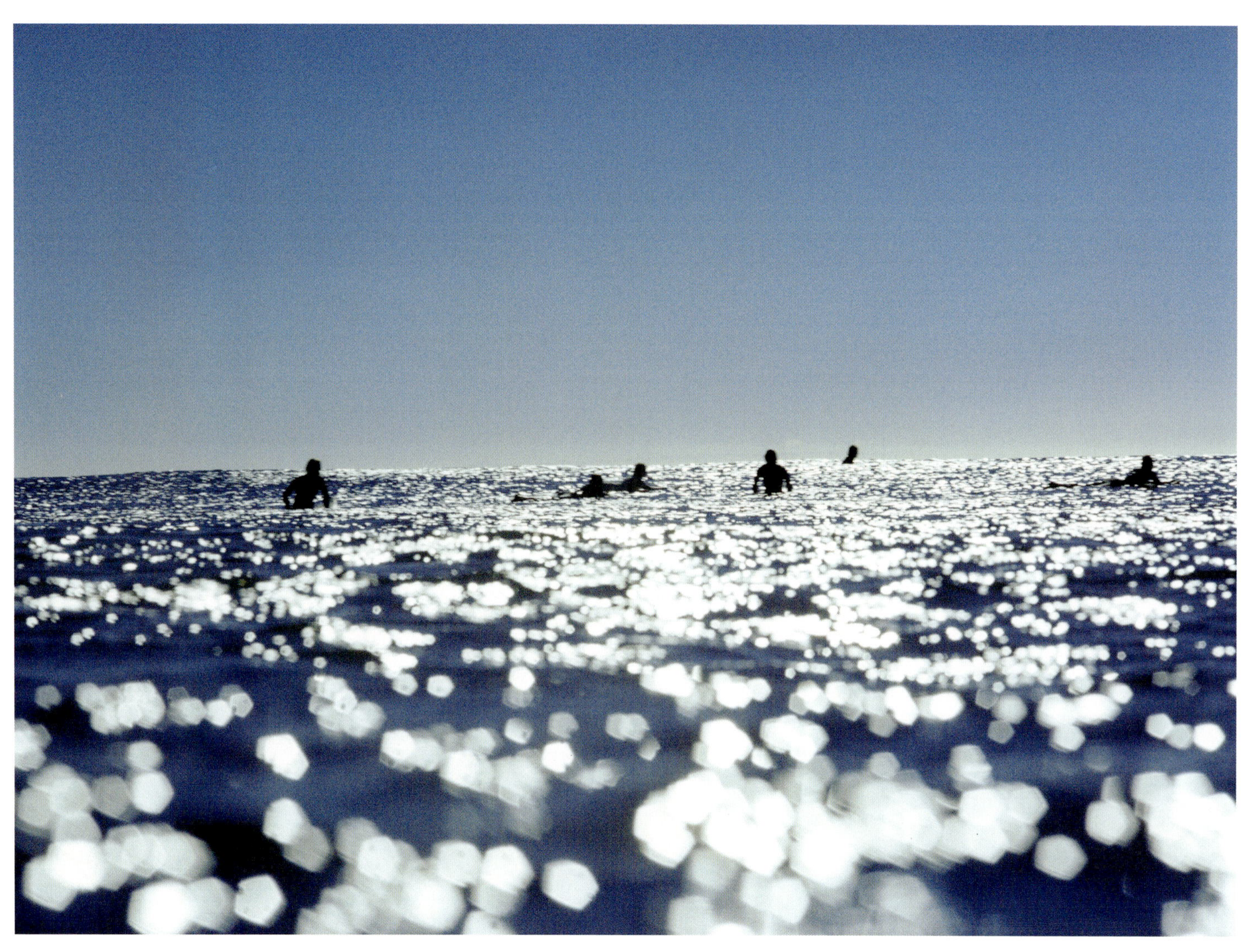

Hollister Ranch, Santa Barbara, CA 1972

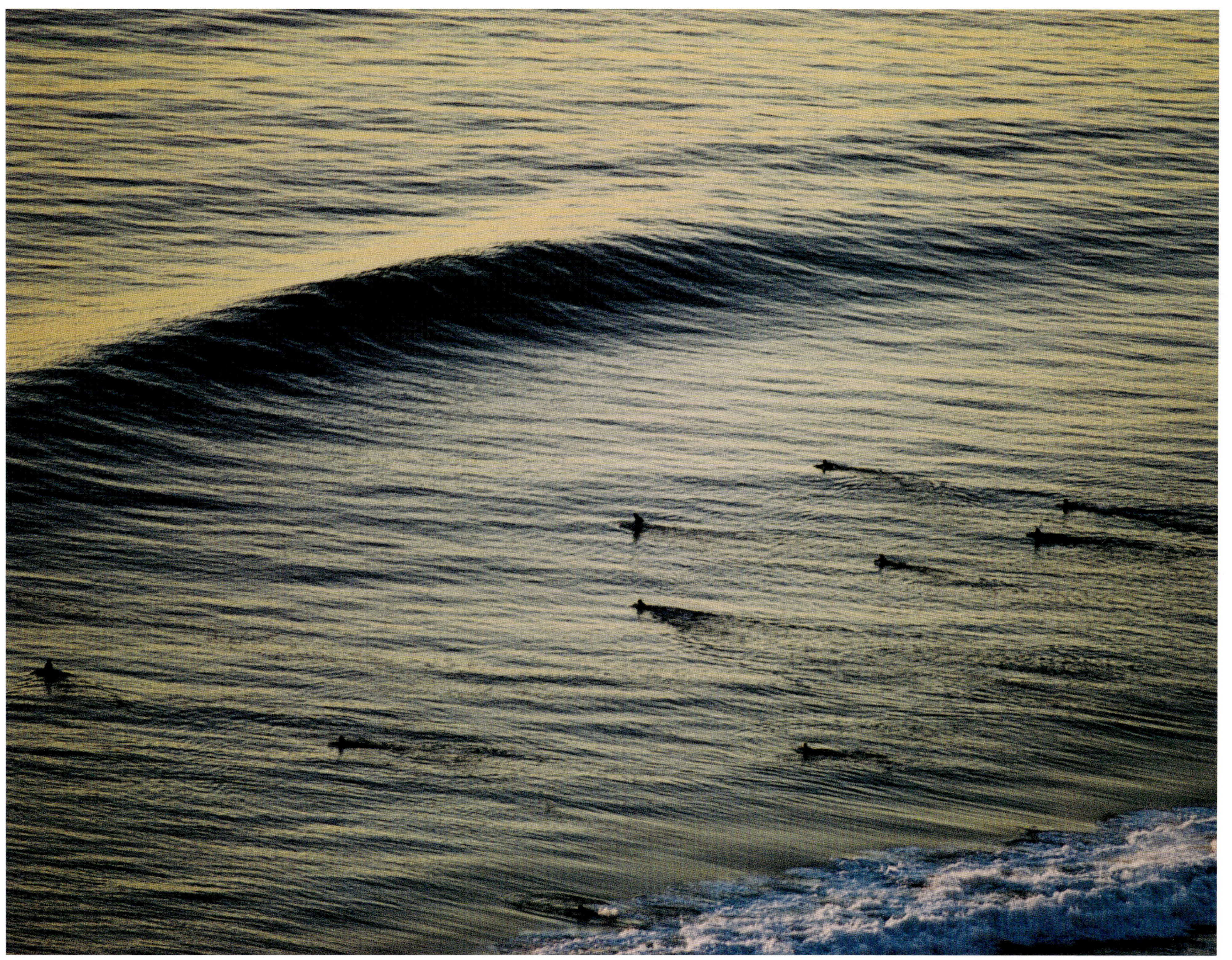

Blacks Beach, La Jolla, CA 1972

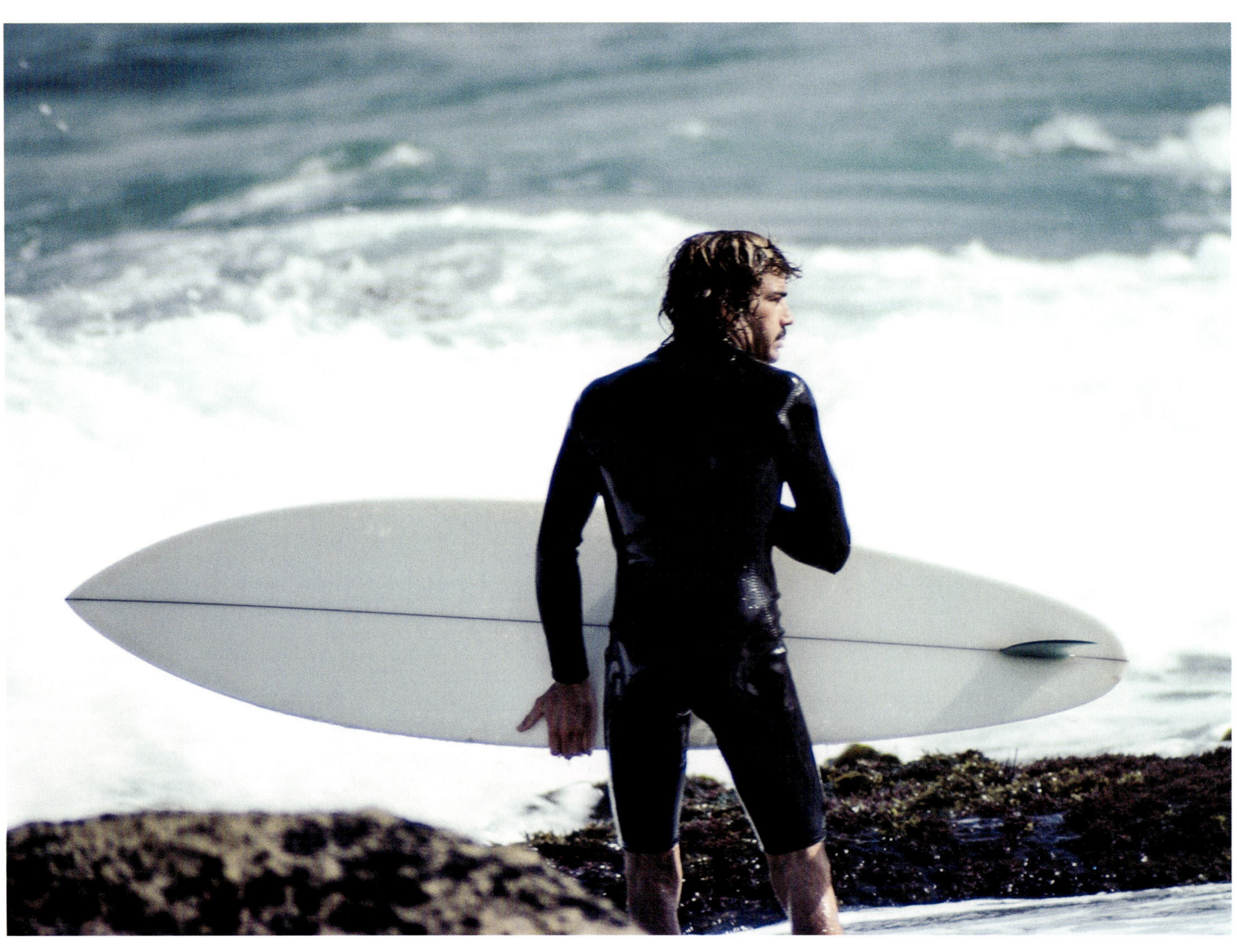

Michael Peterson, Johanna, Victoria, Australia 1976

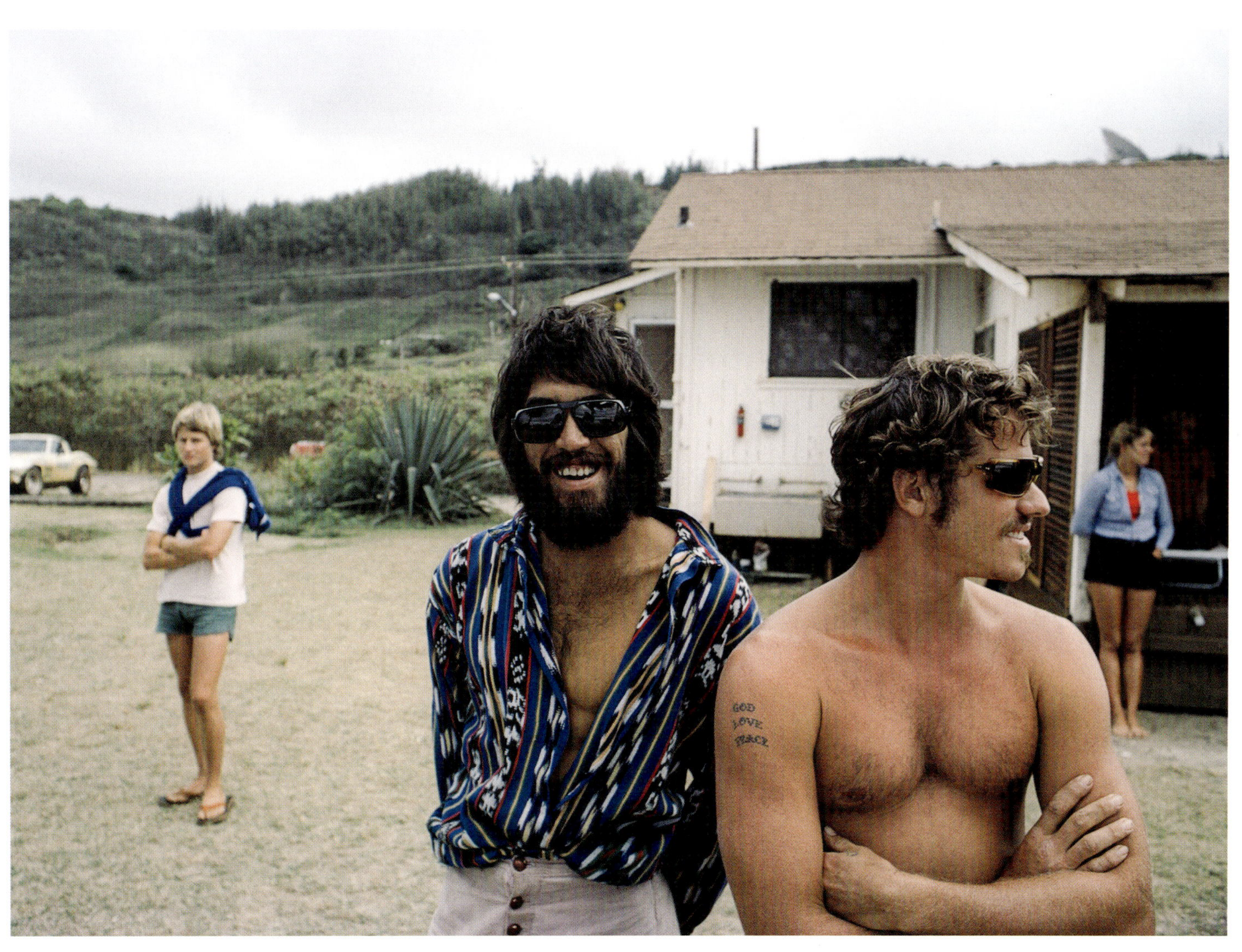

Glenn Kaulukukui, "Fast Eddie" Rothman, Sunset Beach, Oahu, HI 1976

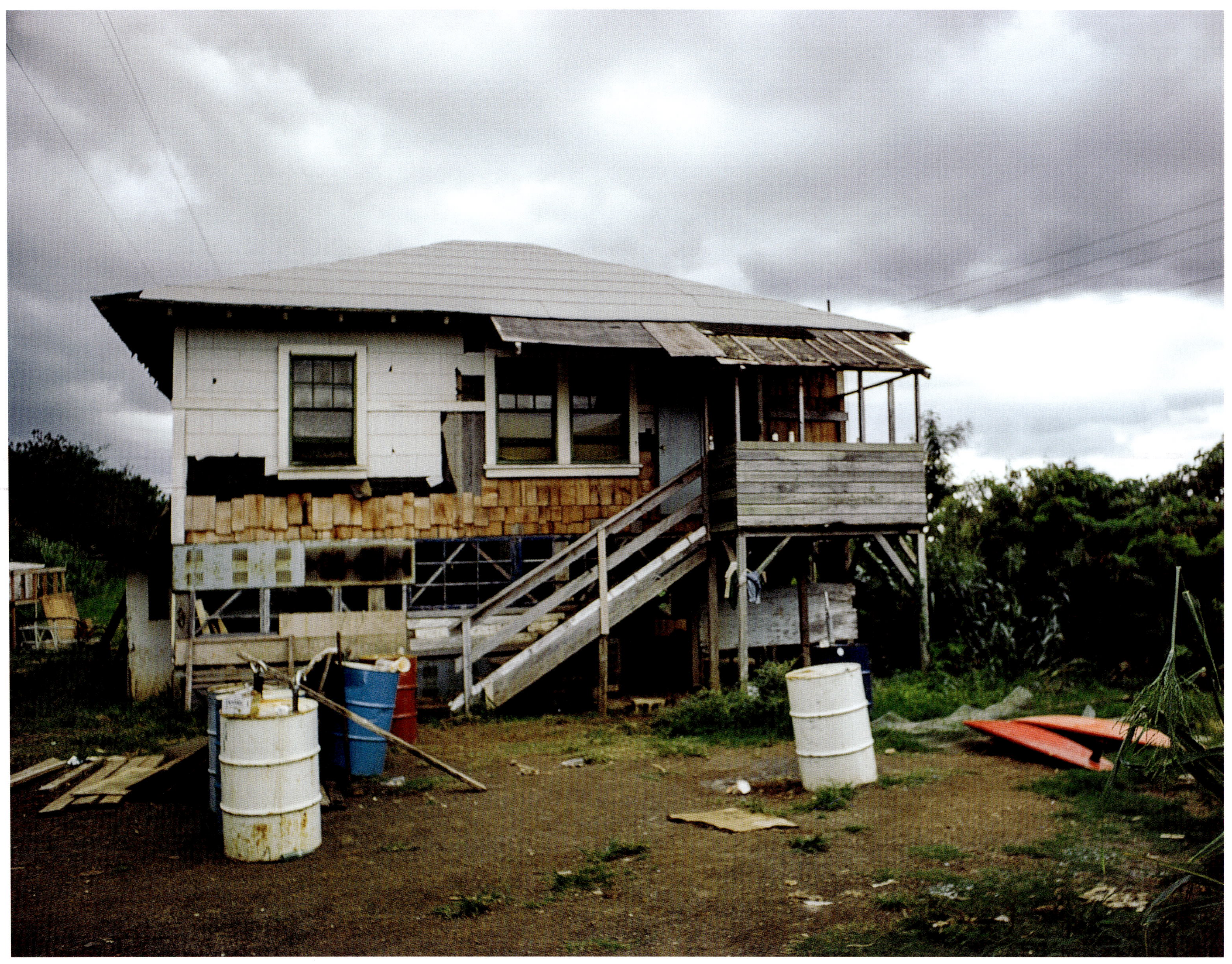

Bummer Hill, North Shore, Oahu, HI 1971

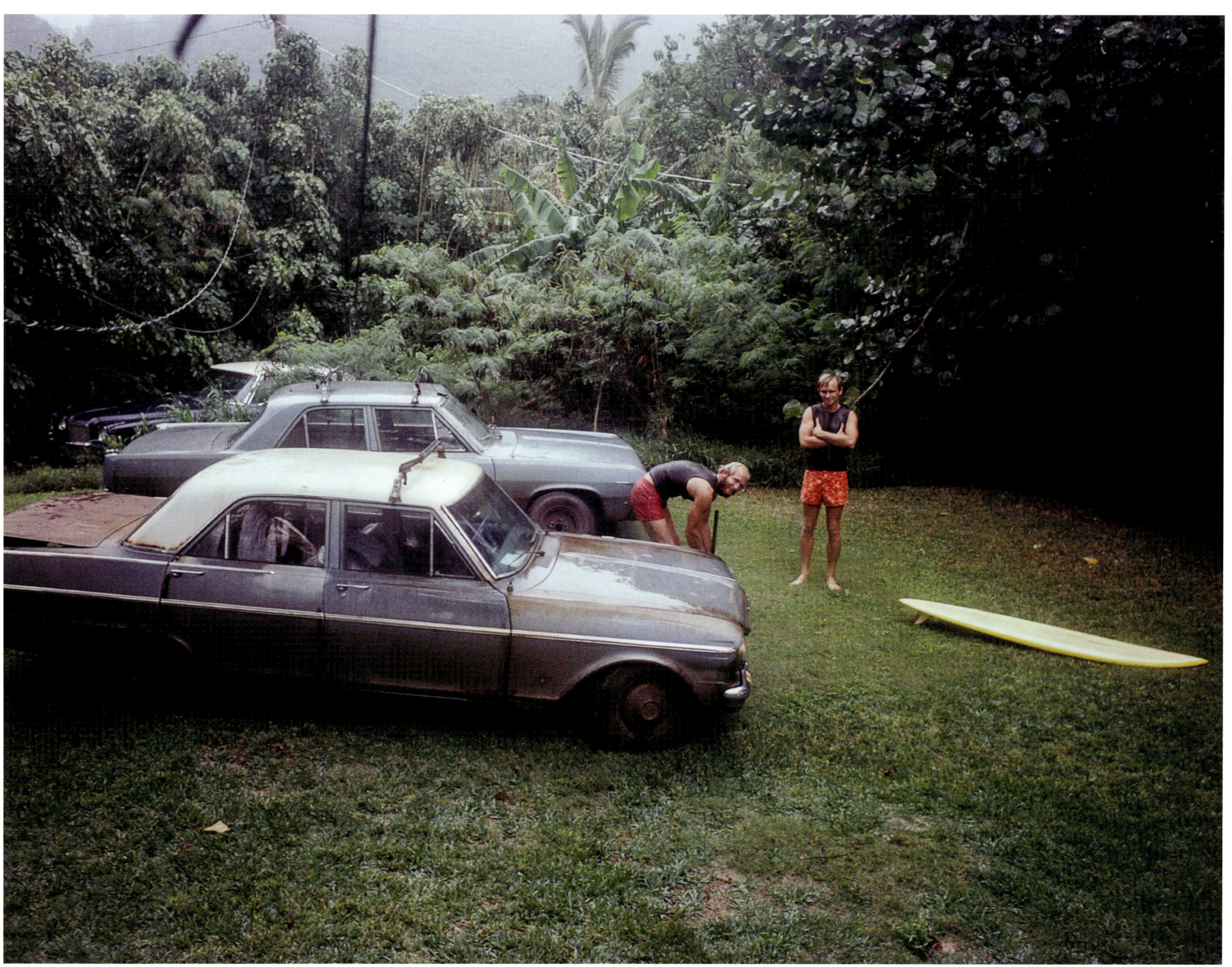

Bill Sikler and friend, Pipeline, Oahu, HI 1979

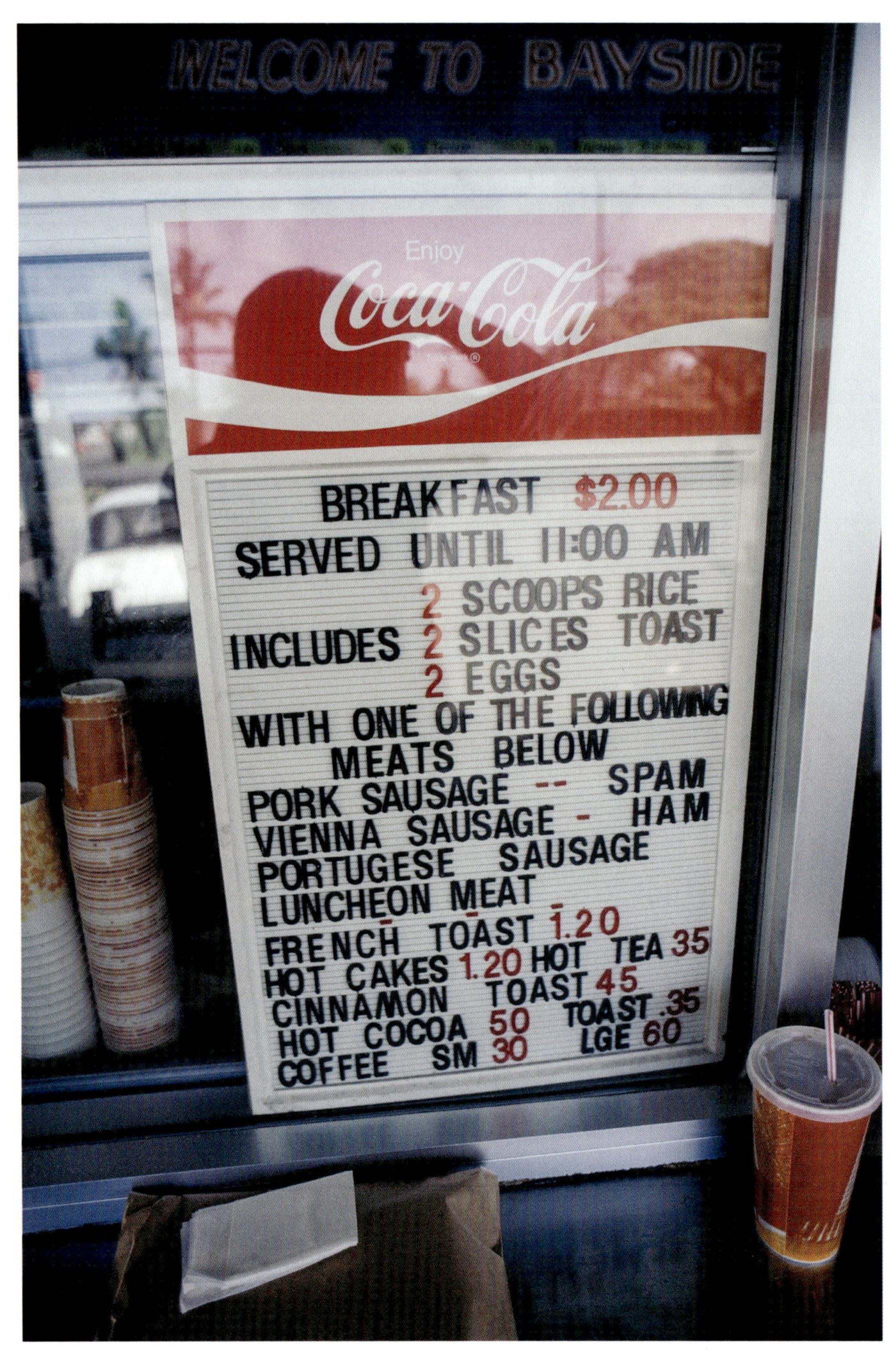

Waianae, Oahu, HI 1979

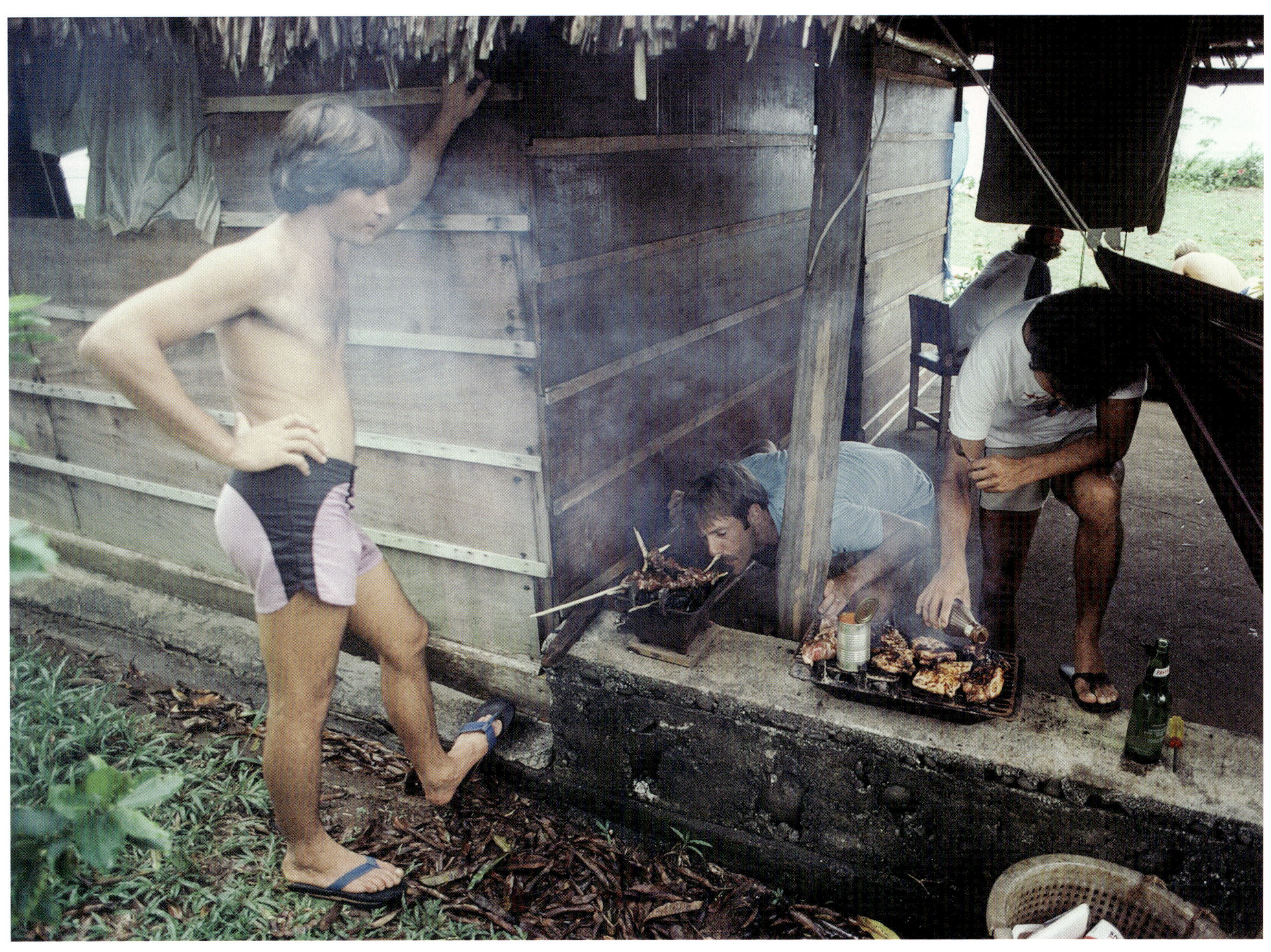

Ken Meyers, Tom Pool, Richard Icaza, Catalina, Panama 1979

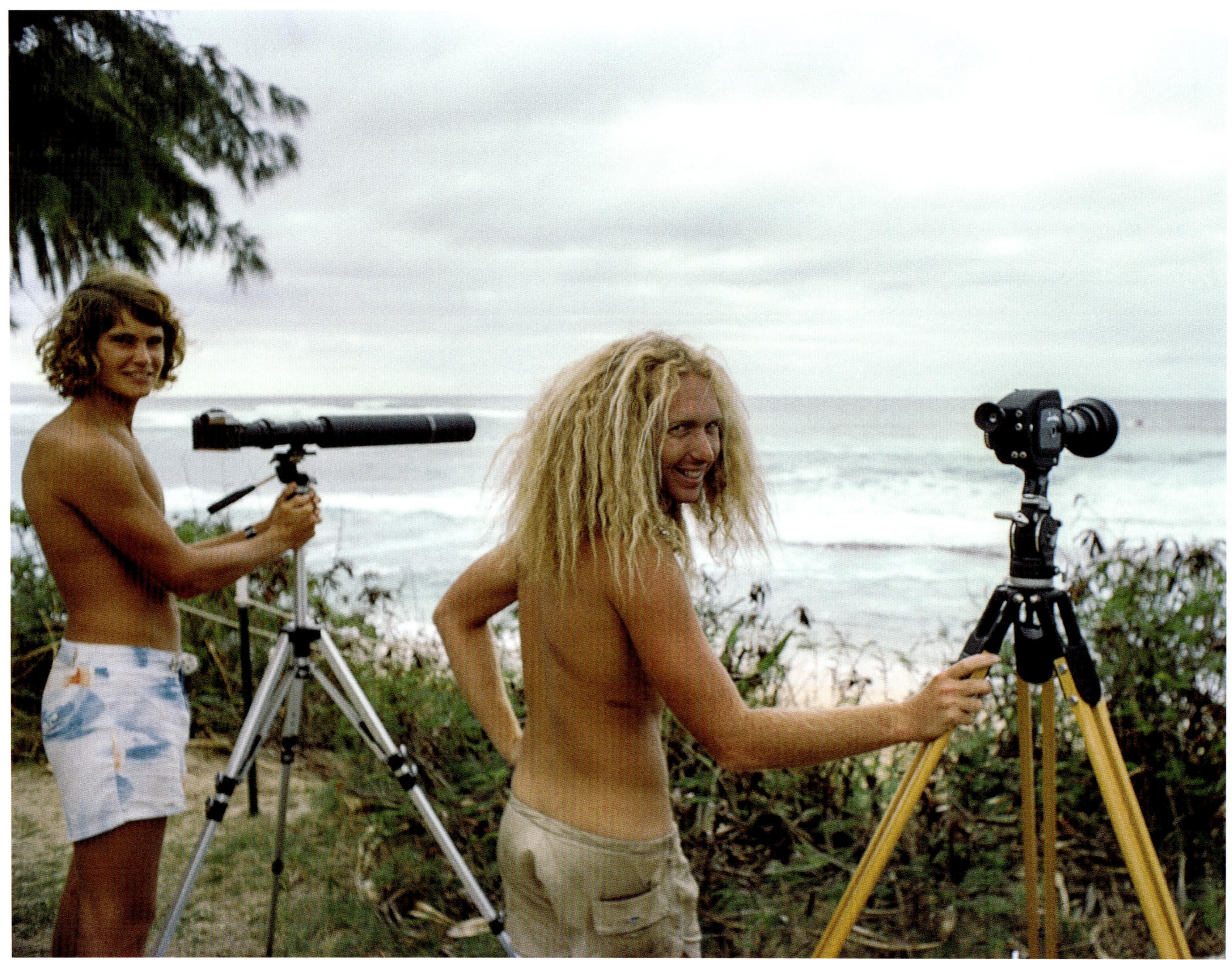

Sunset Beach, Oahu, HI 1976

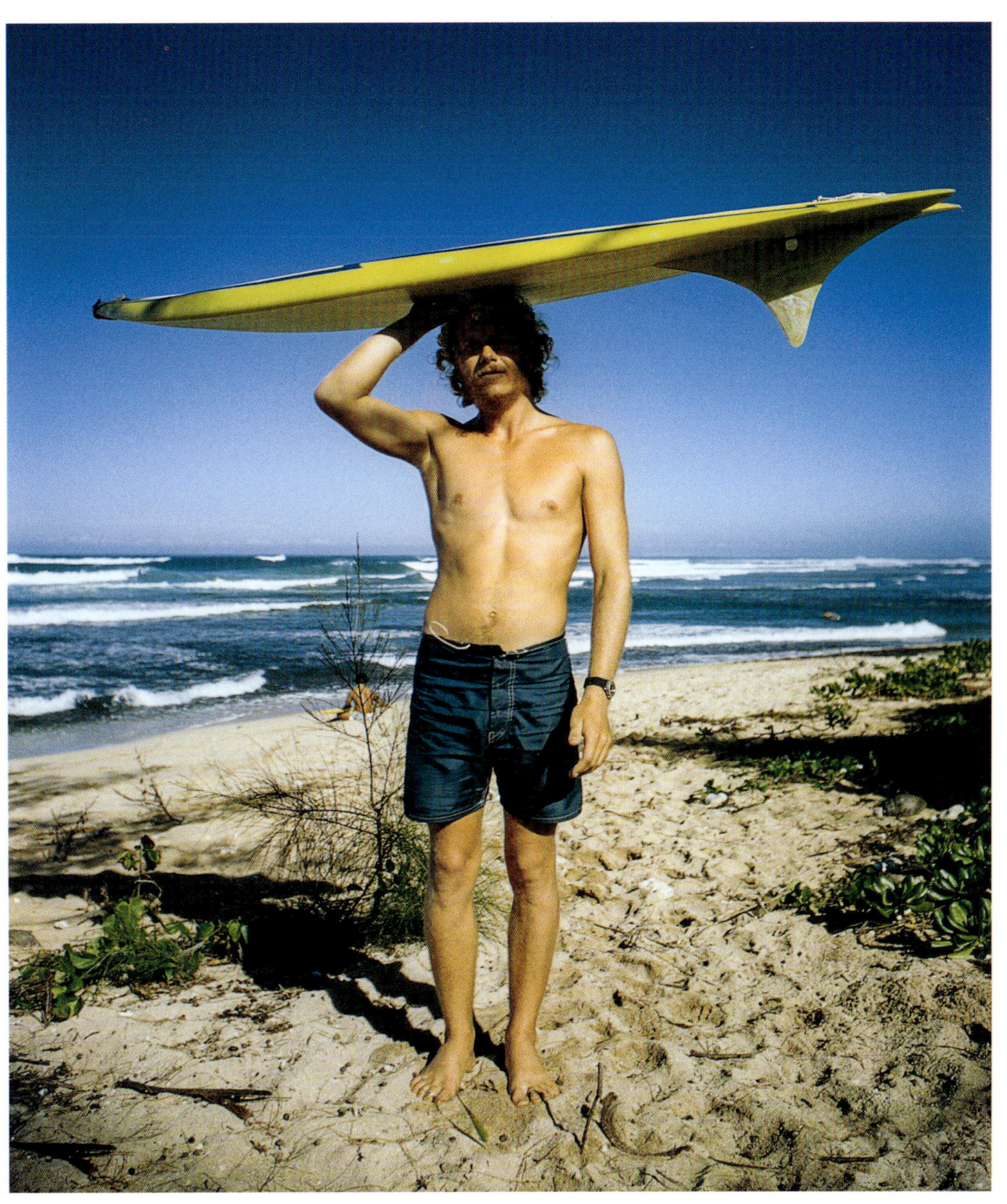

Steve Seebold, Velzyland, Oahu, HI 1973

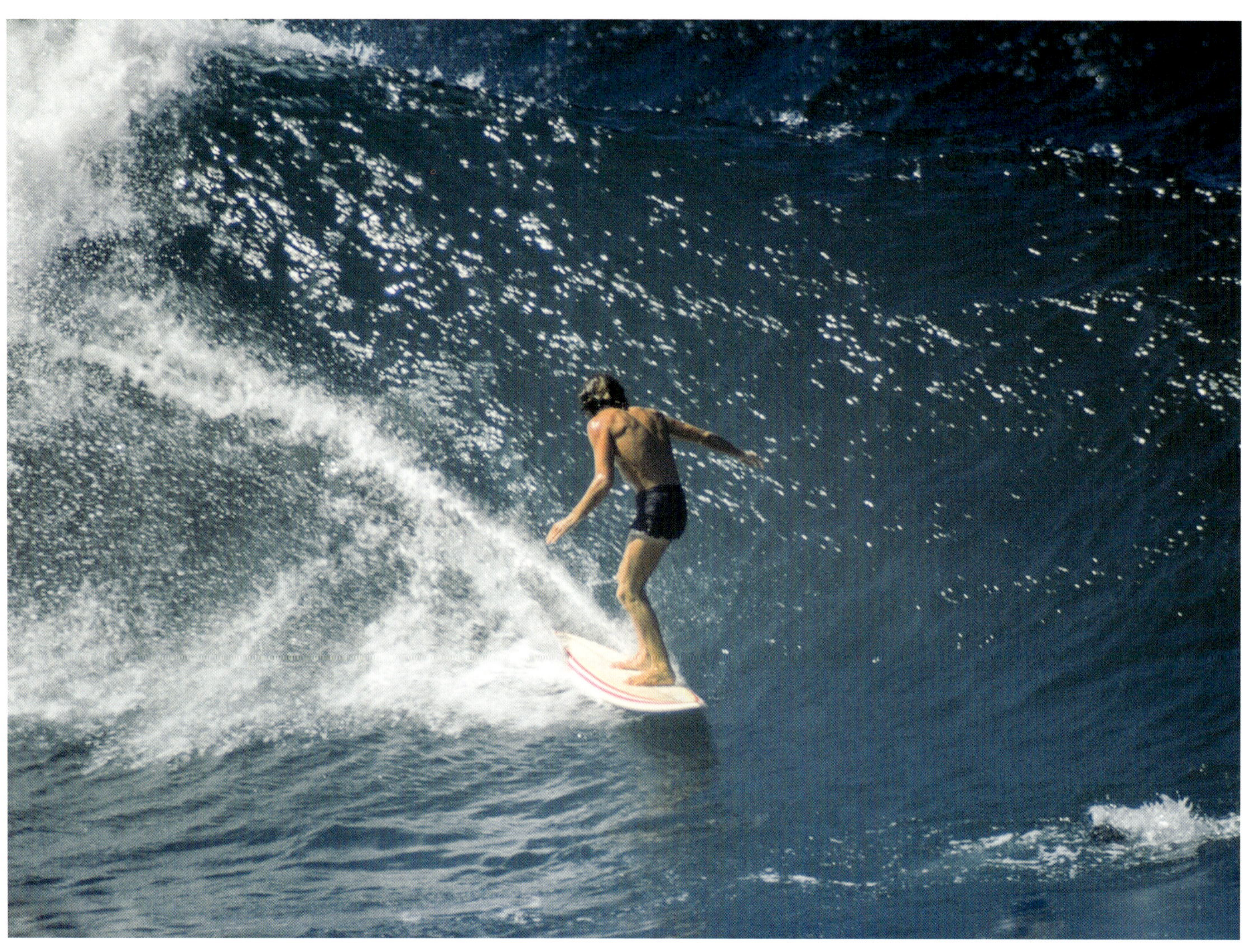

Craig “Owl” Chapman, Pipeline, Oahu, HI 1975

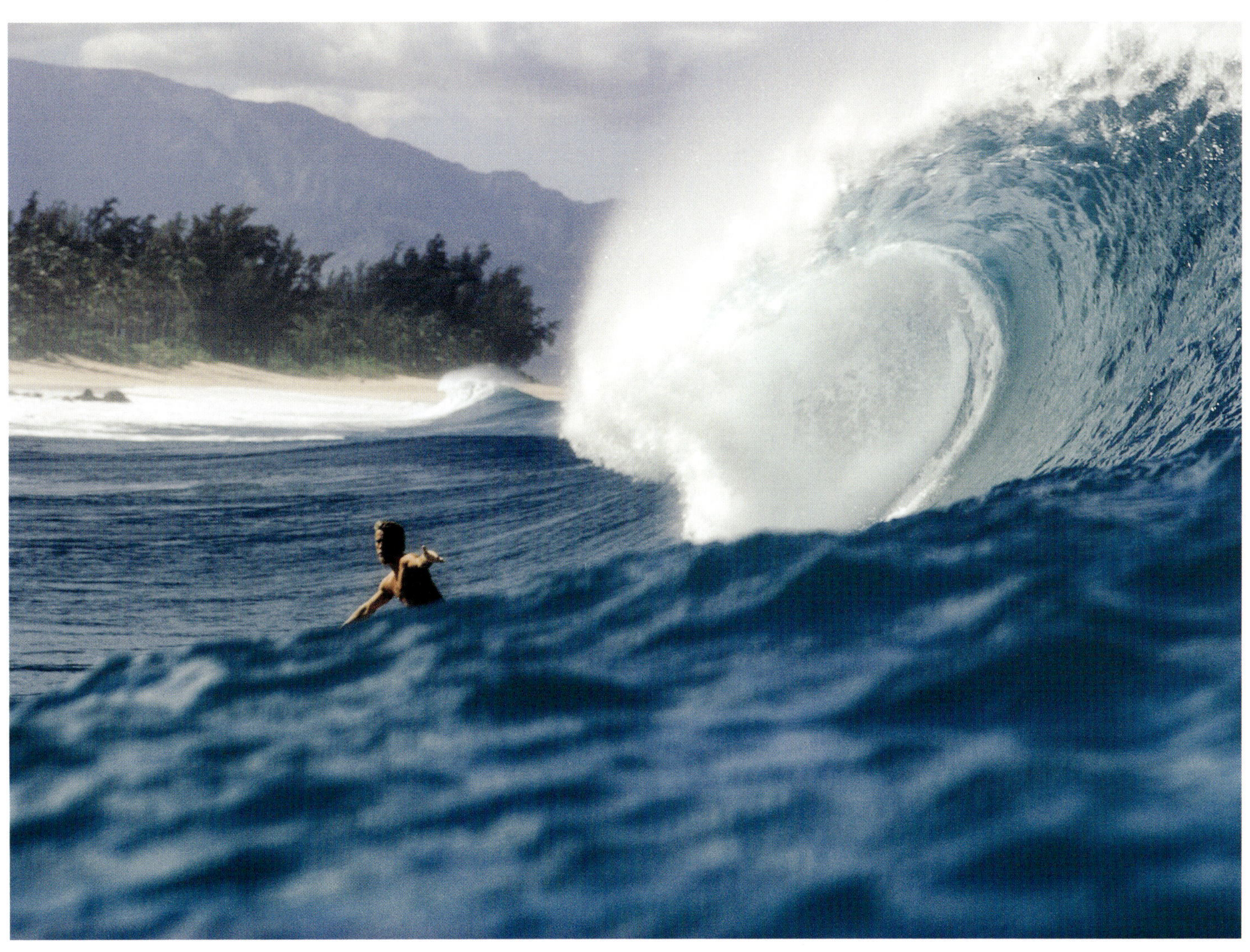

Braxton Grizzard, Pipeline, Oahu, HI 1973

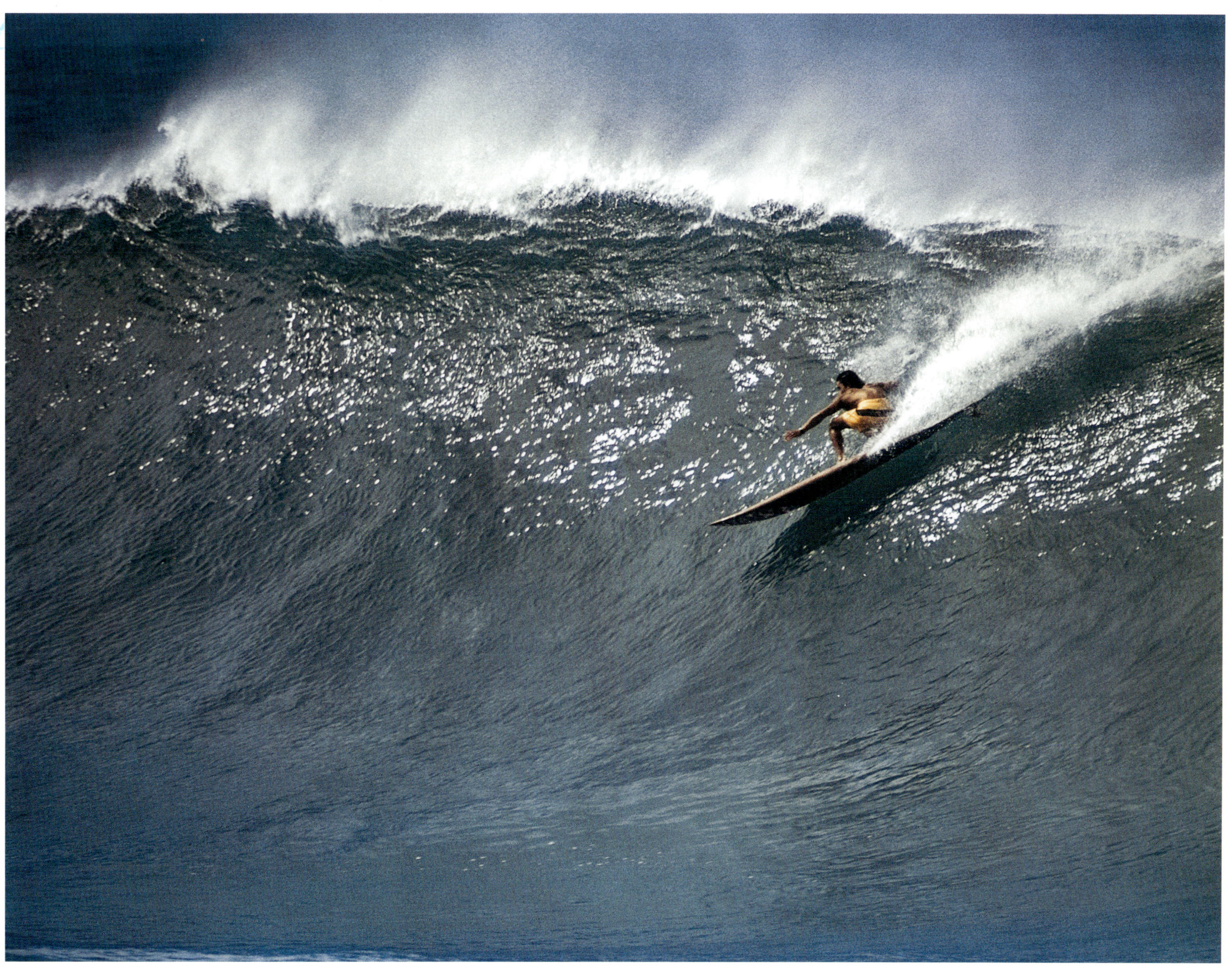

Reno Abellira, Waimea Bay, Oahu, HI 1973

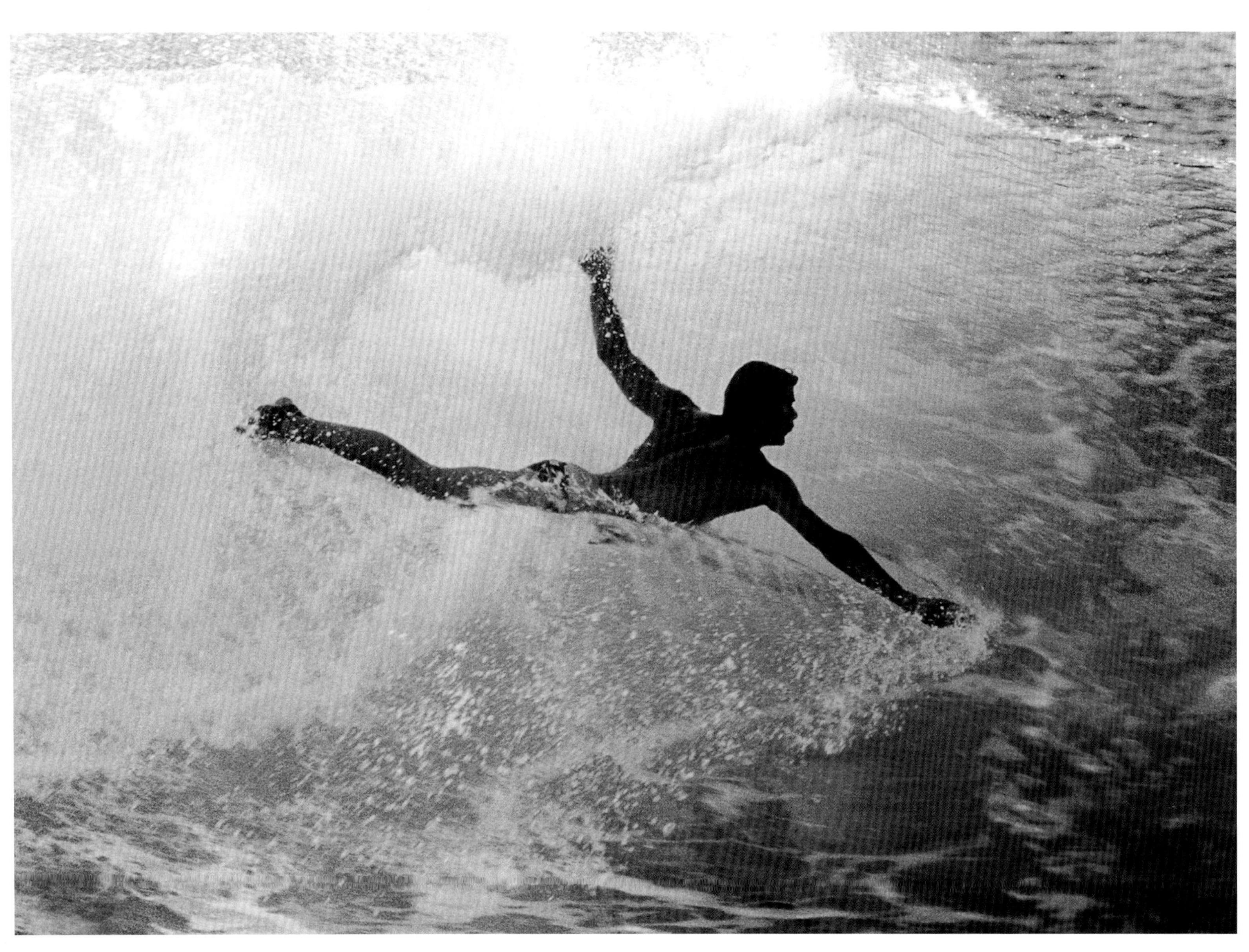

Glen" Redwings" Whitford, Pipeline, Oahu, HI 1977

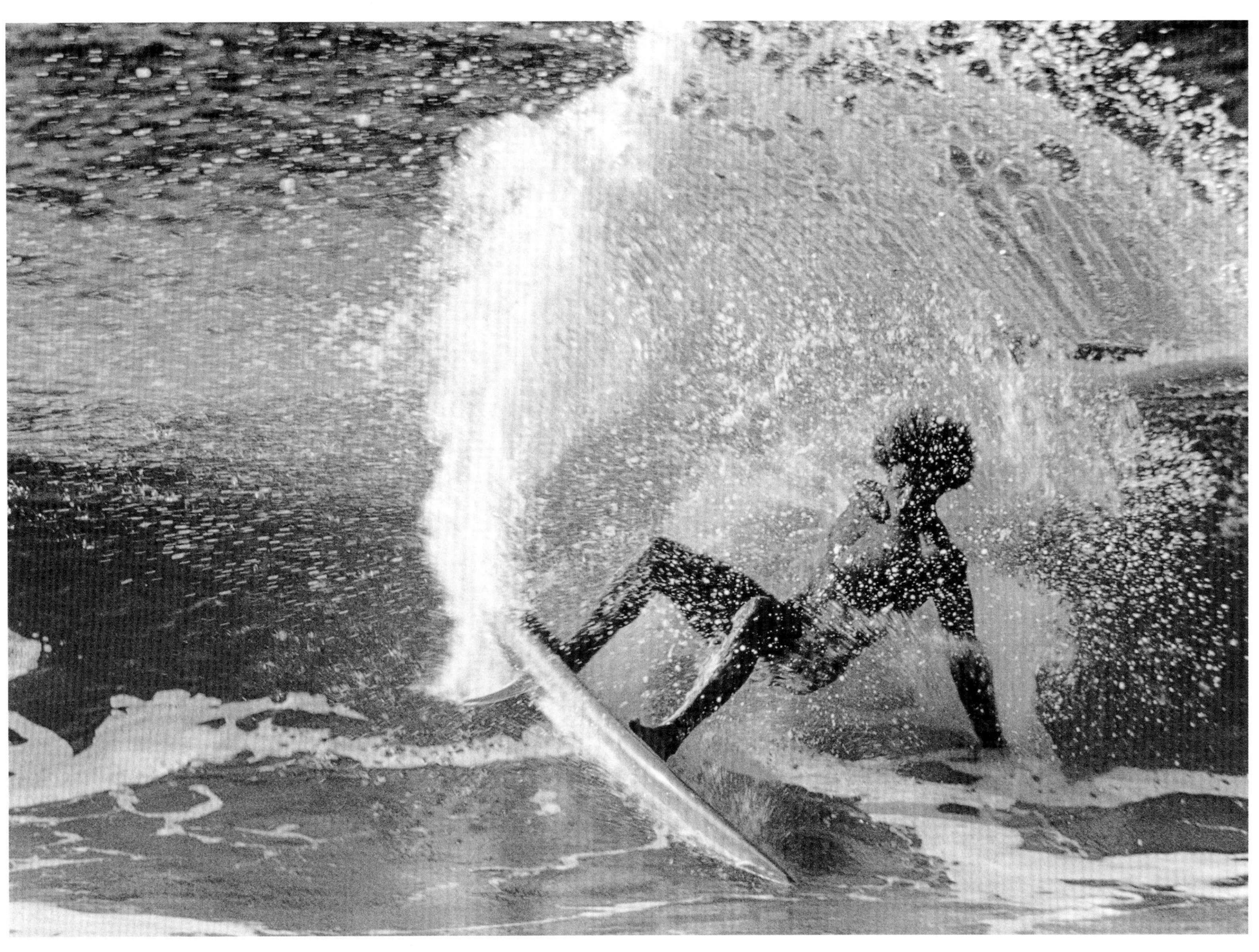

Buttons Kaluhiokalani, Off The Wall, Oahu, HI 1978

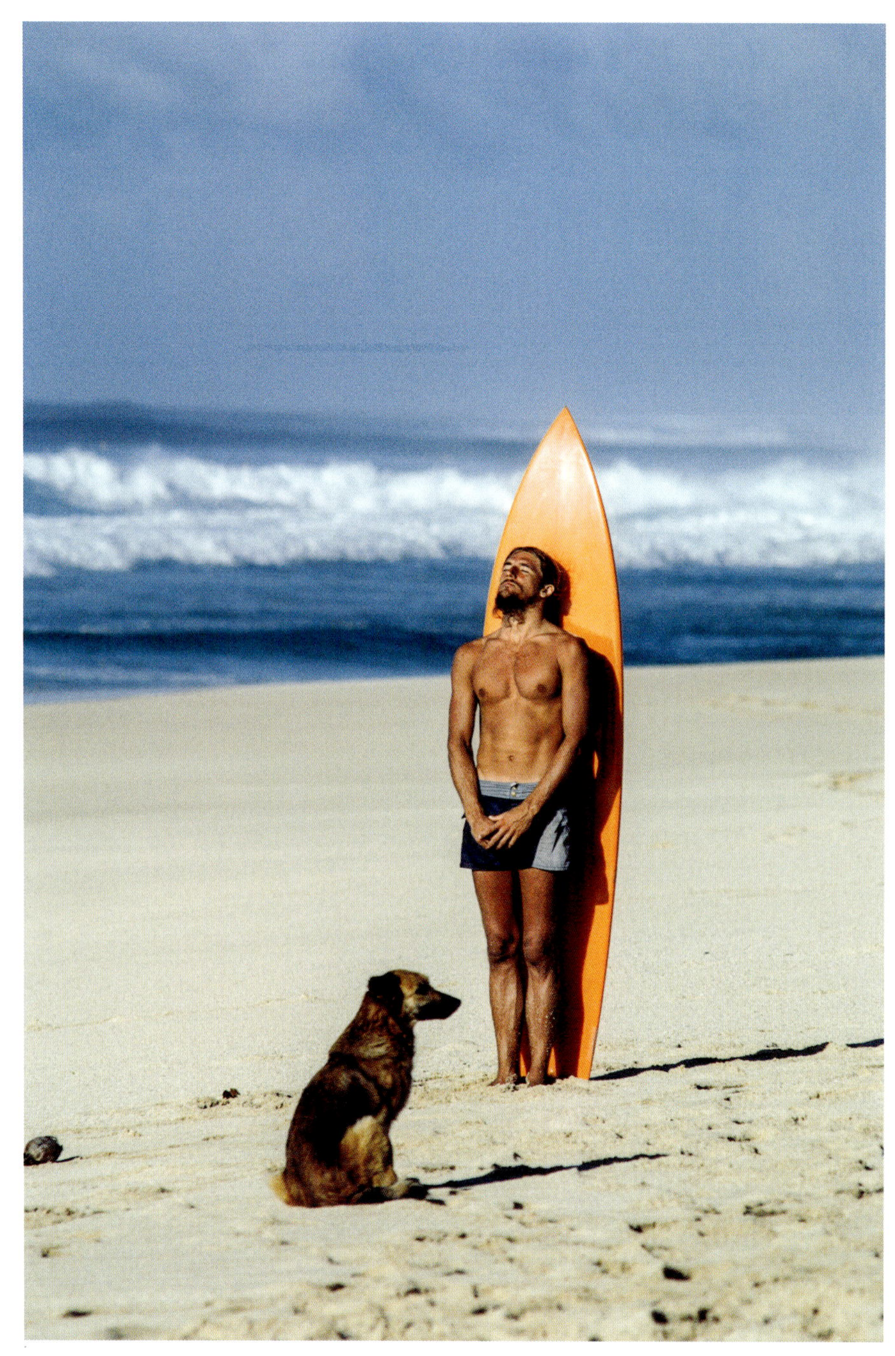

Meditate, Pipeline, Oahu, HI 1979

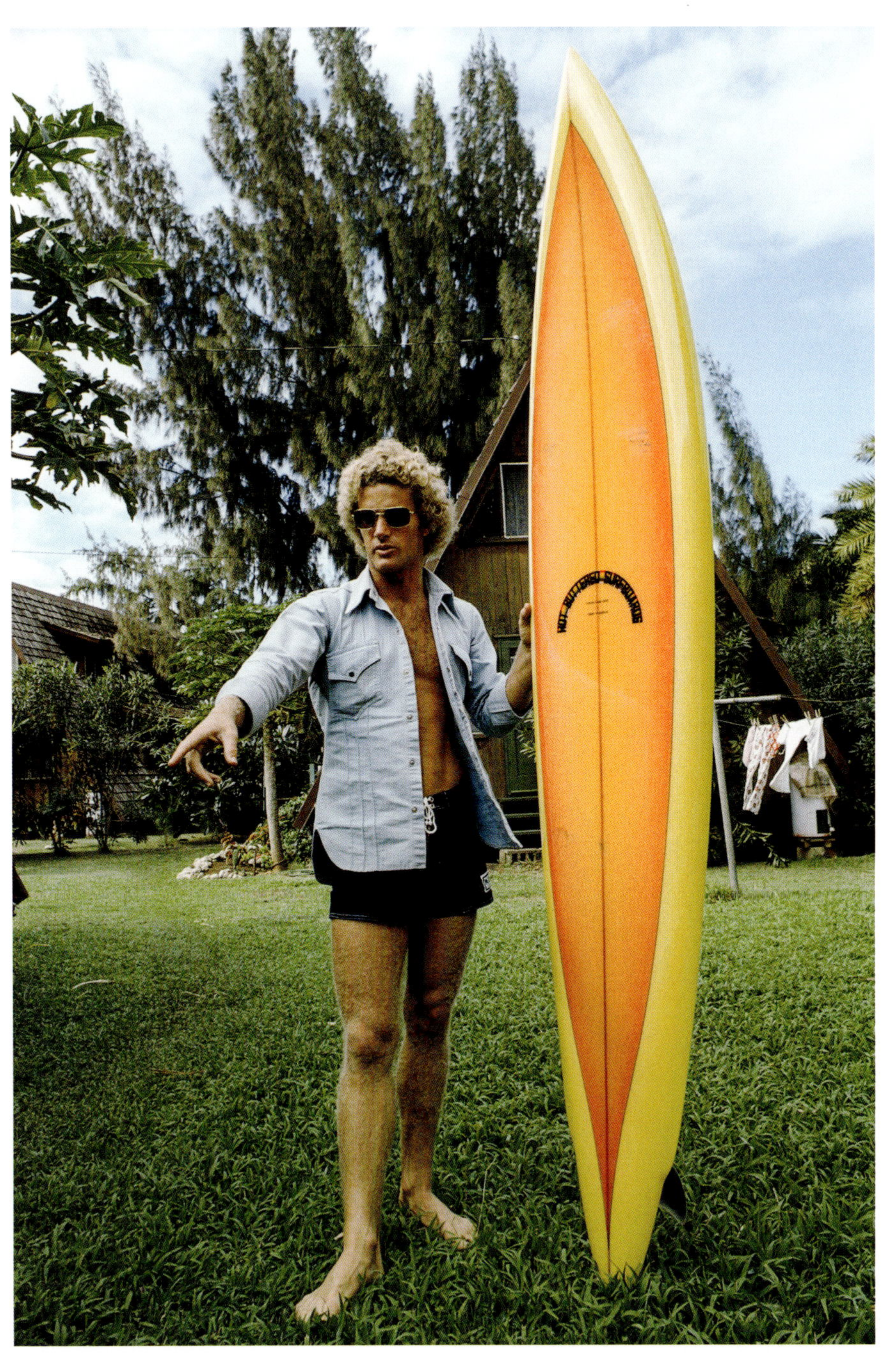

Terry Fitzgerald, Rocky Point, Oahu, HI 1975

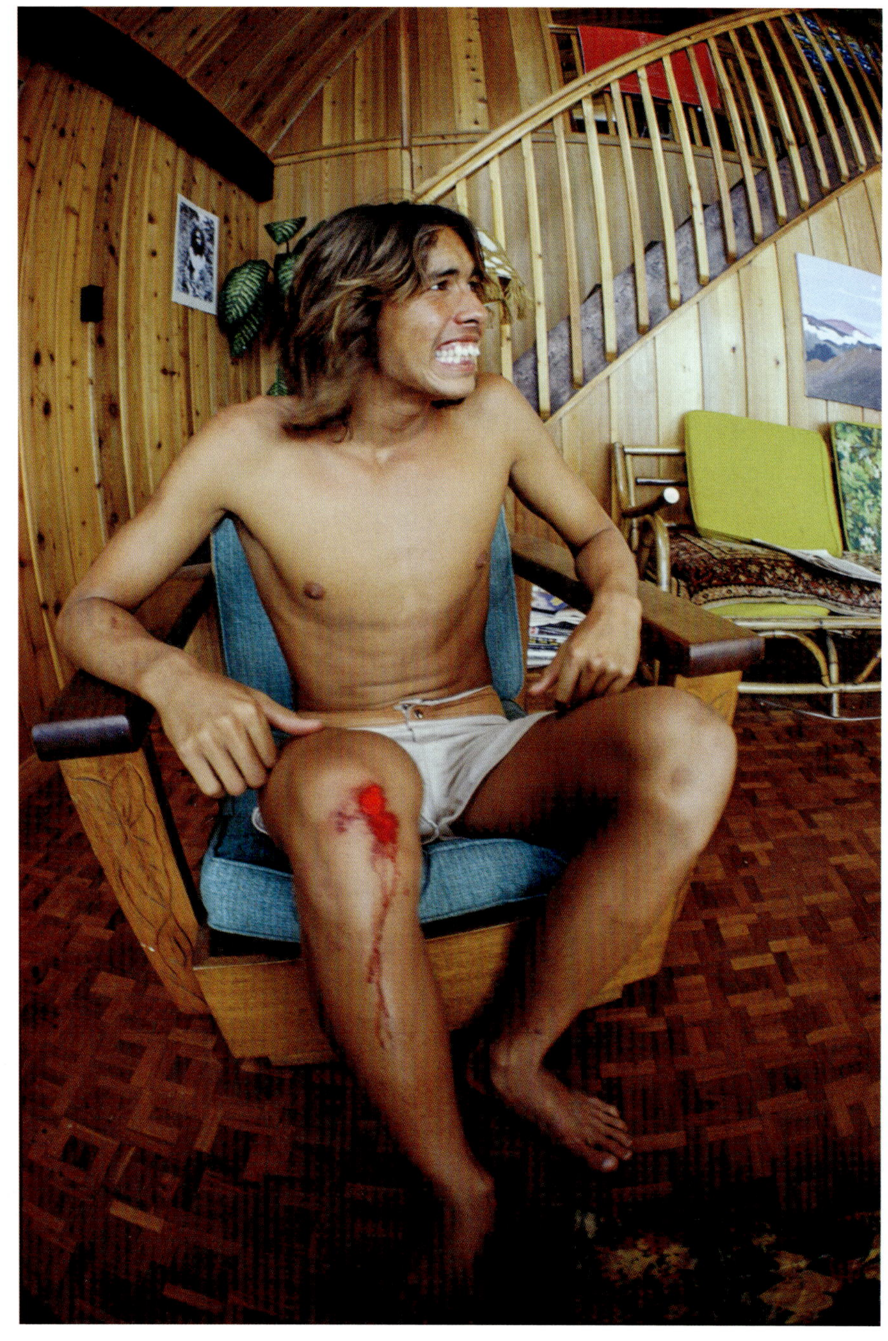

Mark Liddell, Off The Wall, Oahu, HI 1975

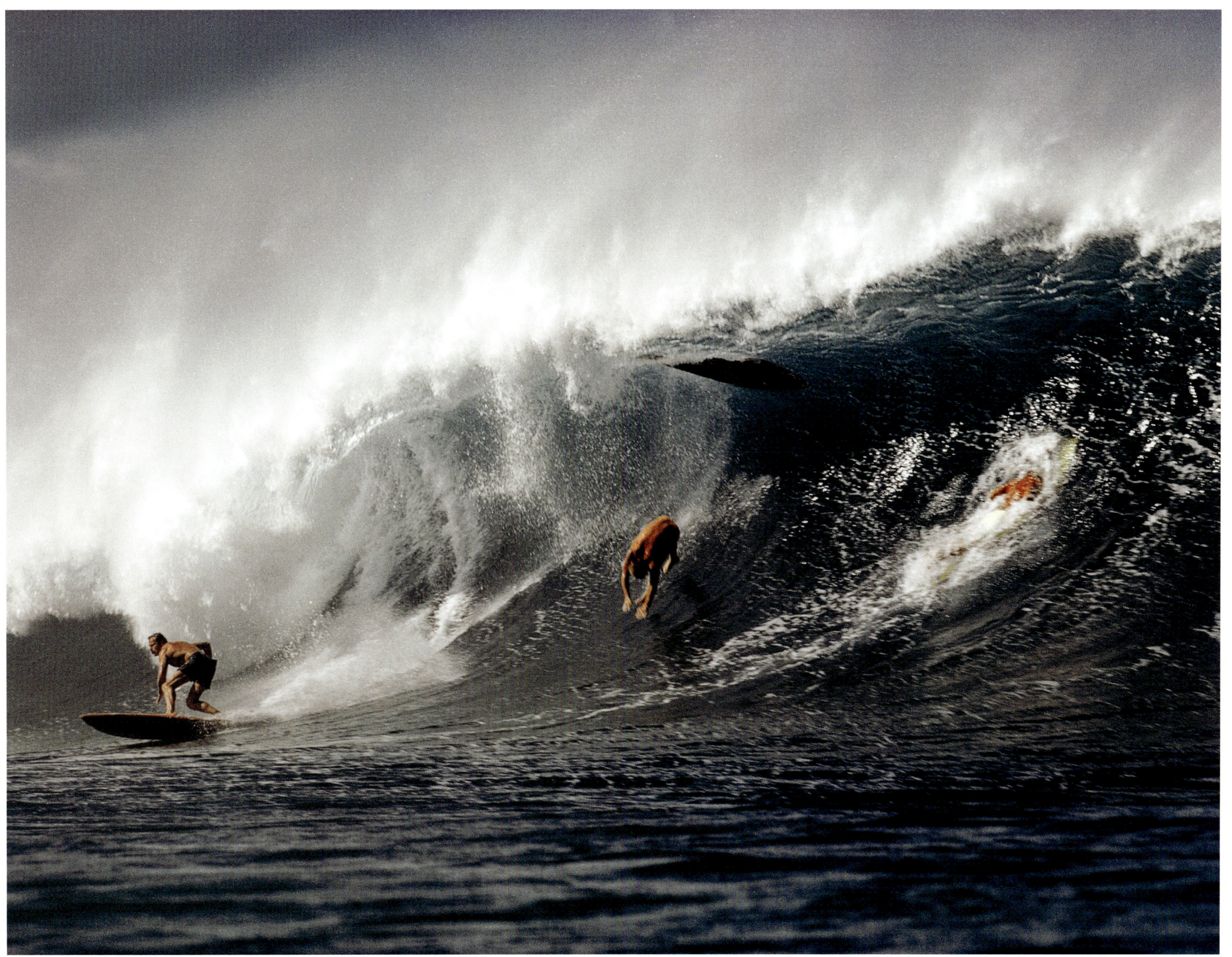

Low Tide, Pipeline, Oahu, HI 1973

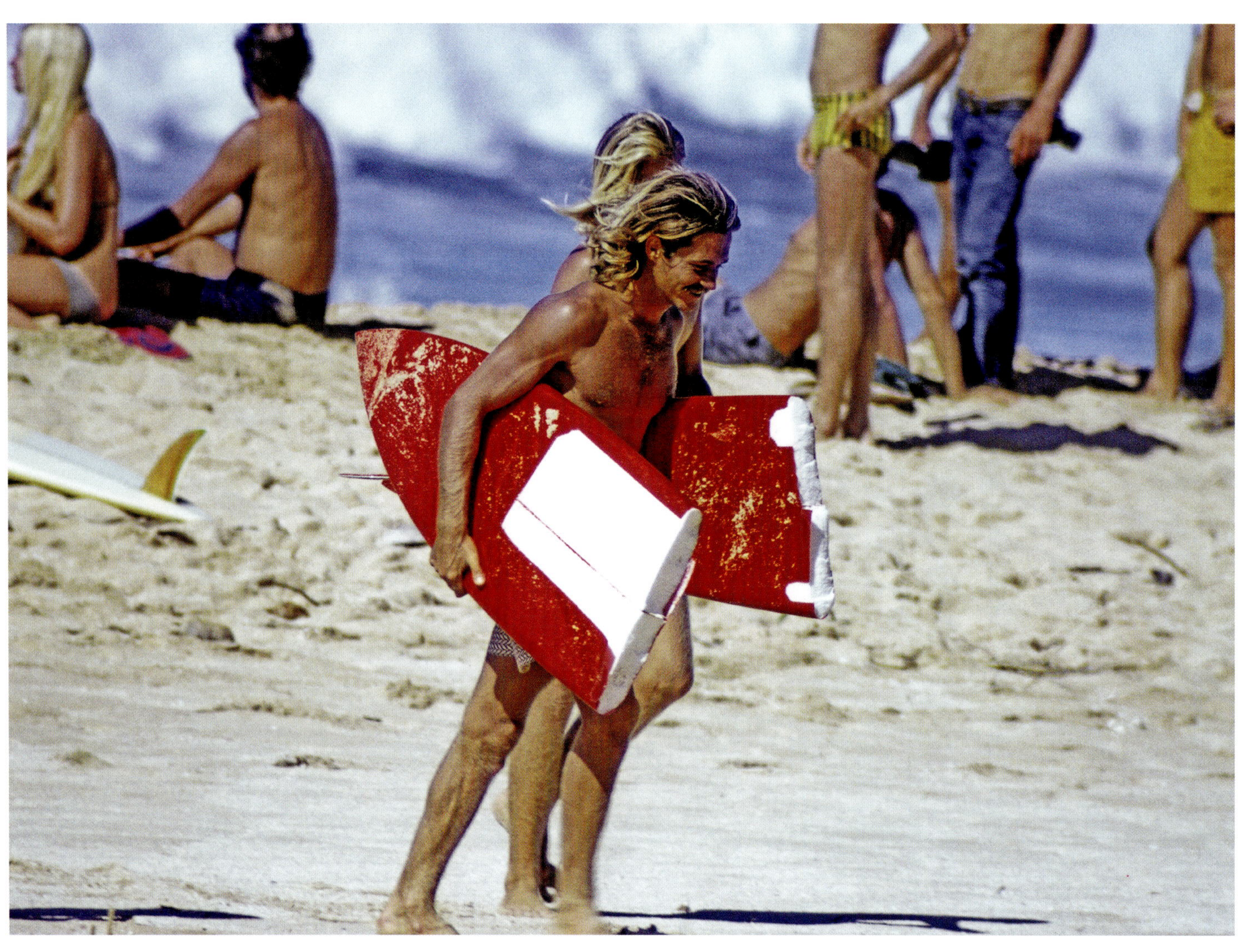

Roger Kincaid, Pipeline, Oahu, HI 1973

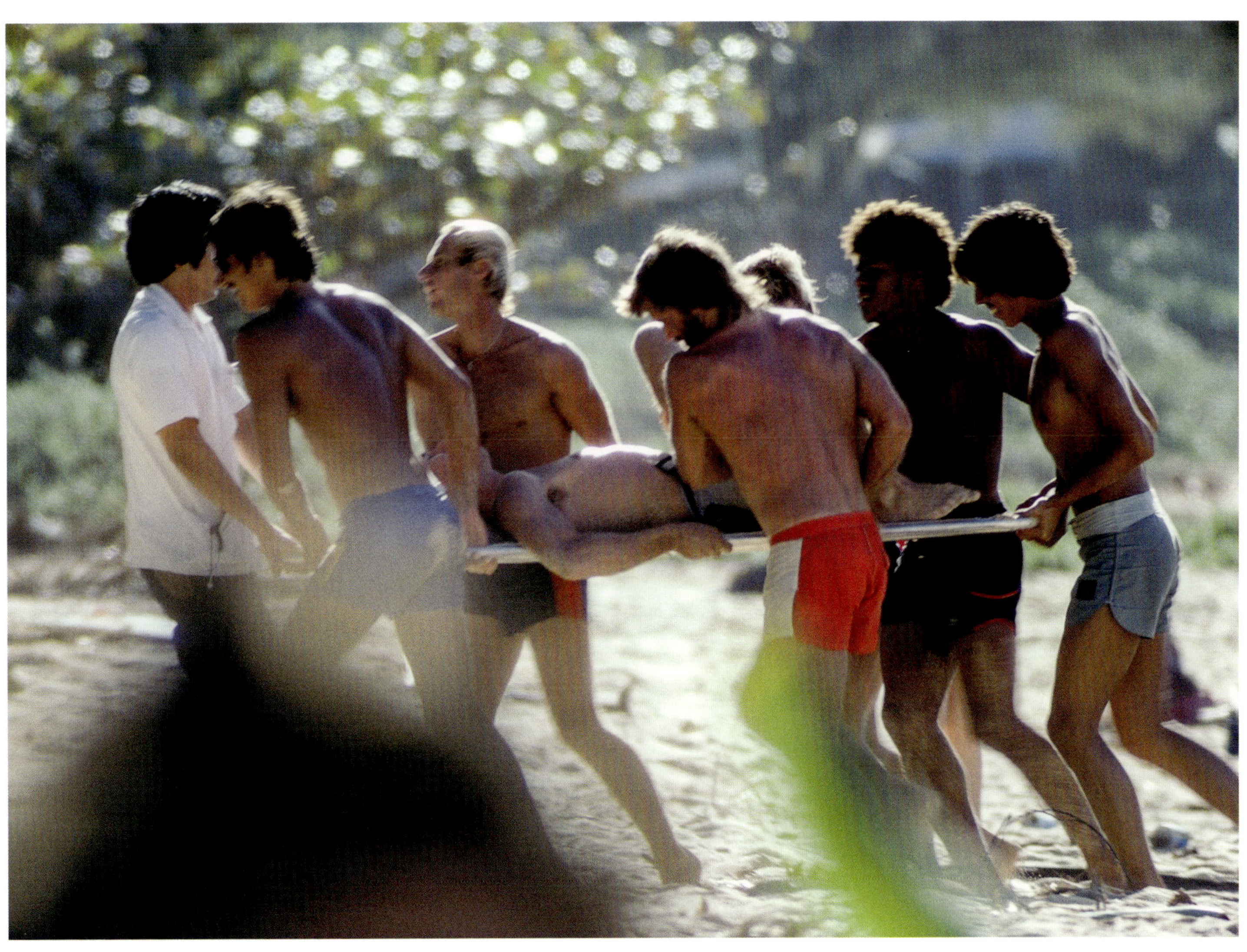

Rescue with Bernie Baker, Ken Bradshaw, Buttons Kaluhiokalani, Mark Liddell, Pipeline, Oahu, HI 1979

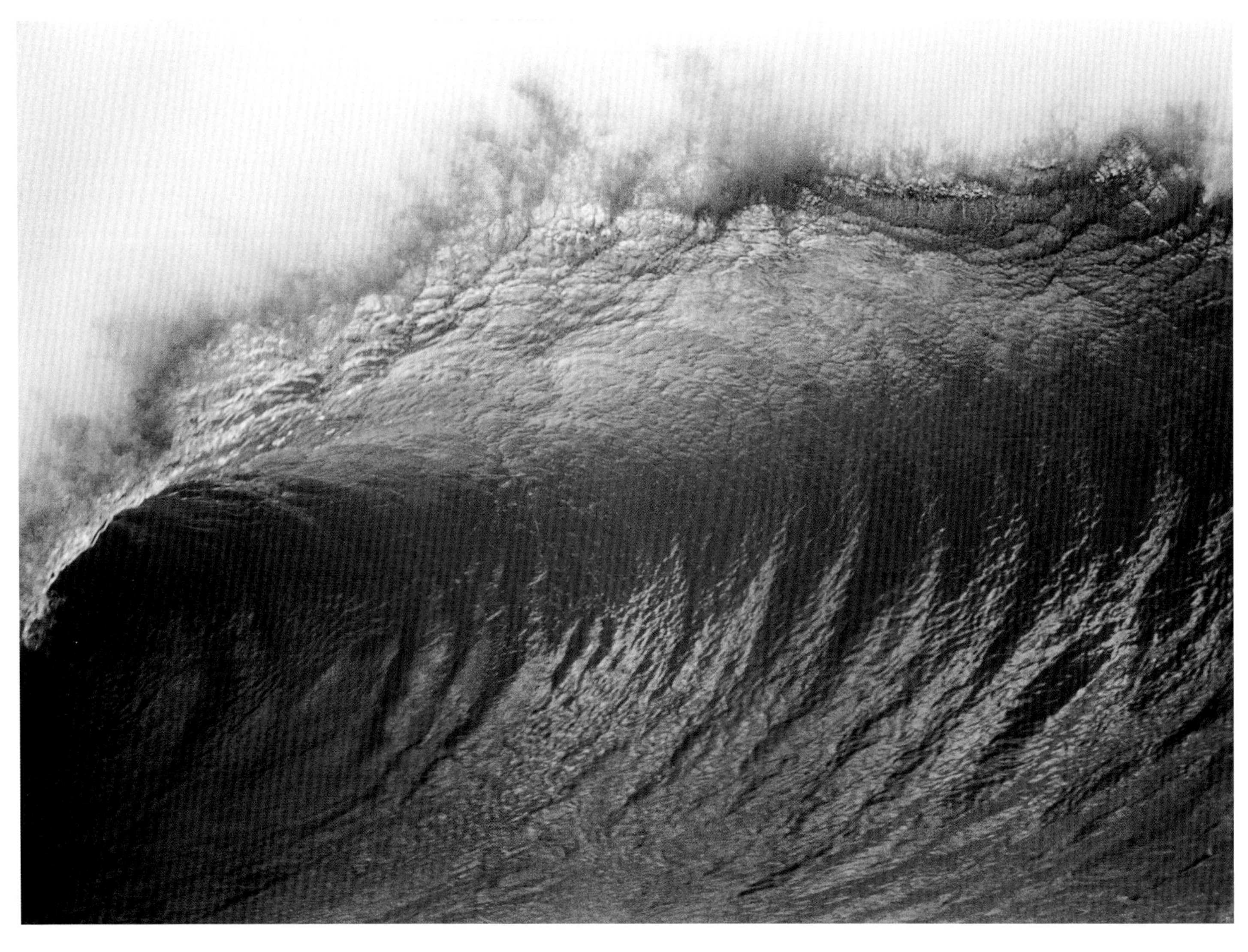

Pipeline, Oahu, HI 1971

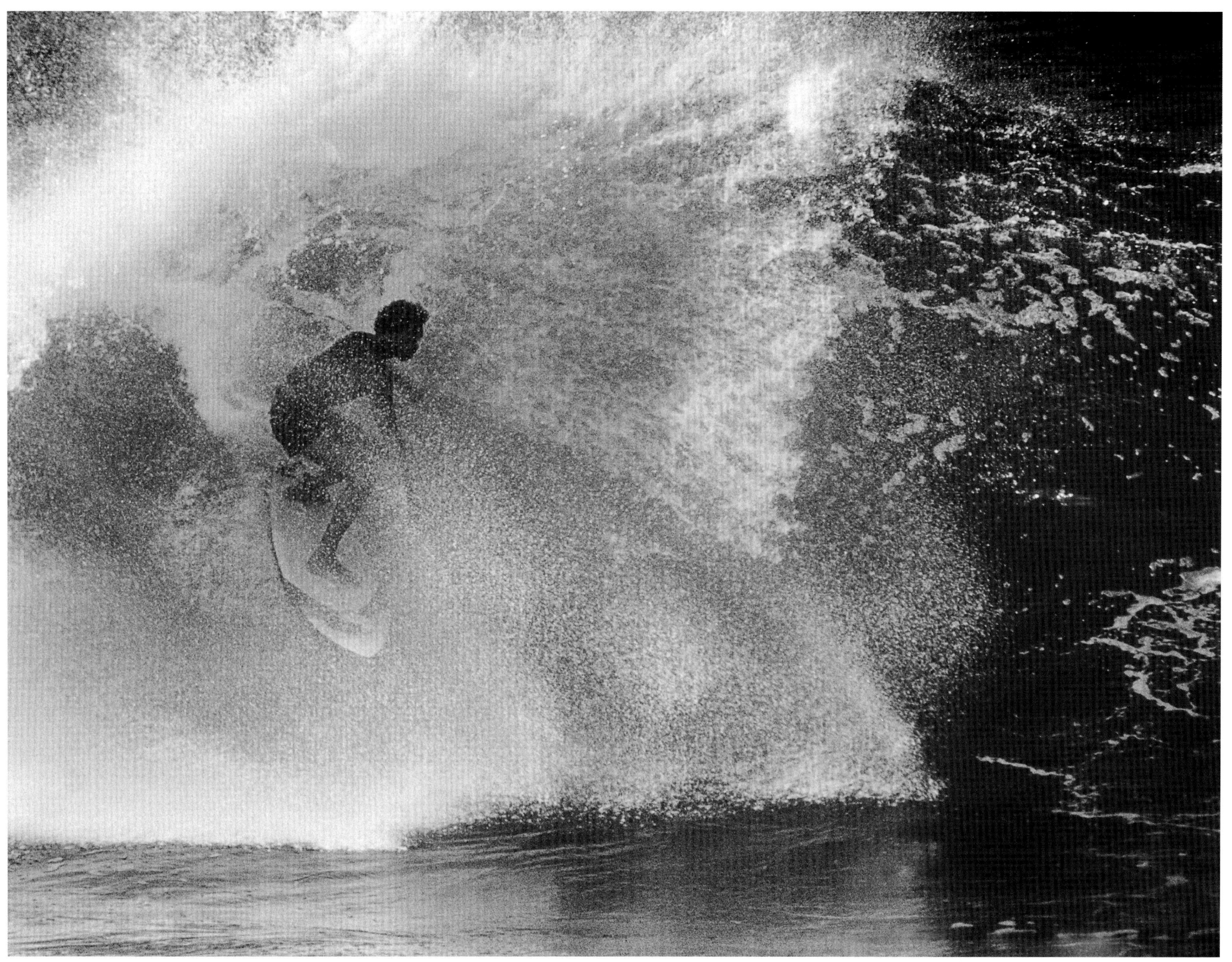

Marvin Foster, Pipeline, Oahu, HI 1979

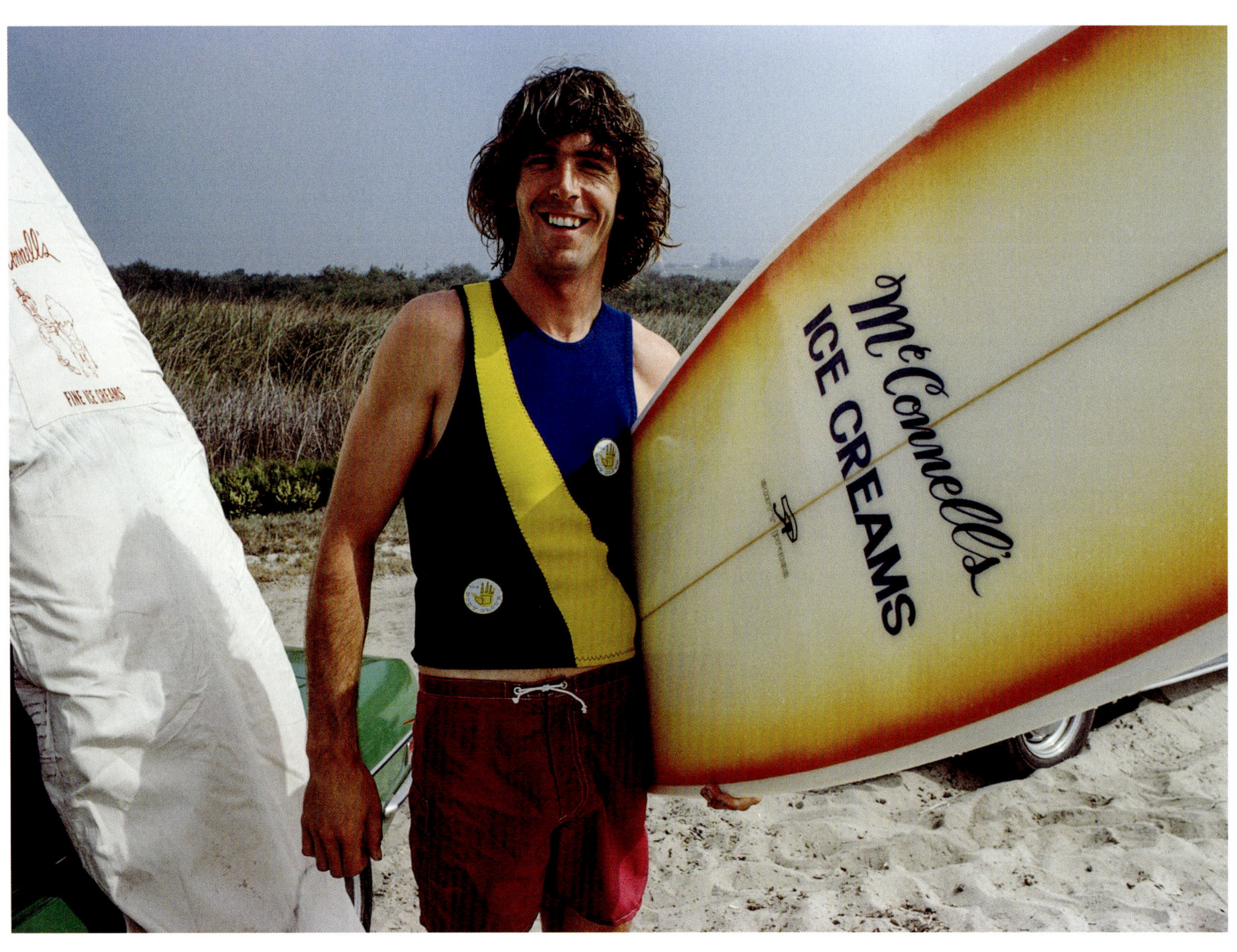

Scott Price, Lower Trestle, San Clemente, ca 1977

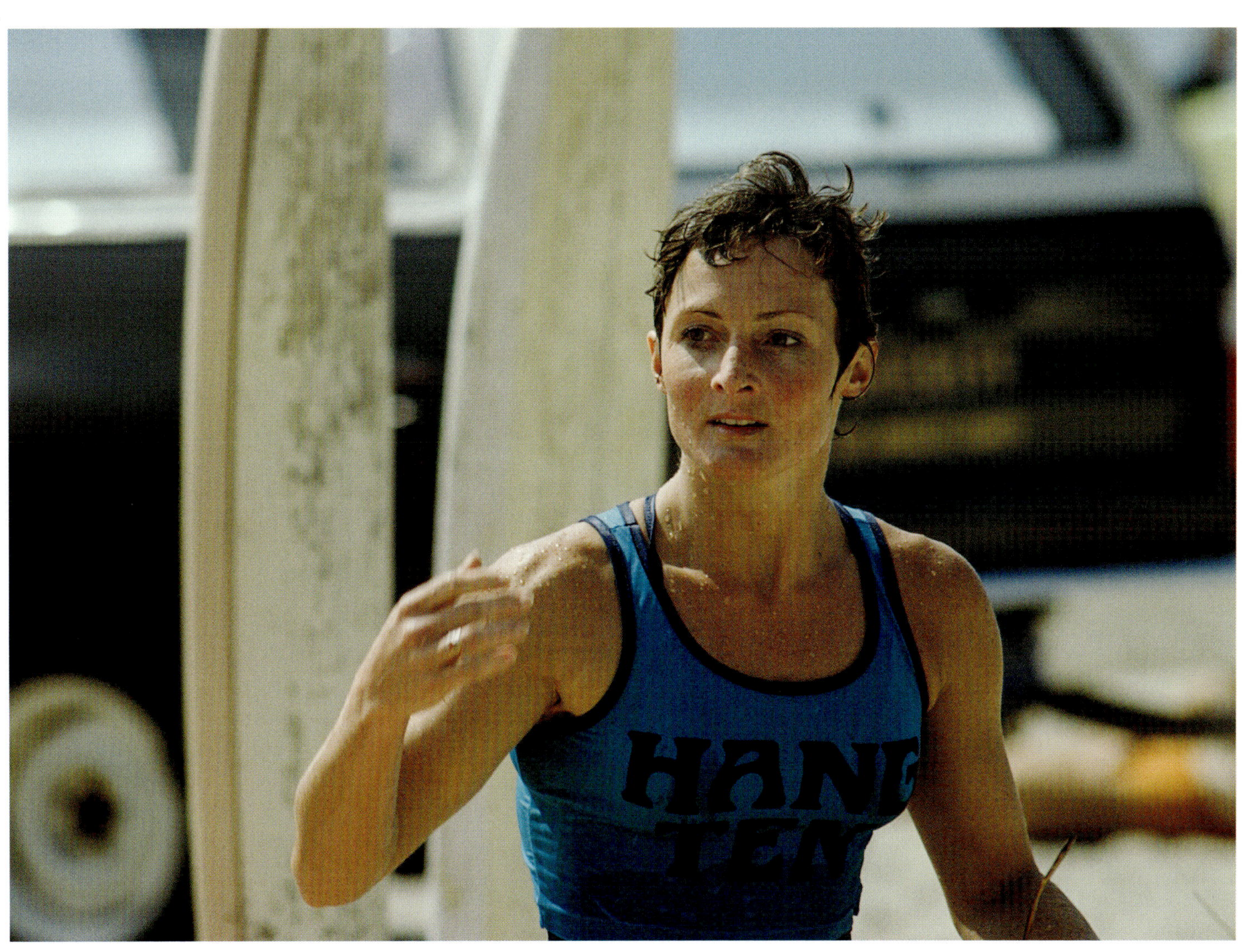

Jericho Poppler Bartlow, Church, San Clemente, CA 1976

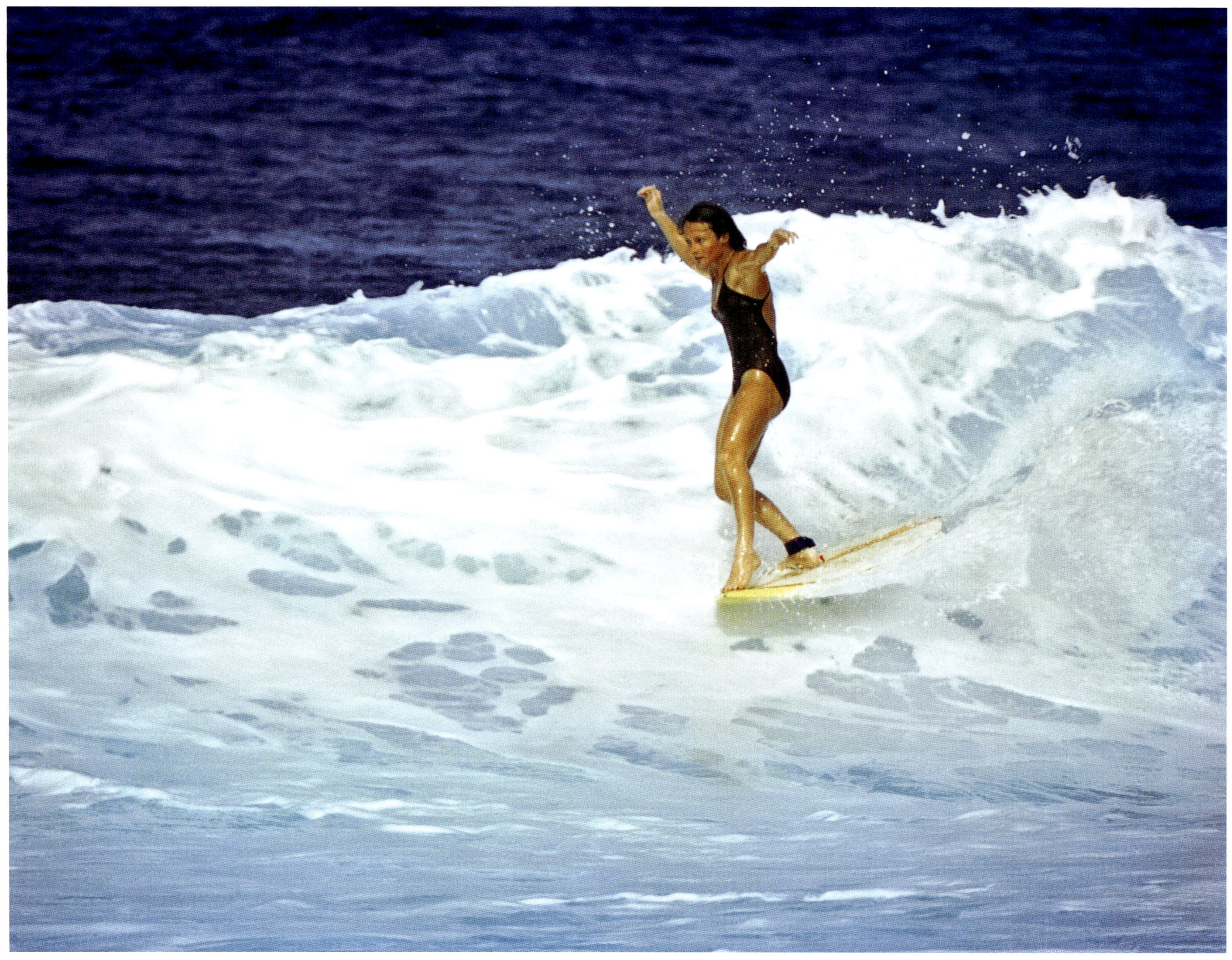

Jericho Poppler Bartlow, Haleiwa, Oahu, HI 1979

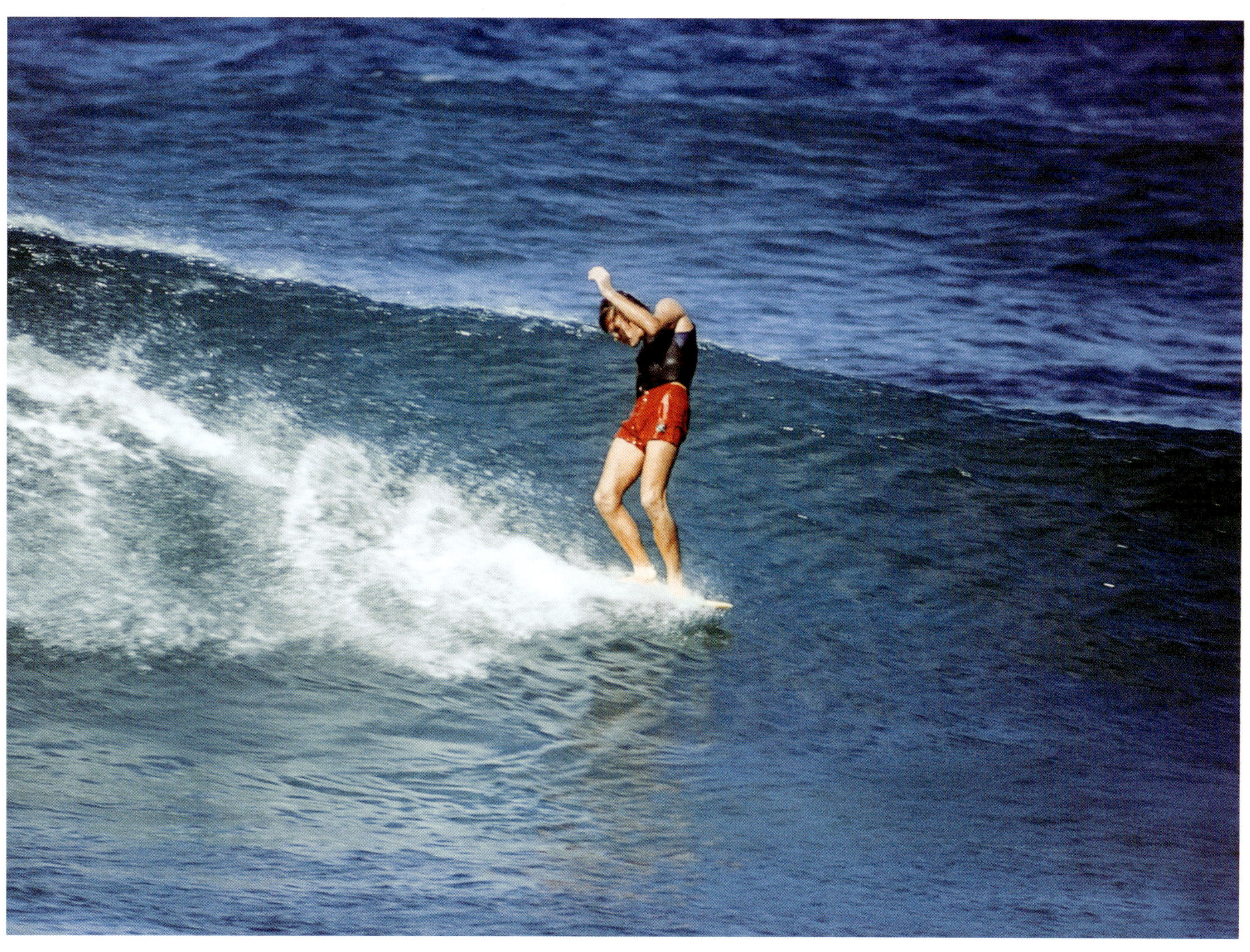

Wayne "Rabbit" Bartholomew, Pipeline, HI 1978

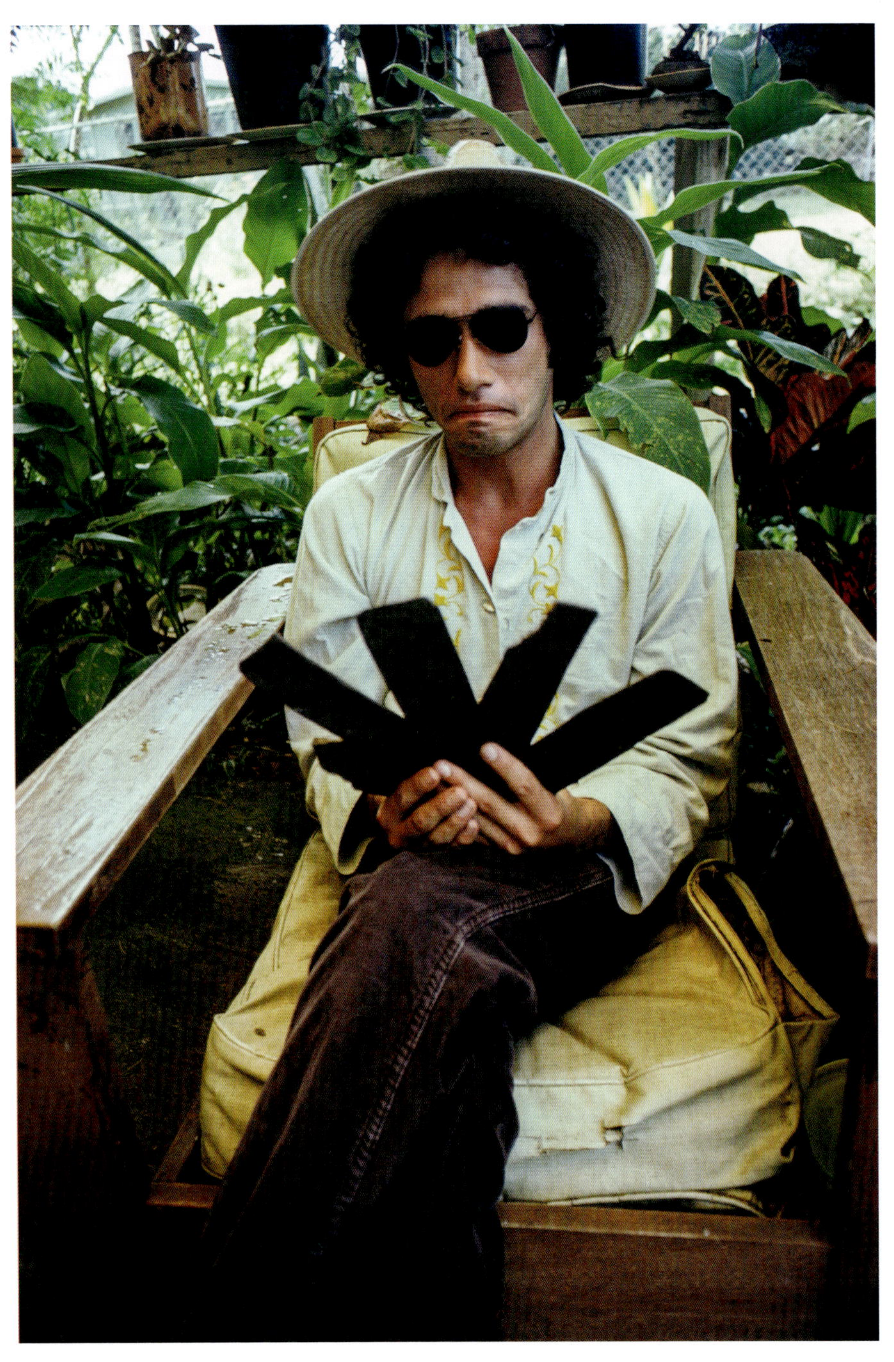

Brotherhood hash, Ke Iki Road, Oahu, HI 1974

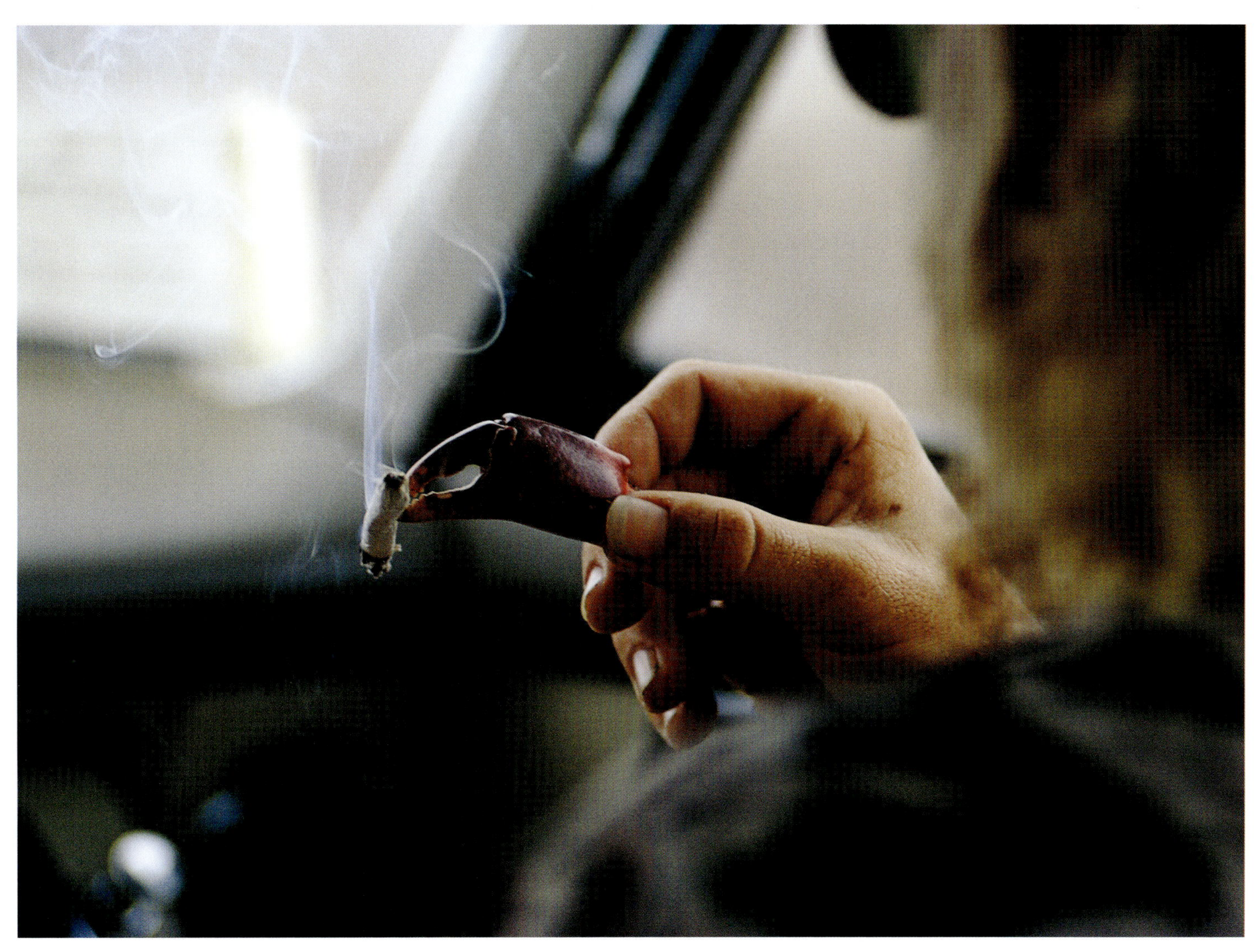

La Jolla Shores, CA 1971

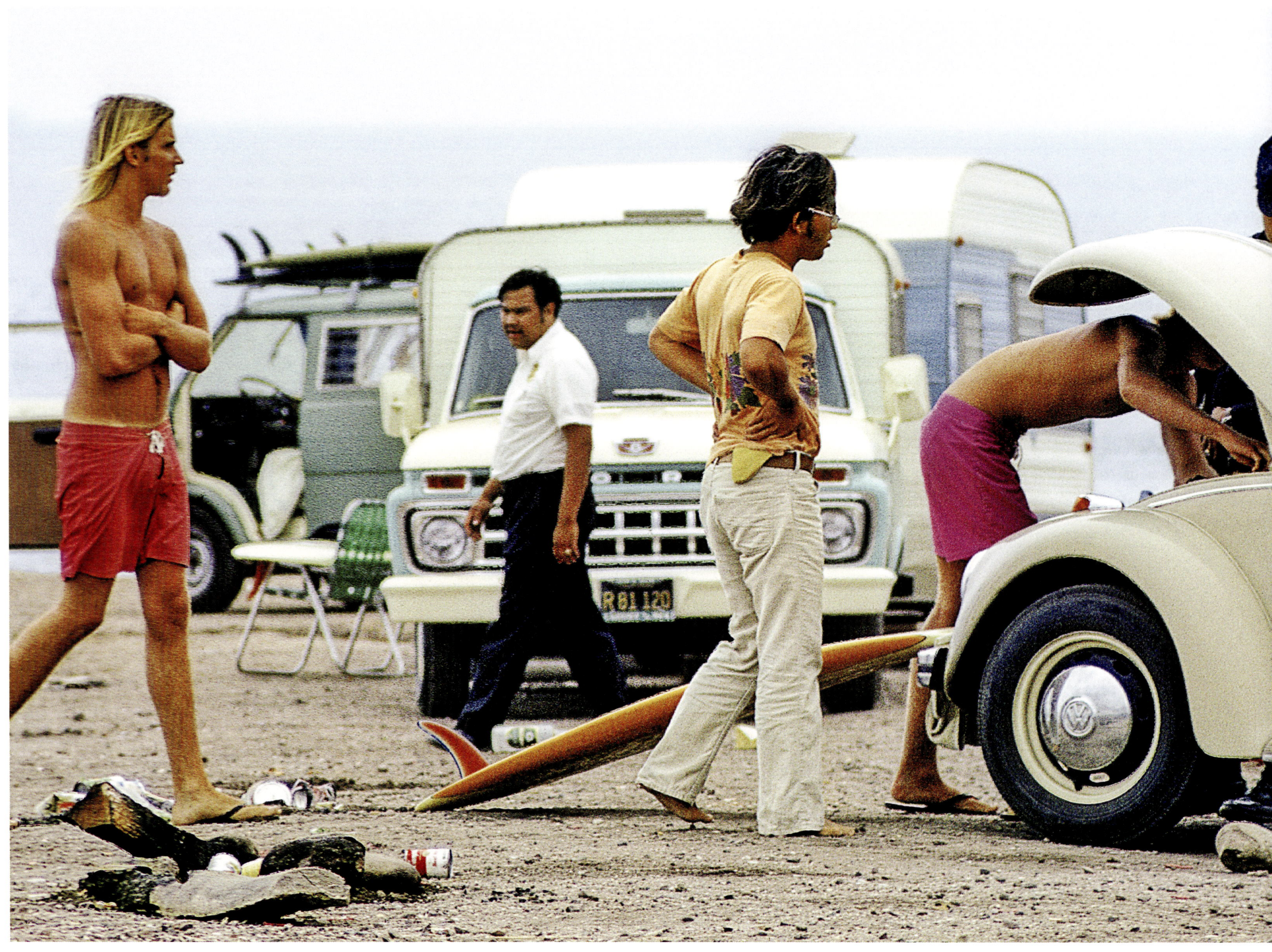

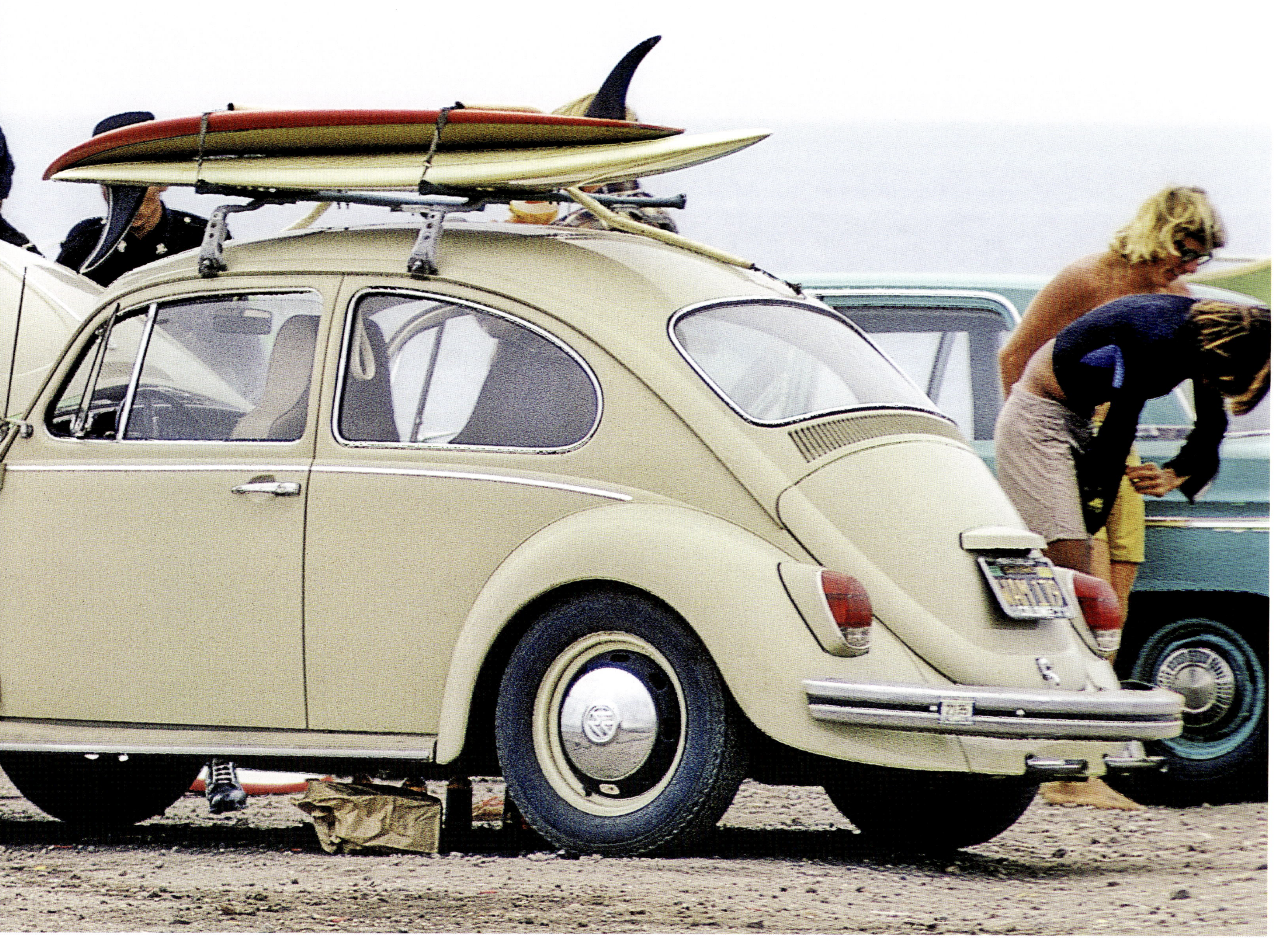

Rousted by fédérales at K38, Baja California 1972

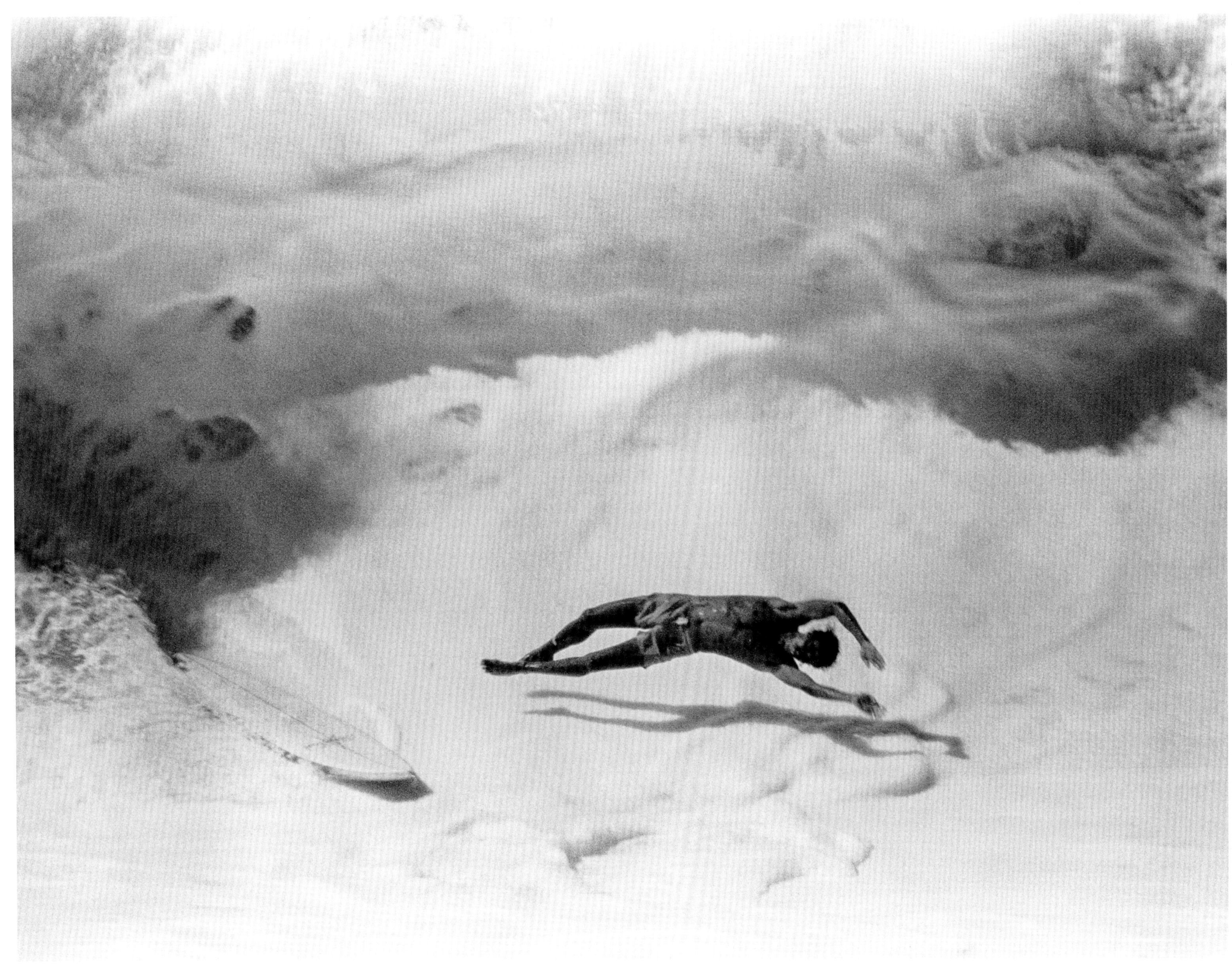

Basement Please, Pipeline, Oahu, HI 1974

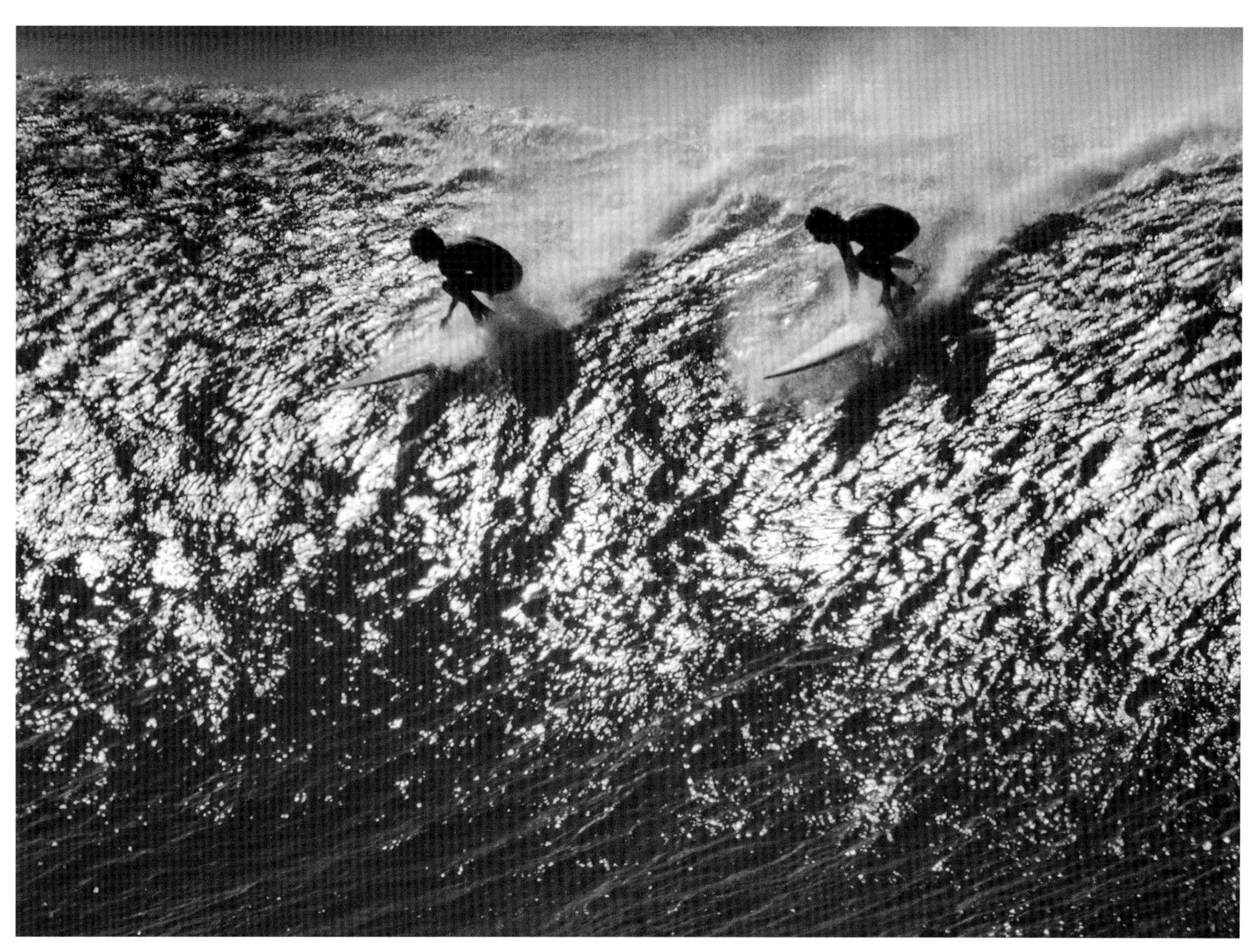

Waimea Bay, Oahu, HI 1977

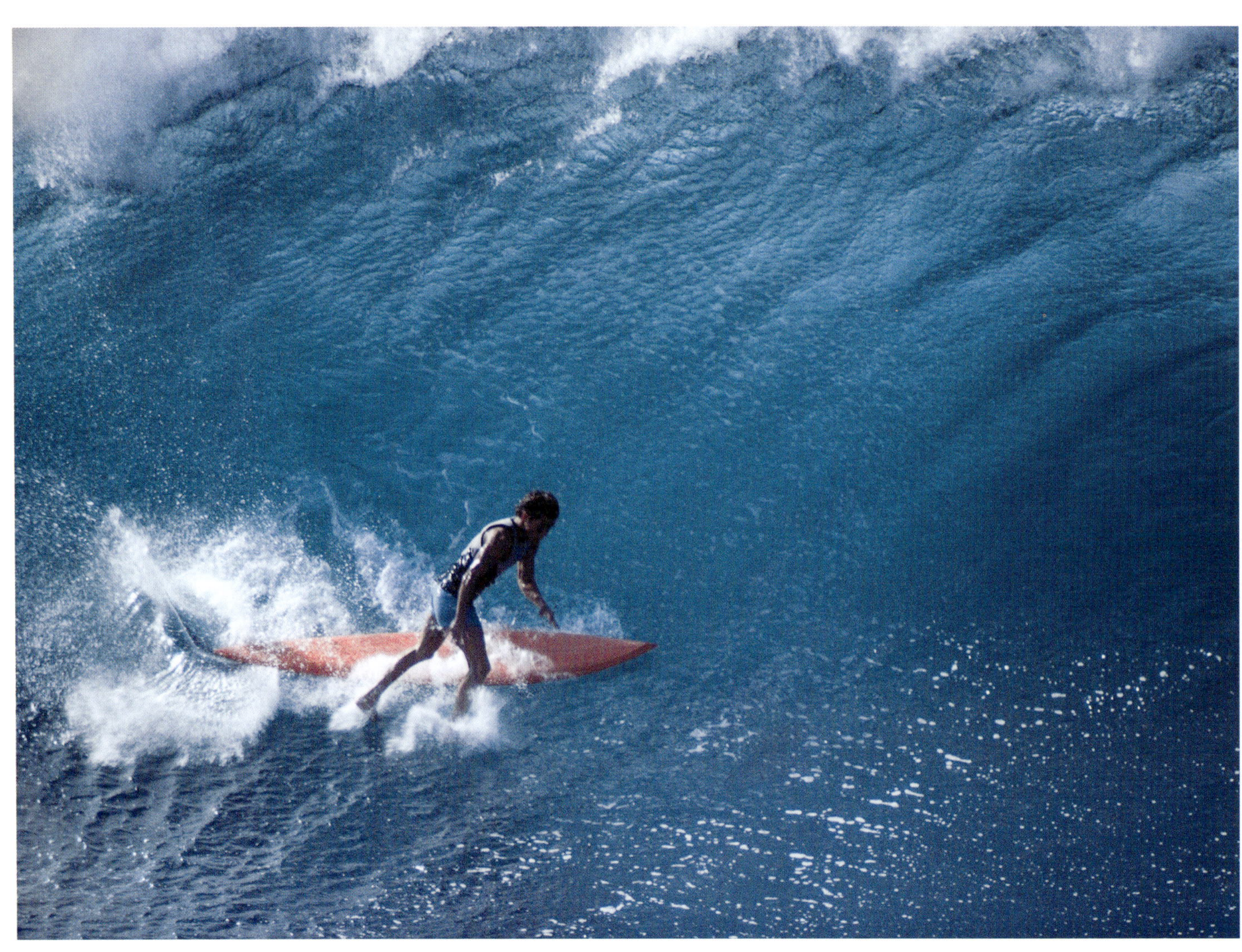

Tony Brinkworth, Pipeline, Oahu, HI 1978

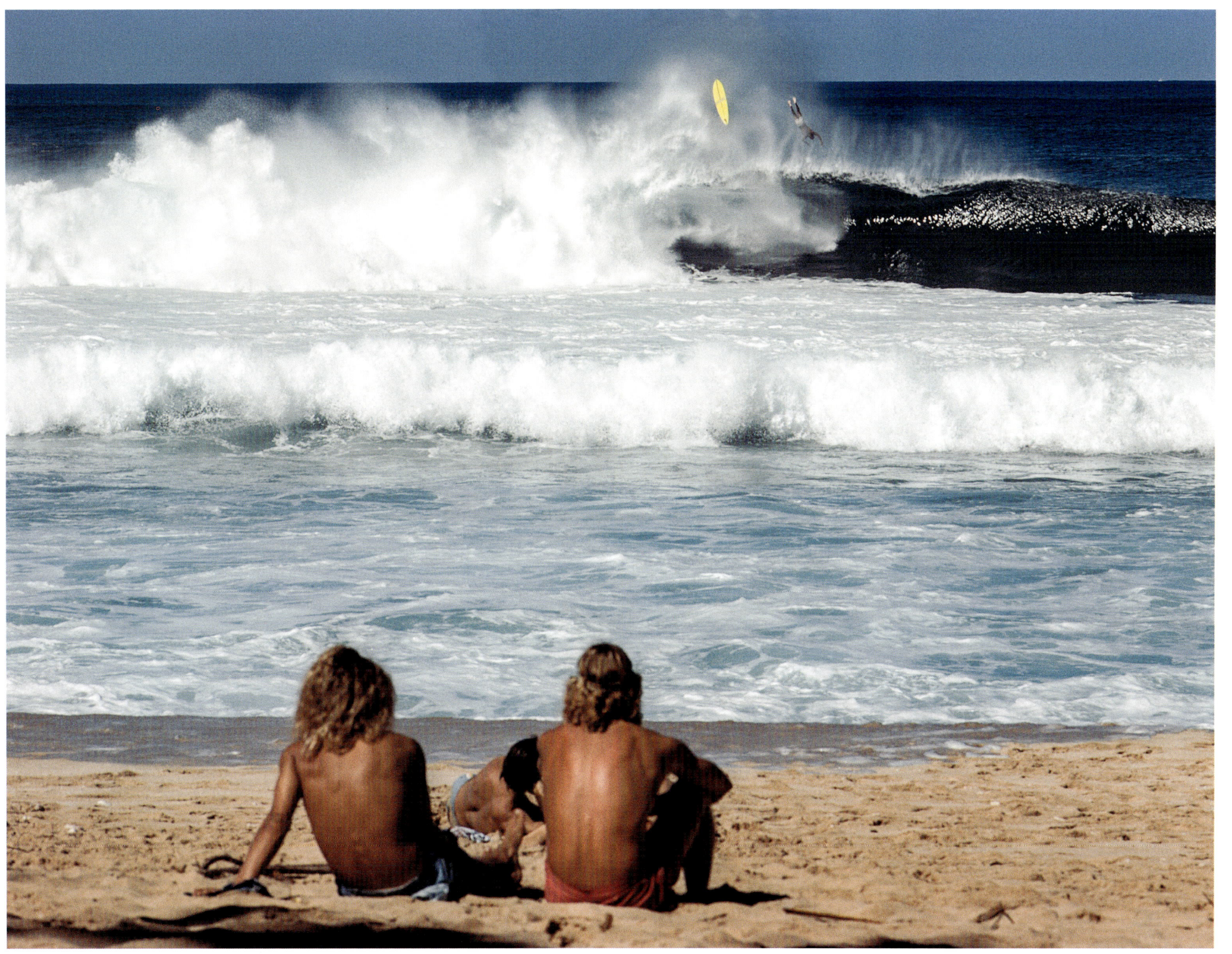

Pipeline, Oahu, HI 1974

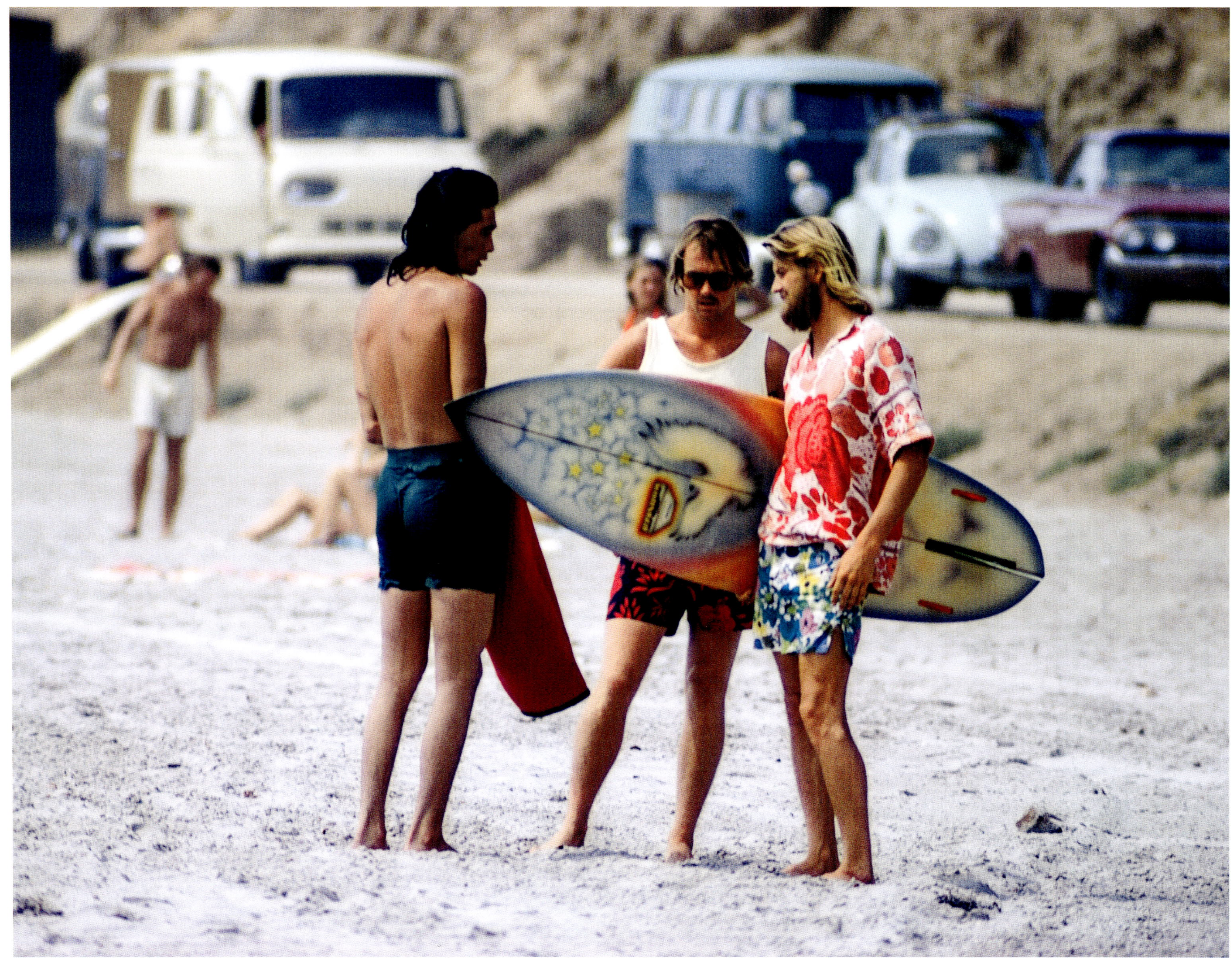

David Nuuhiwa, Greg Person, Les Potts, Salt Creek, Dana Point, CA 1971

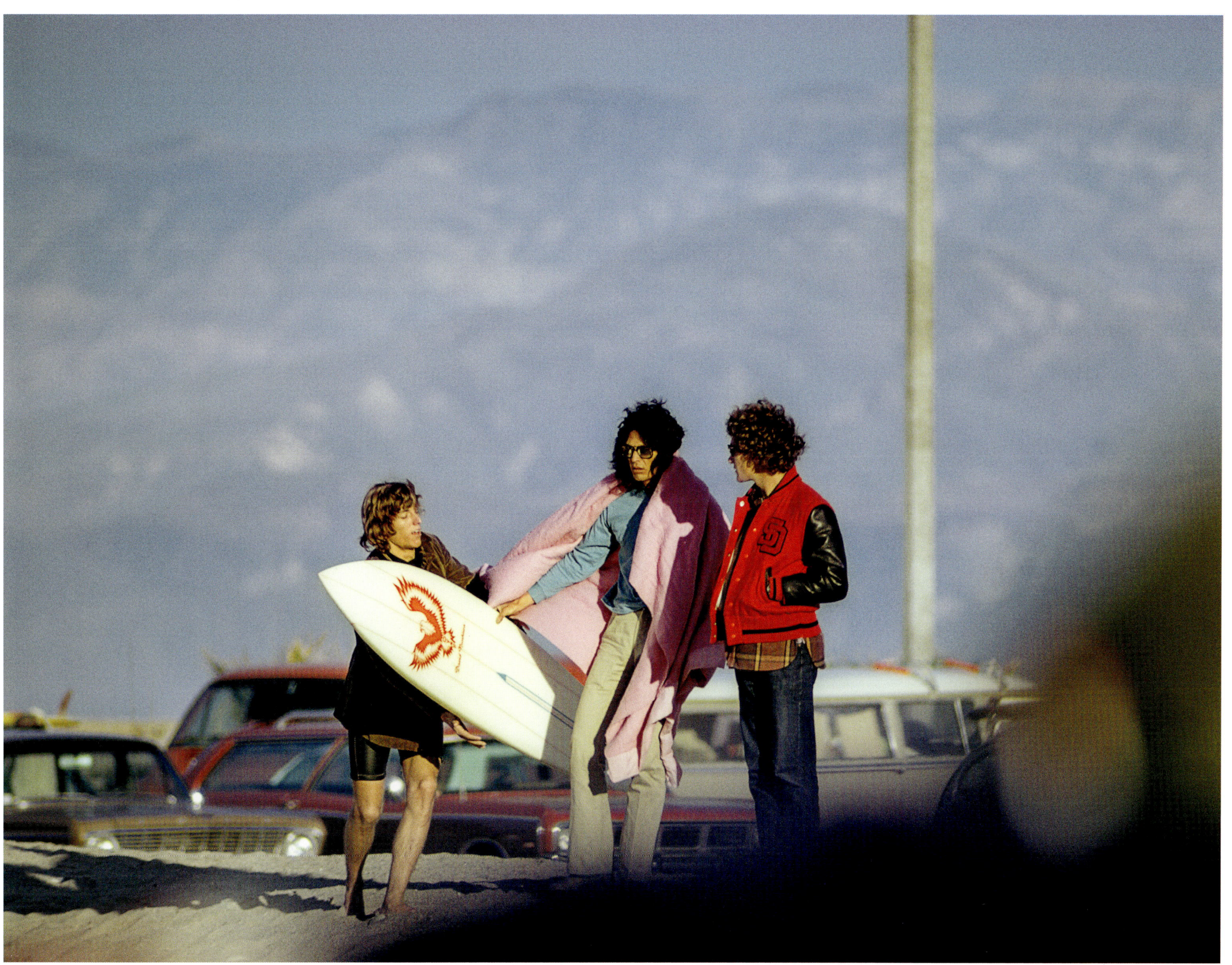

David Nuuhiwa, Alan Rich, Oxnard, CA 1971

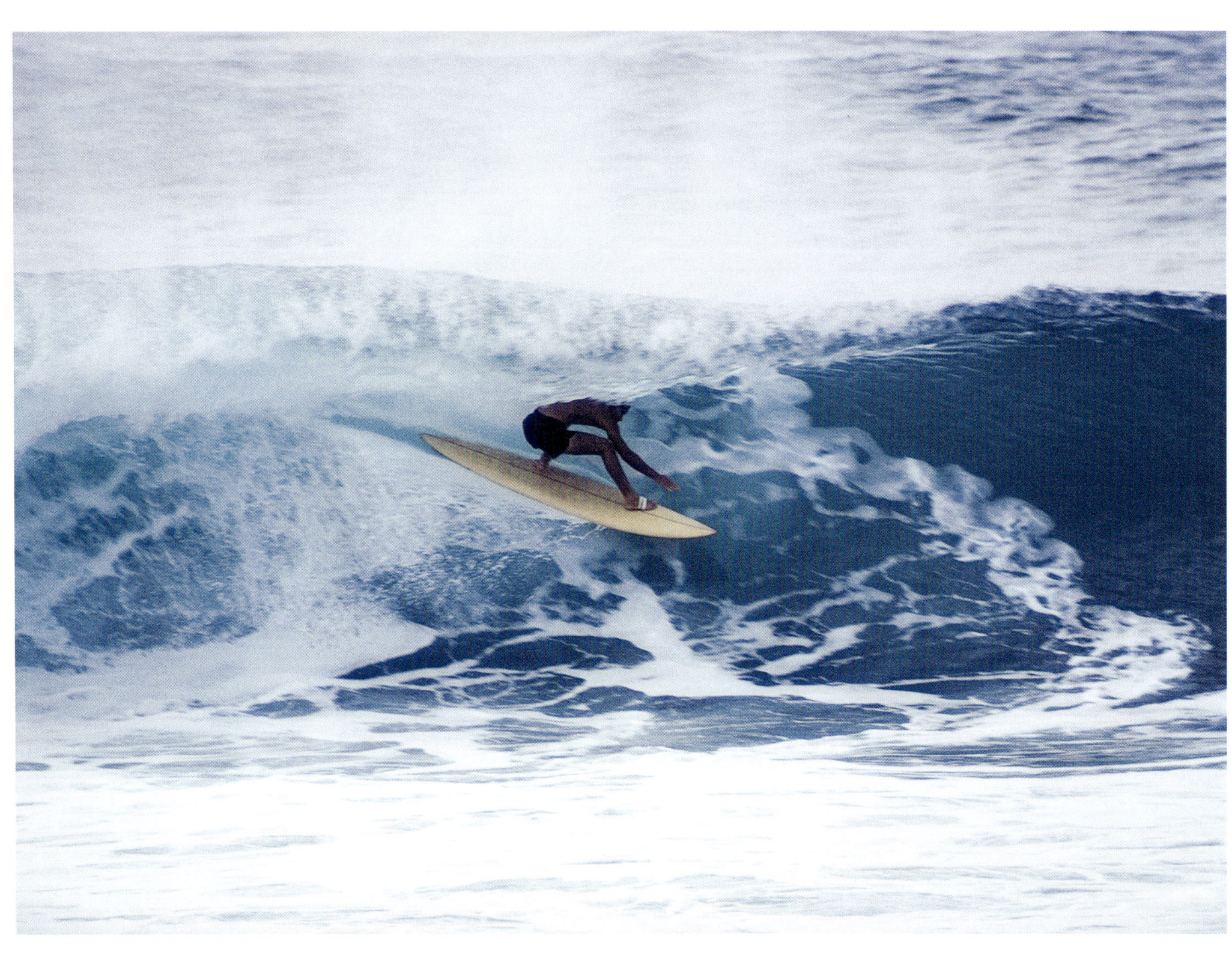

Gerry Lopez, Pipeline, Oahu, HI 1971

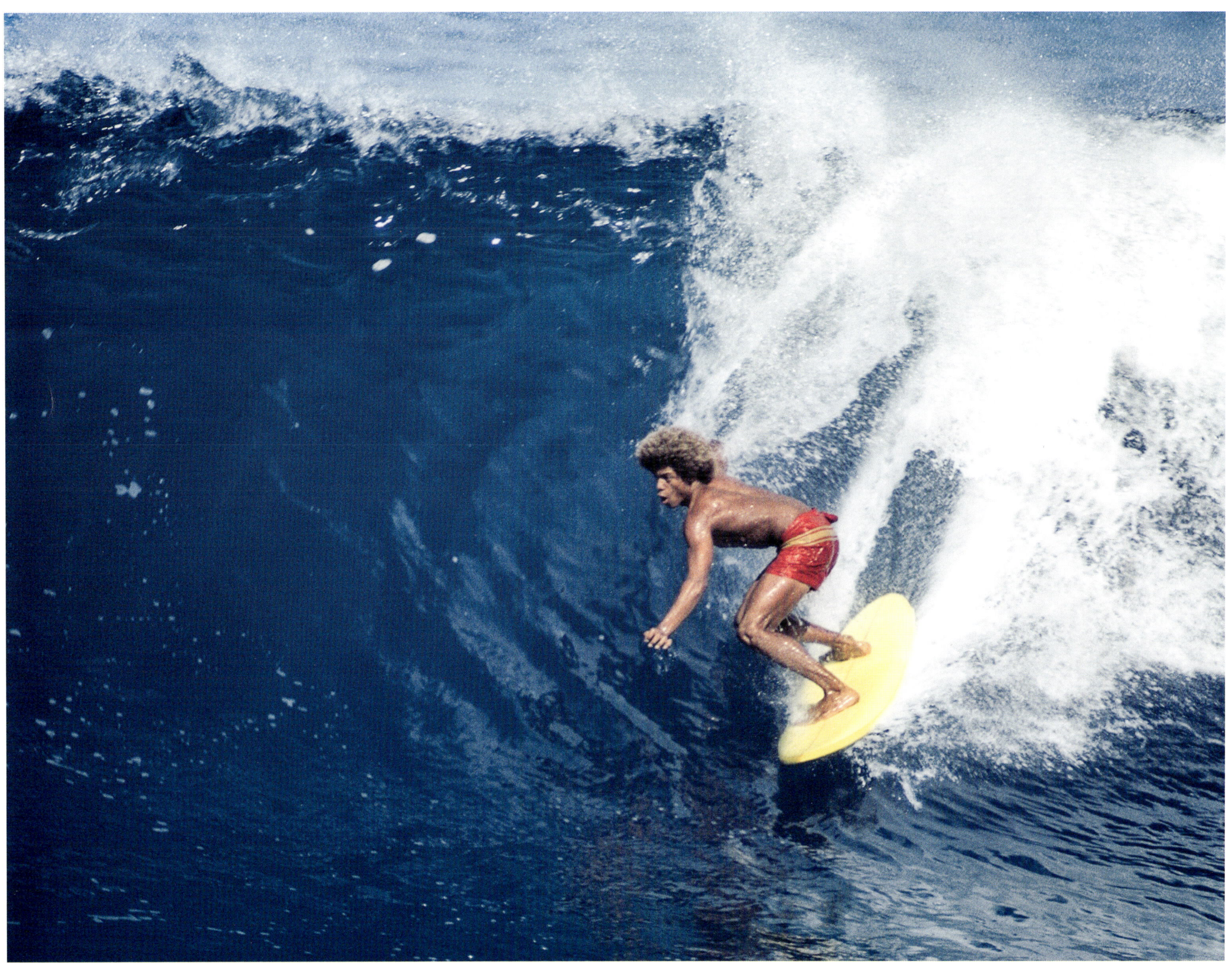

Buttons Kaluhiokalani, Backdoor, Oahu, HI 1978

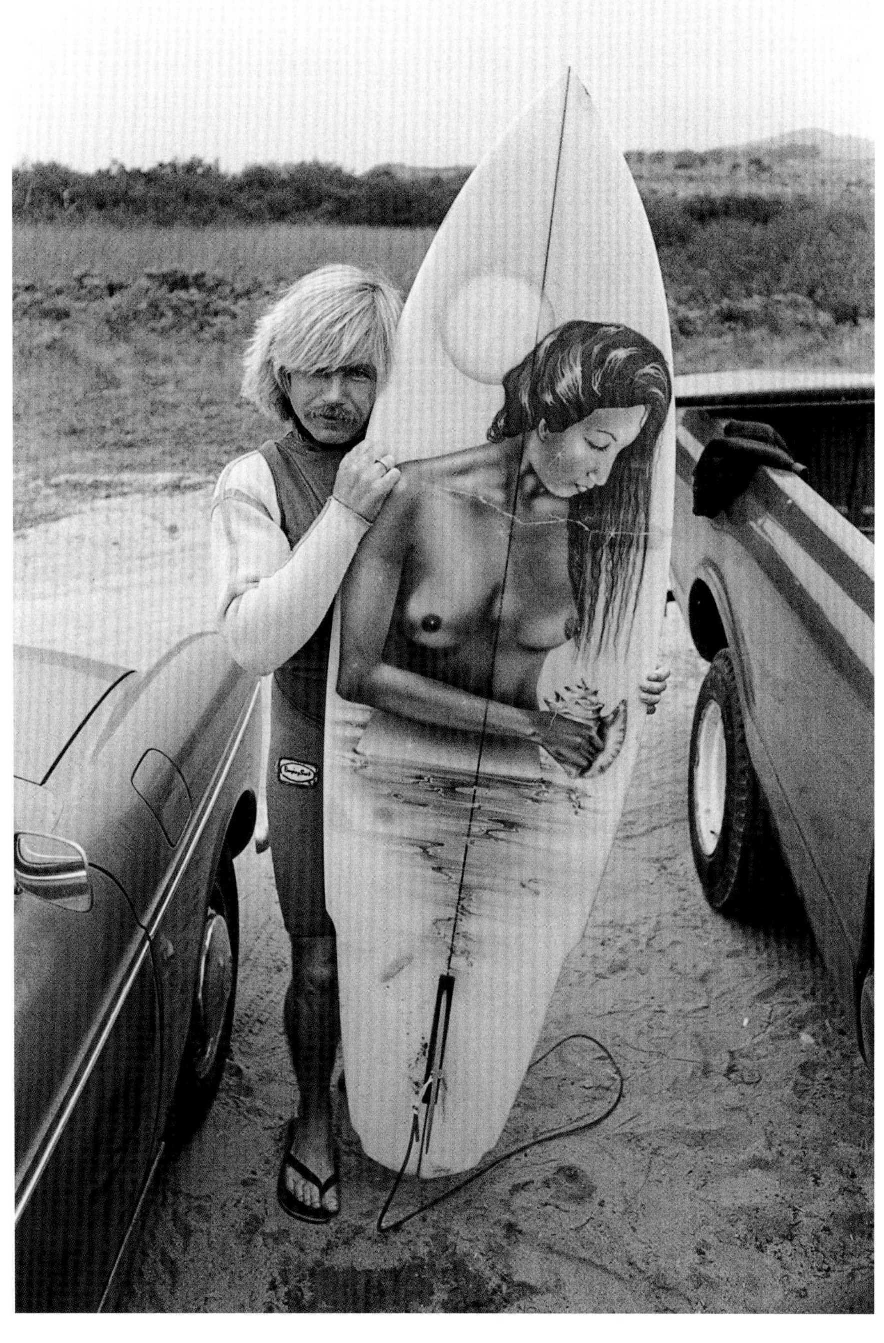

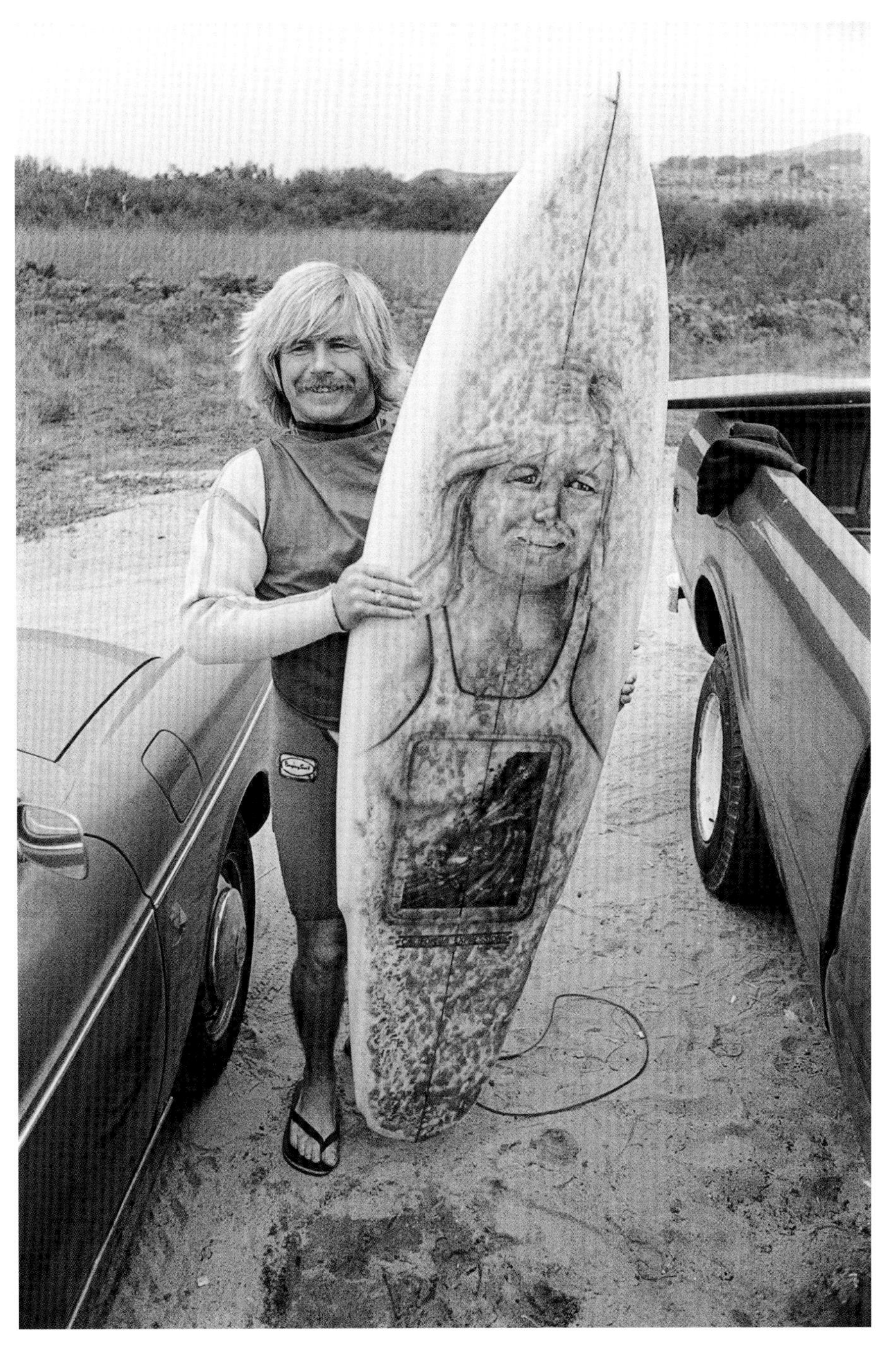

Mike Purpus, Lower Trestle, San Clemente, CA 1977

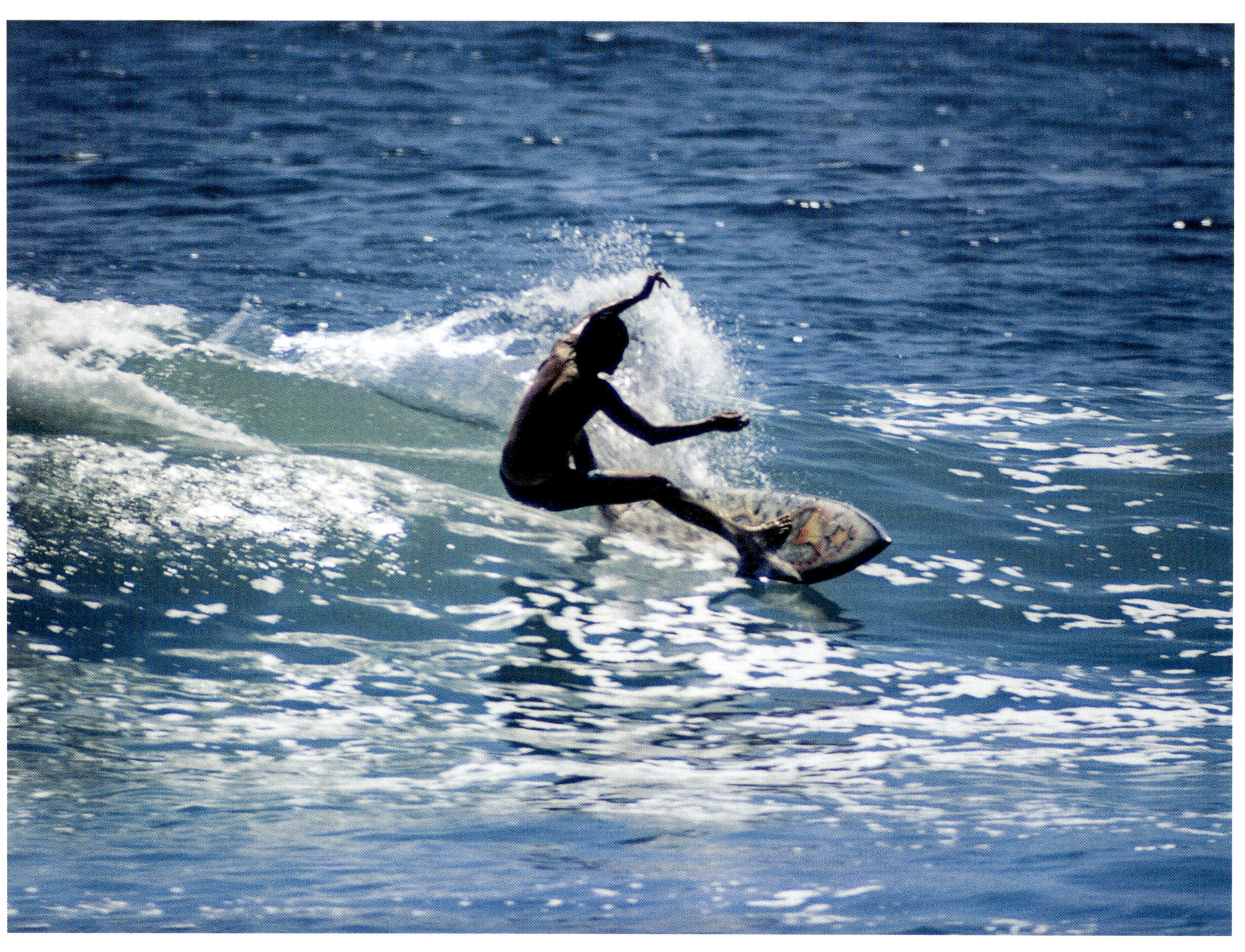

David Nuuhiwa, Salt Creek, Dana Point, CA 1971

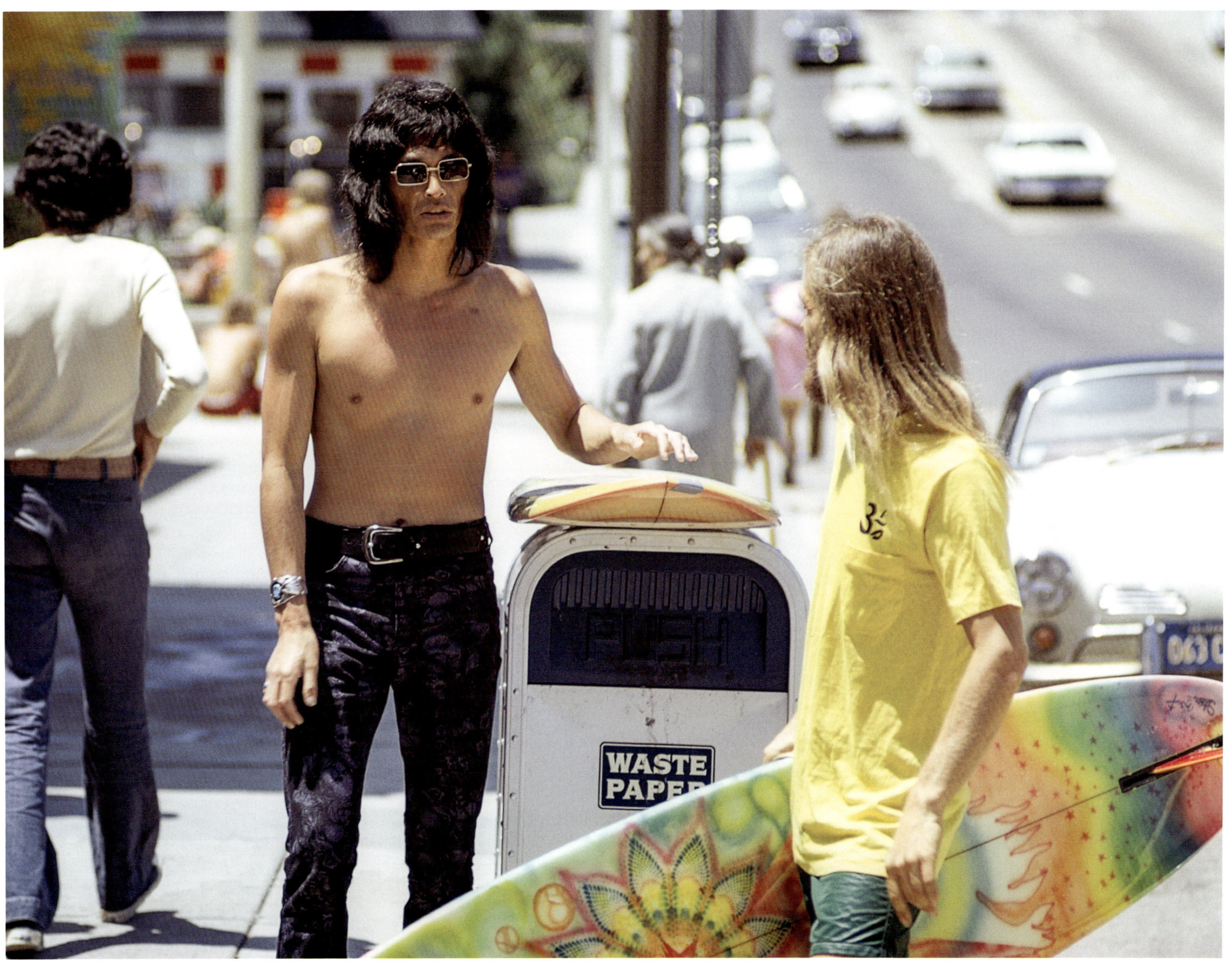

David Nuuhiwa, John Gale, PCH Laguna Beach, CA 1971

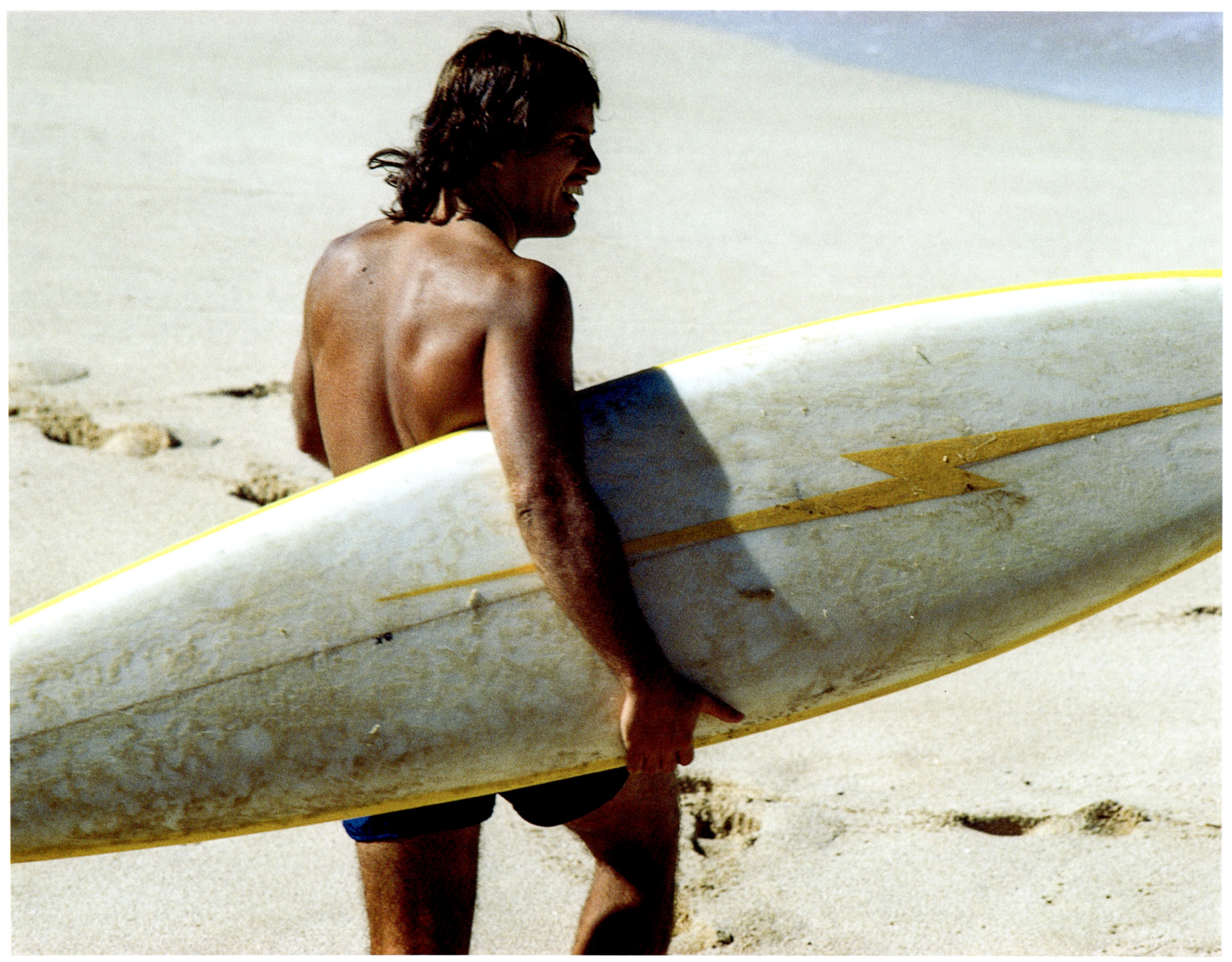

Barry Kanaiaupuni, Rocky Point, Oahu, HI 1976

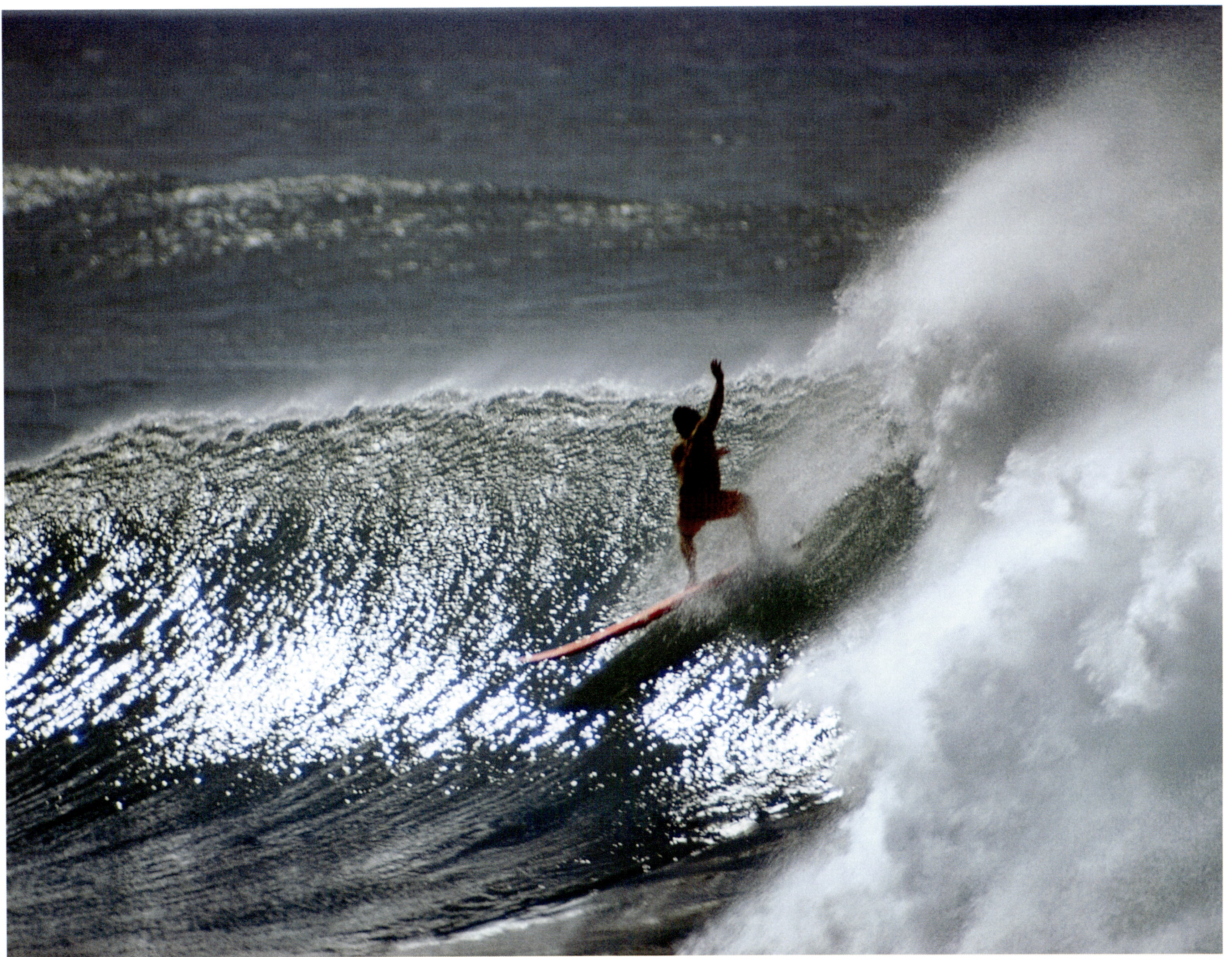

Ben Aipa, Sunset Beach, Oahu, HI 1971

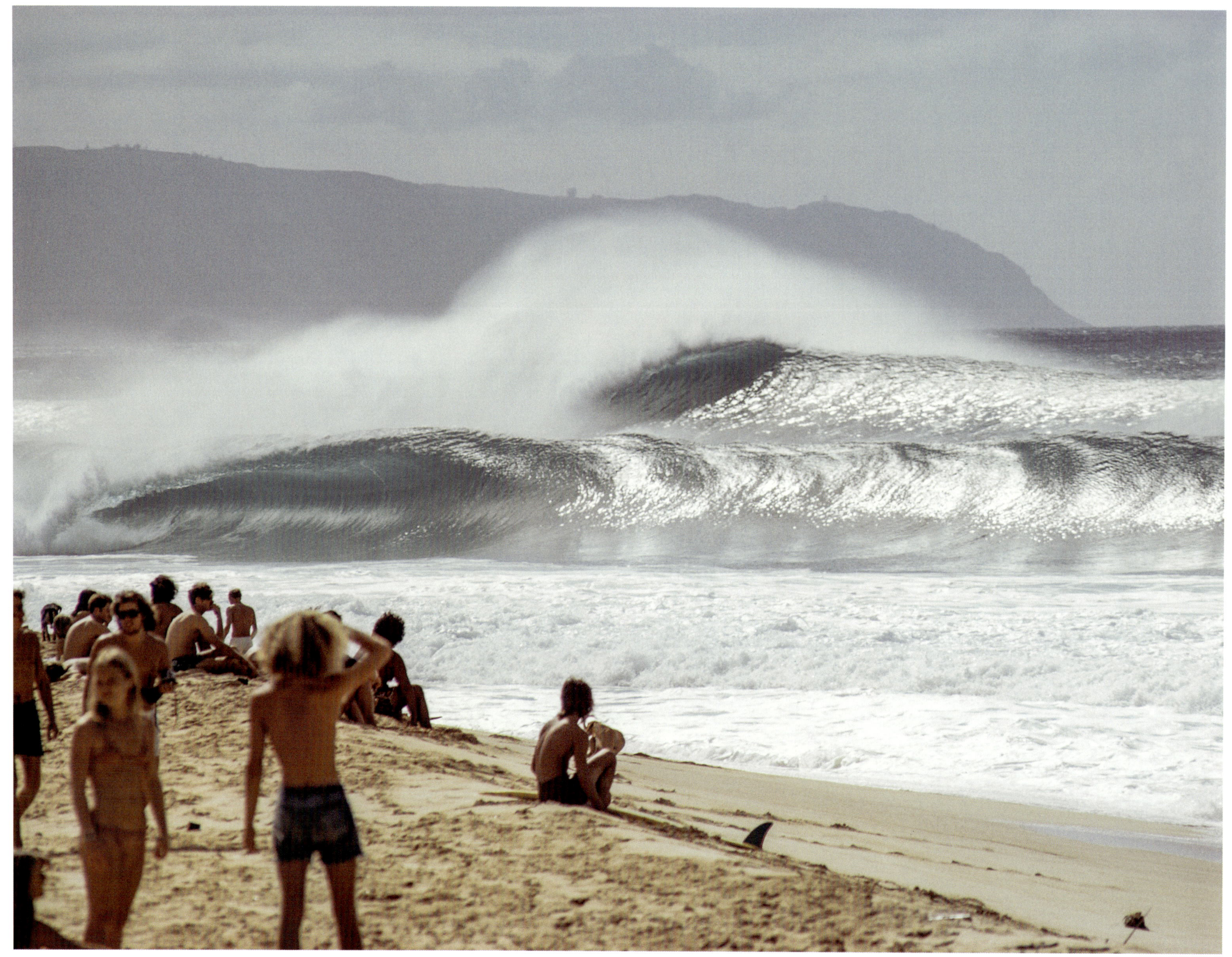

Rockpile, Oahu, HI 1973

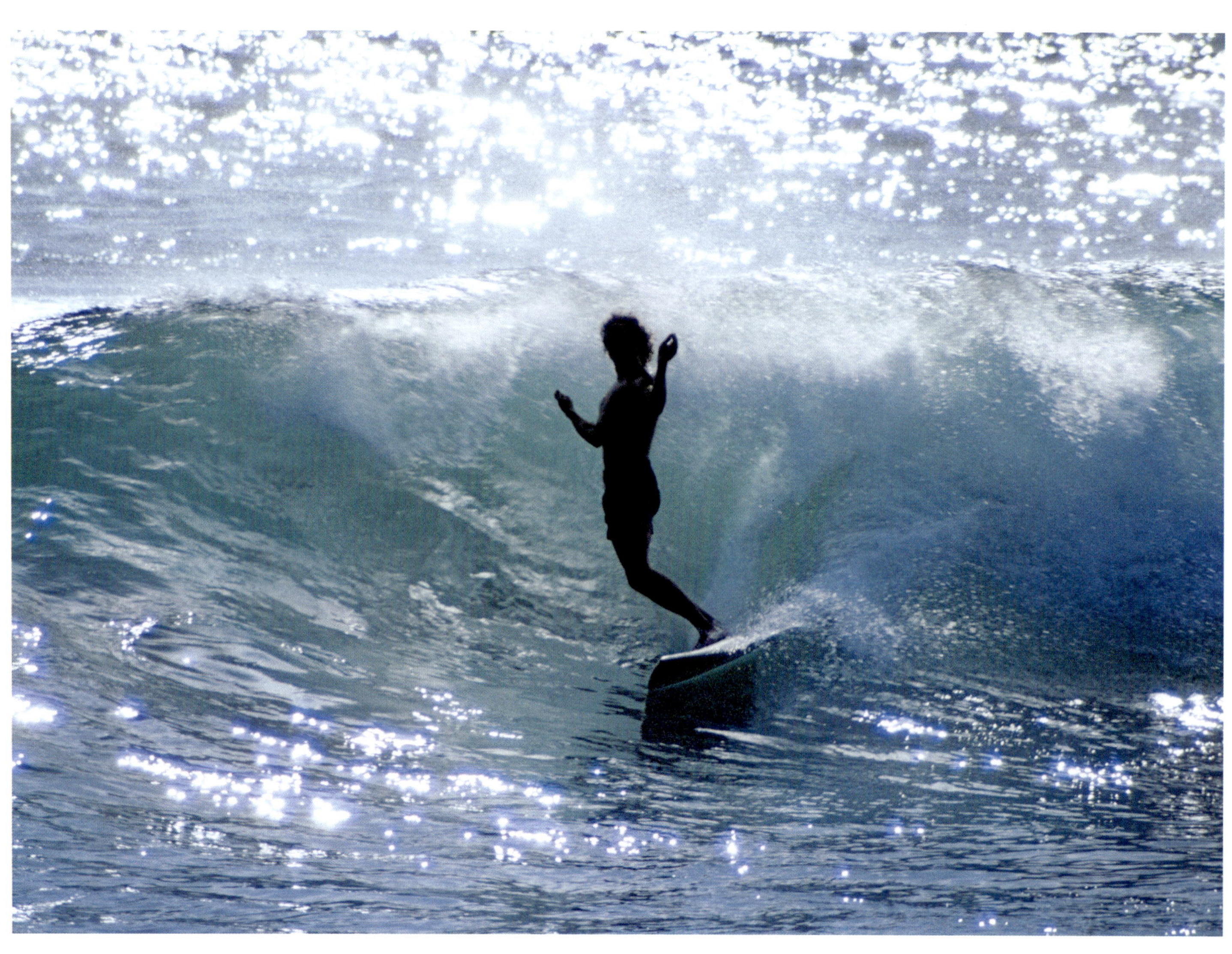

David Rullo, Windansea, La Jolla, CA 1972

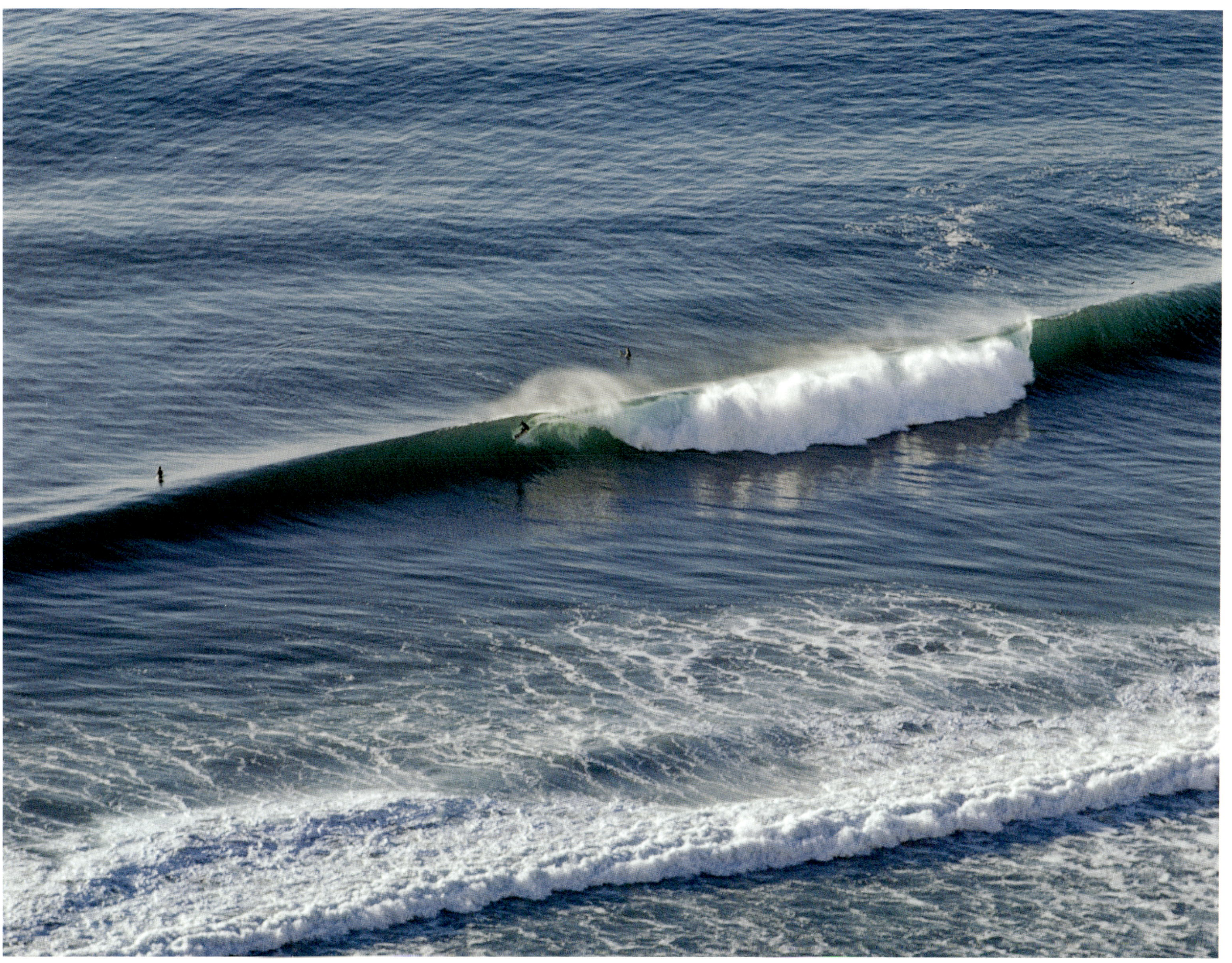

Blacks Beach, La Jolla, CA 1973

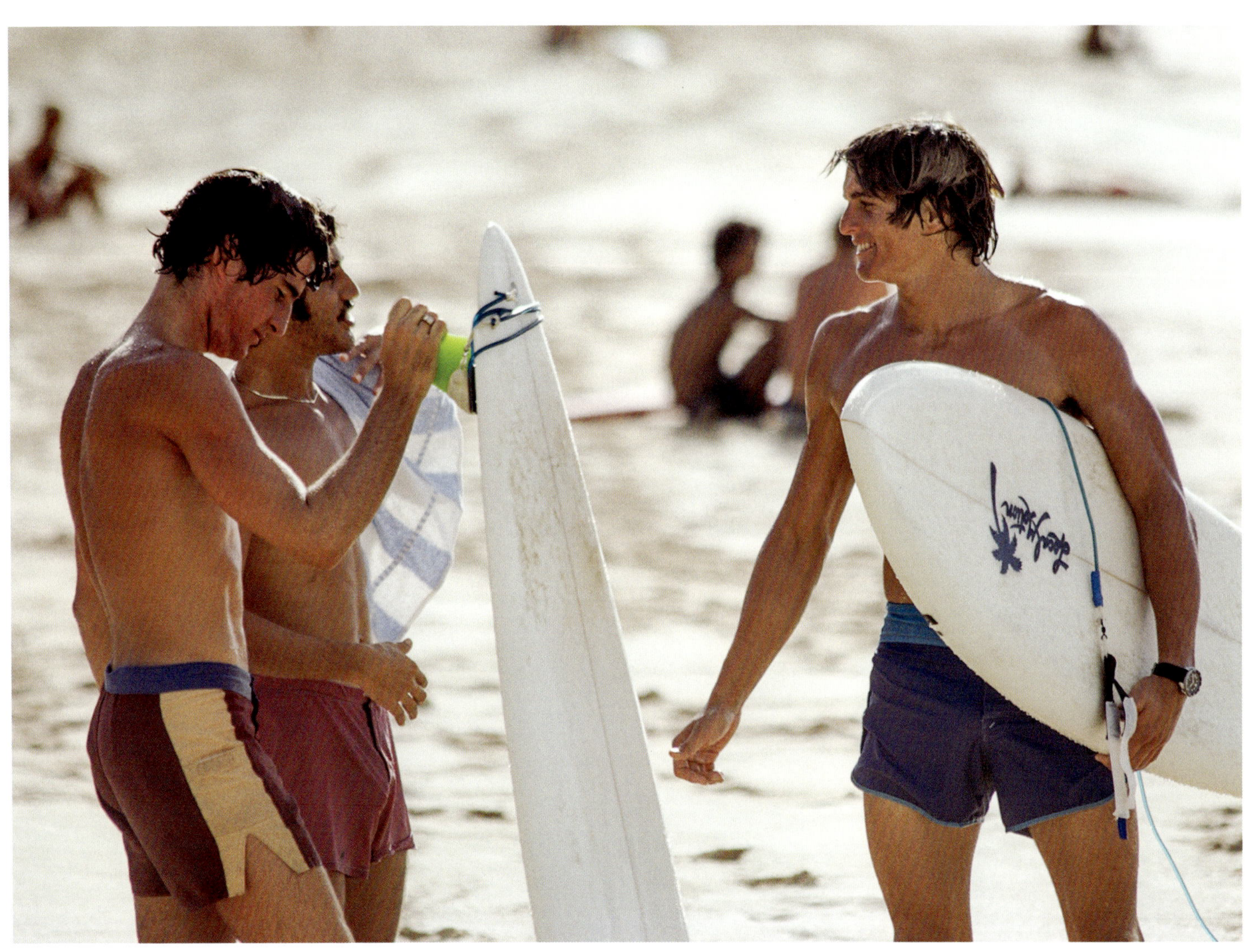

Hans Hedemann, Mike Ho, Buzzy Kerbox, Sunset Beach Oahu, HI 1978

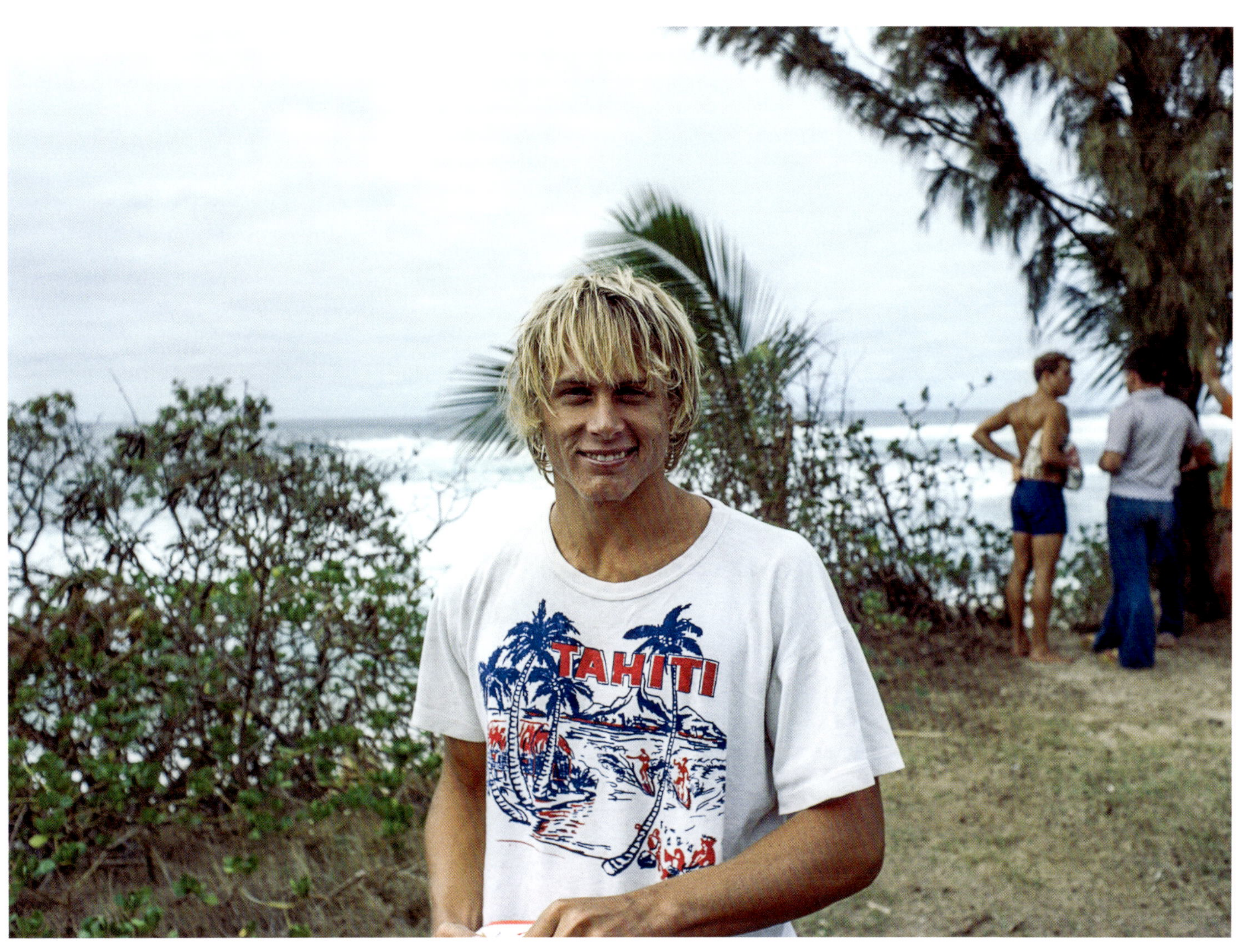

Jackie Dunn, Sunset Beach Oahu, HI 1976

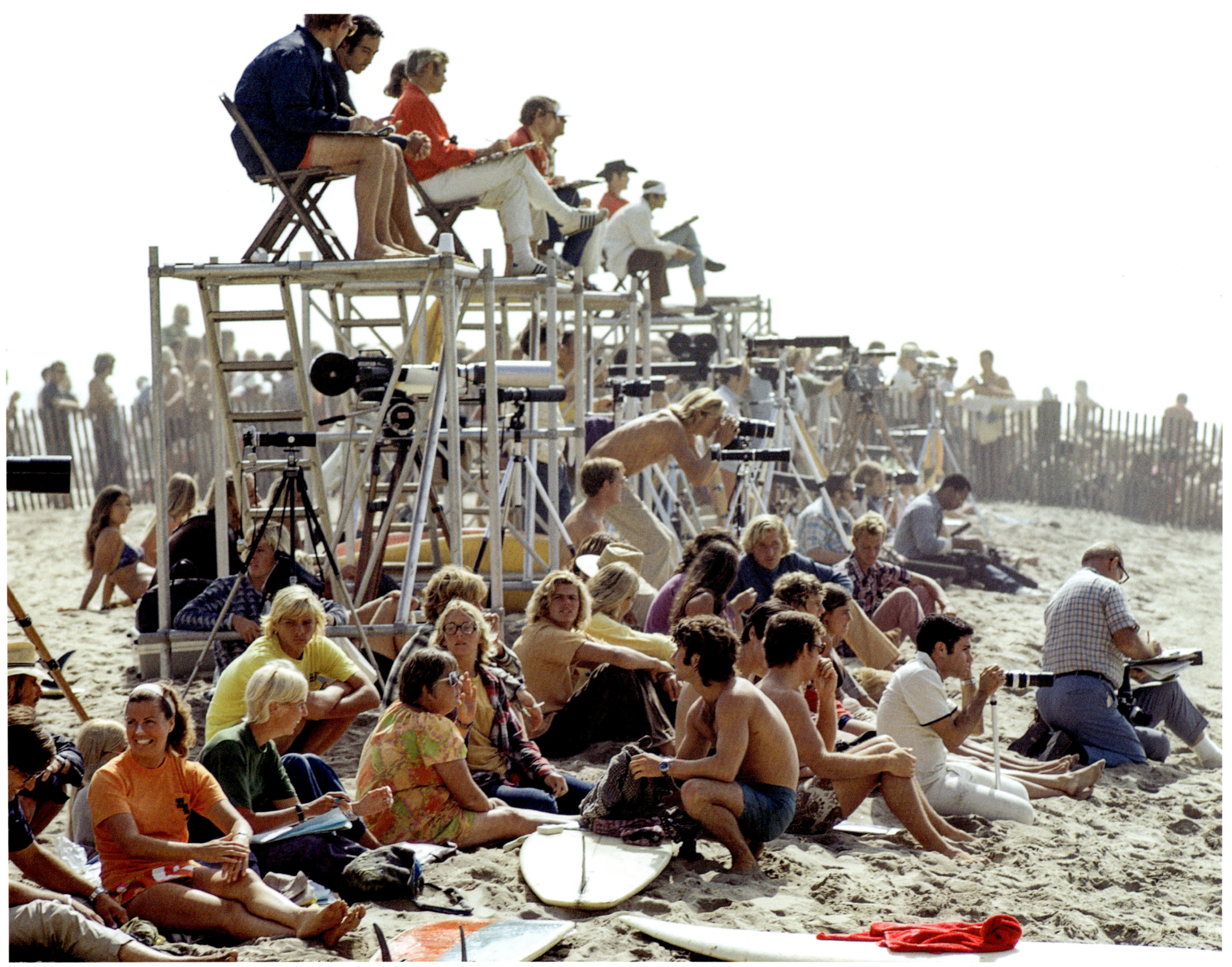

Huntington Beach, CA 1971

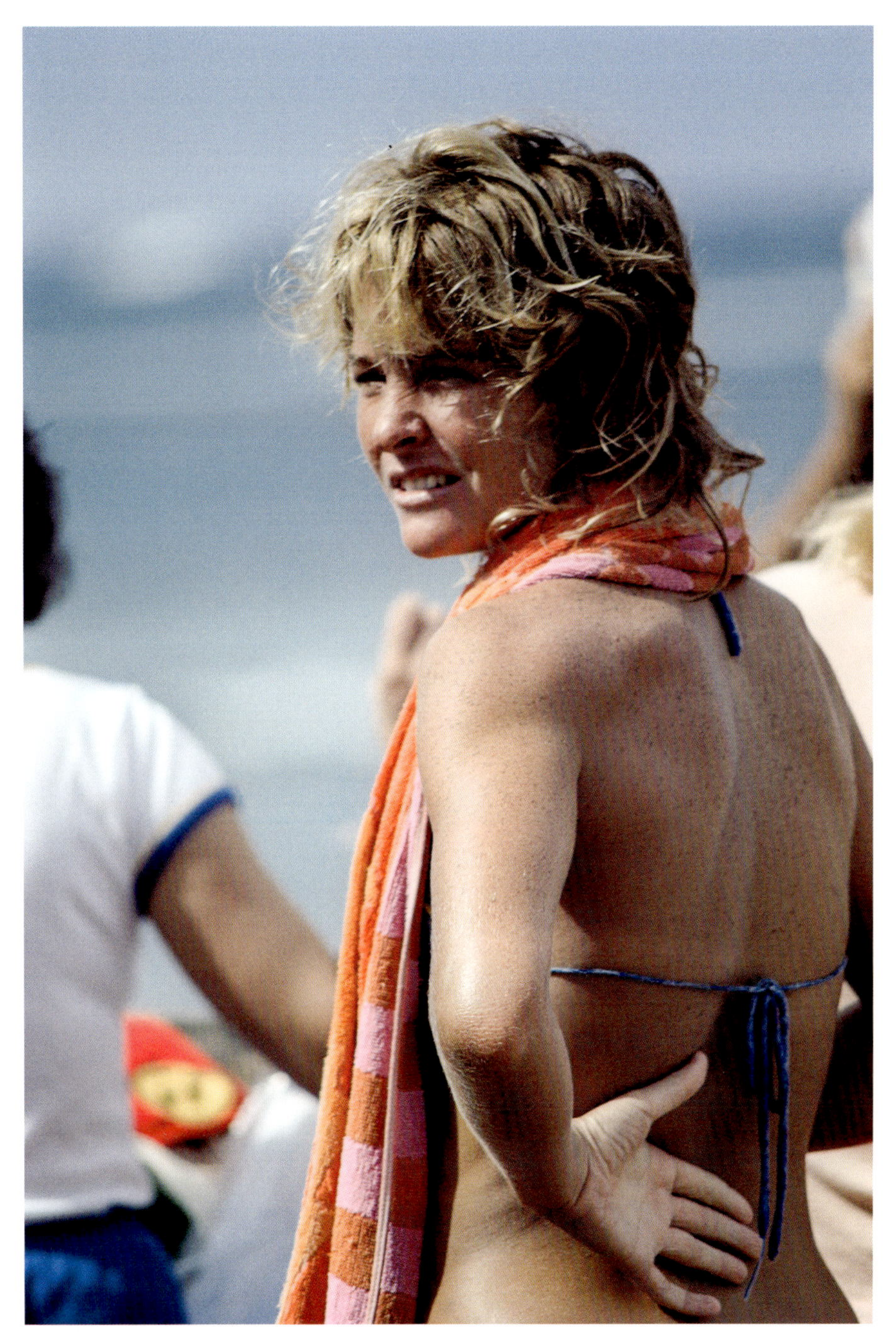

Lynne Boyer, Malibu, CA 1979

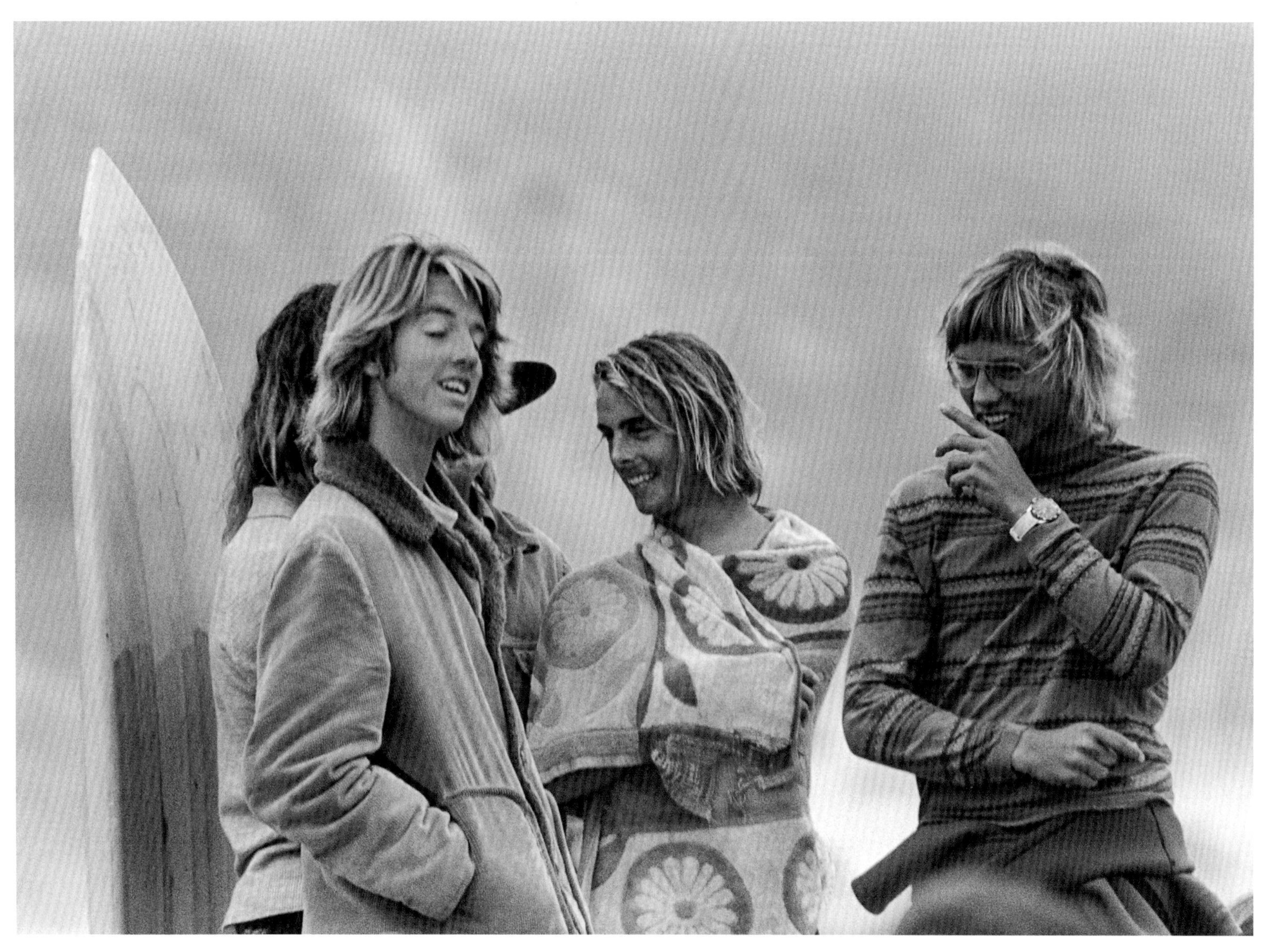

Malibu, CA 1971

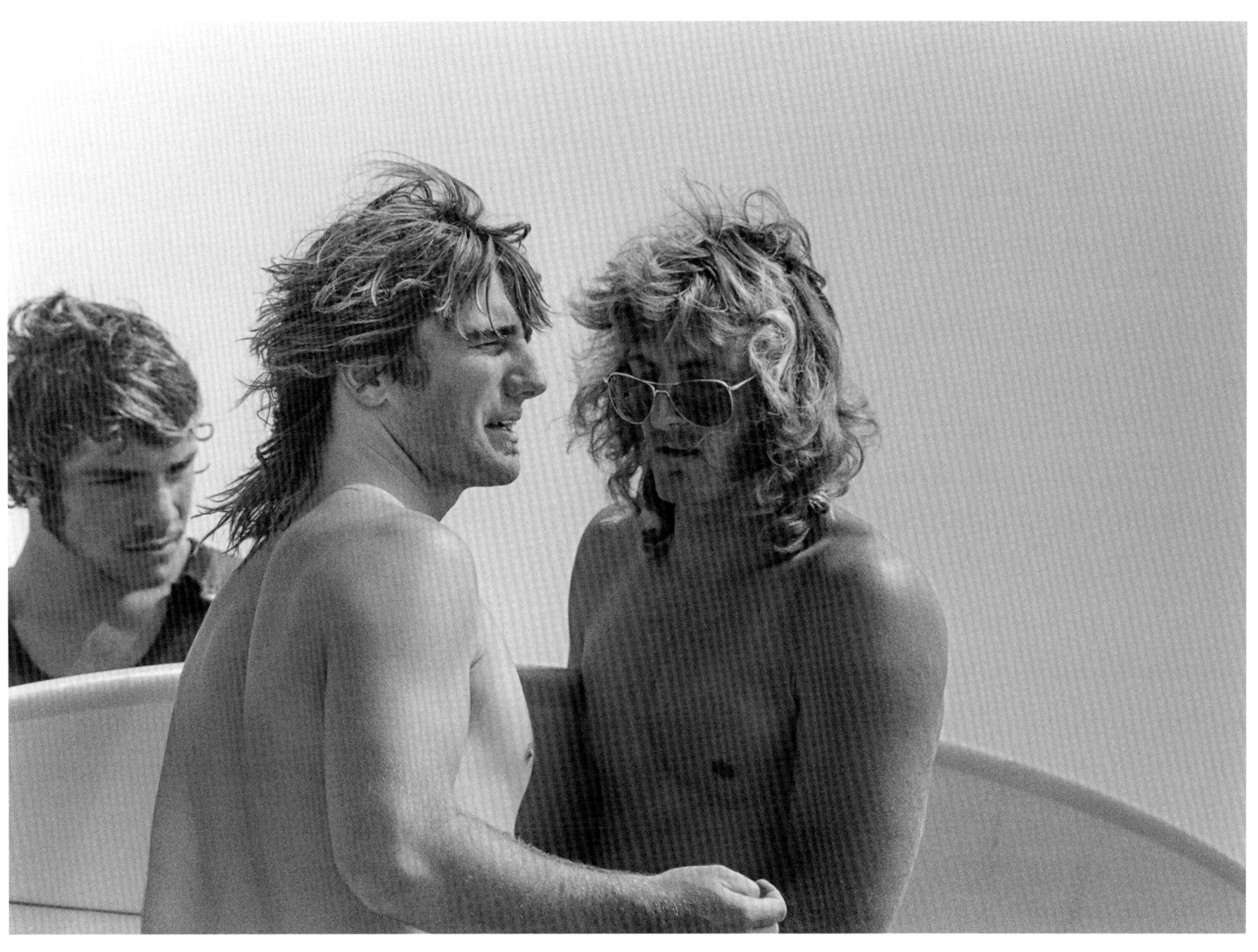

Allen Sarlo, Glen Kennedy, John Thornton, Malibu, CA 1971

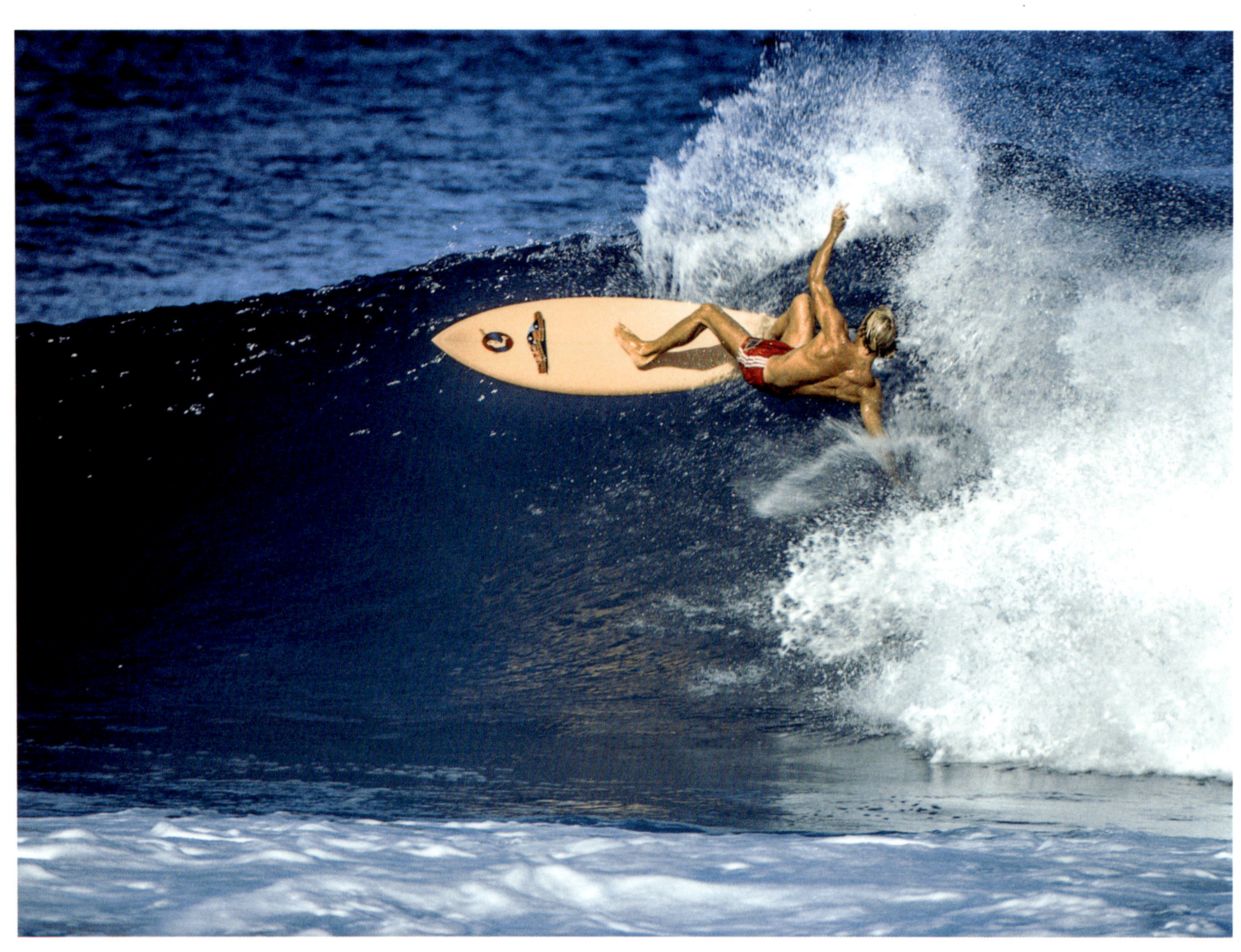

Peter Townend, Off The Wall, Oahu, HI 1976

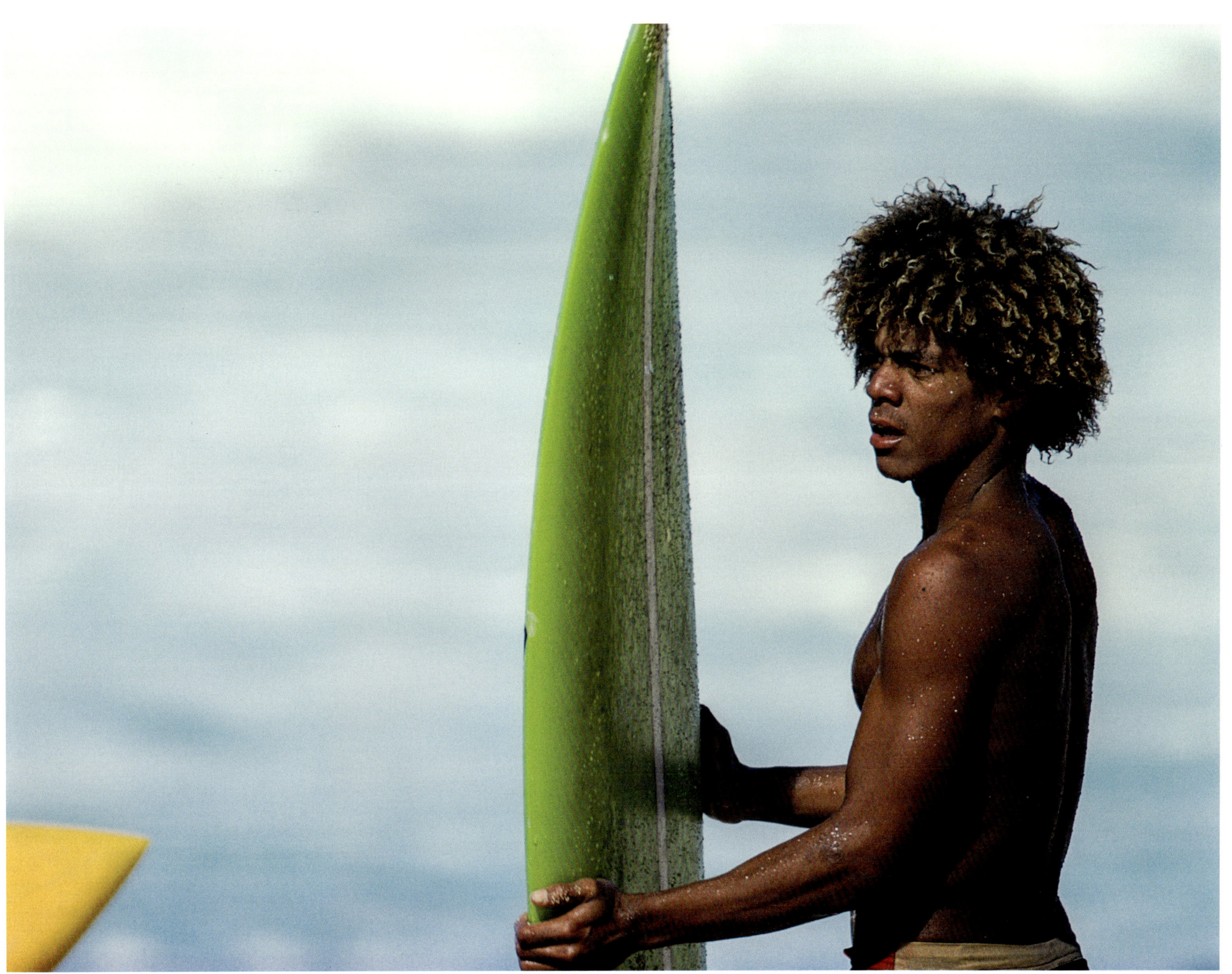

Buttons Kaluhiokalani, Off The Wall, Oahu, HI 1974

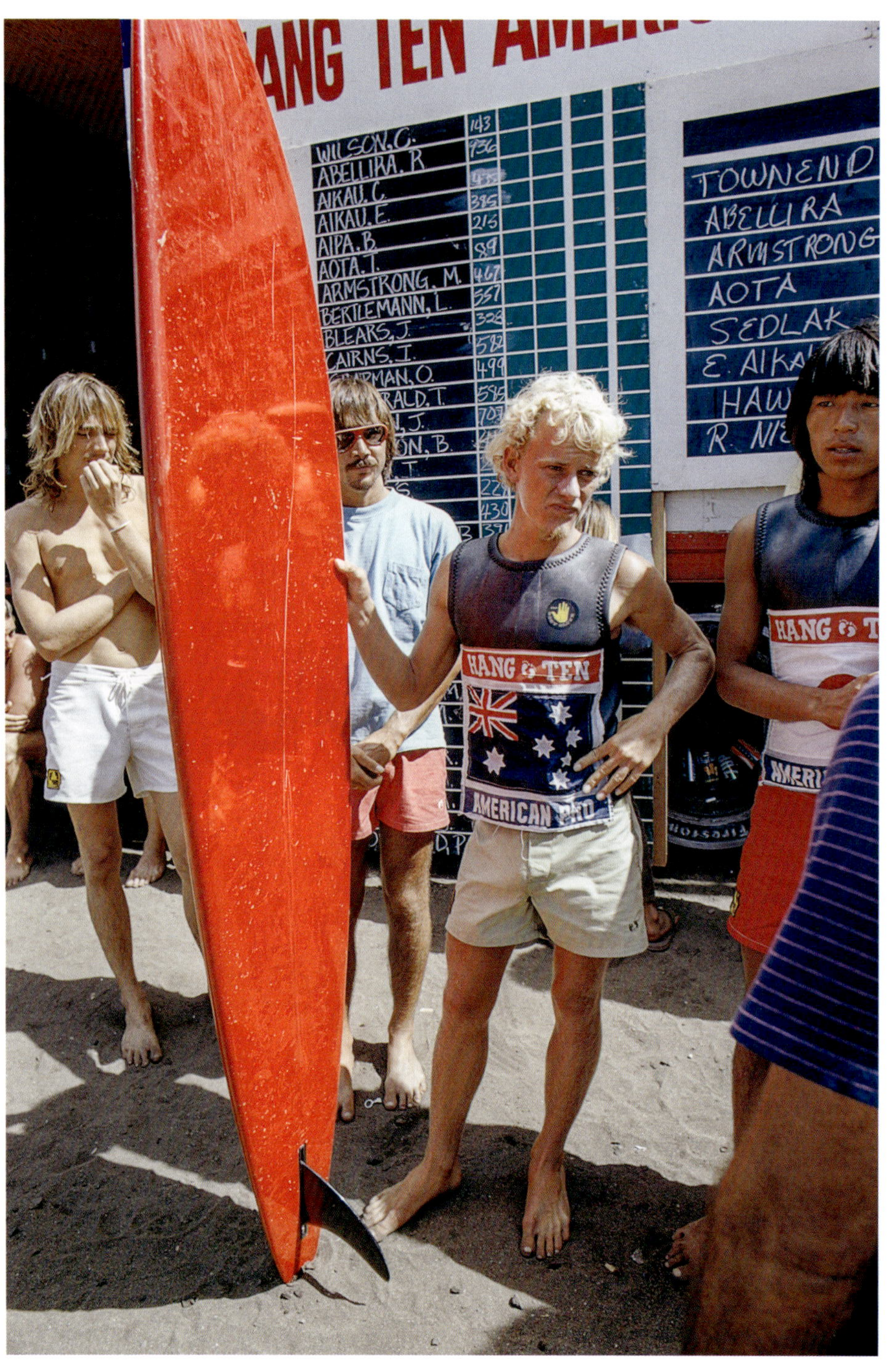

Rory Russell, Gerry Lopez, Peter Townend, Takuji Aota, Sunset Beach , Oahu, HI 1974

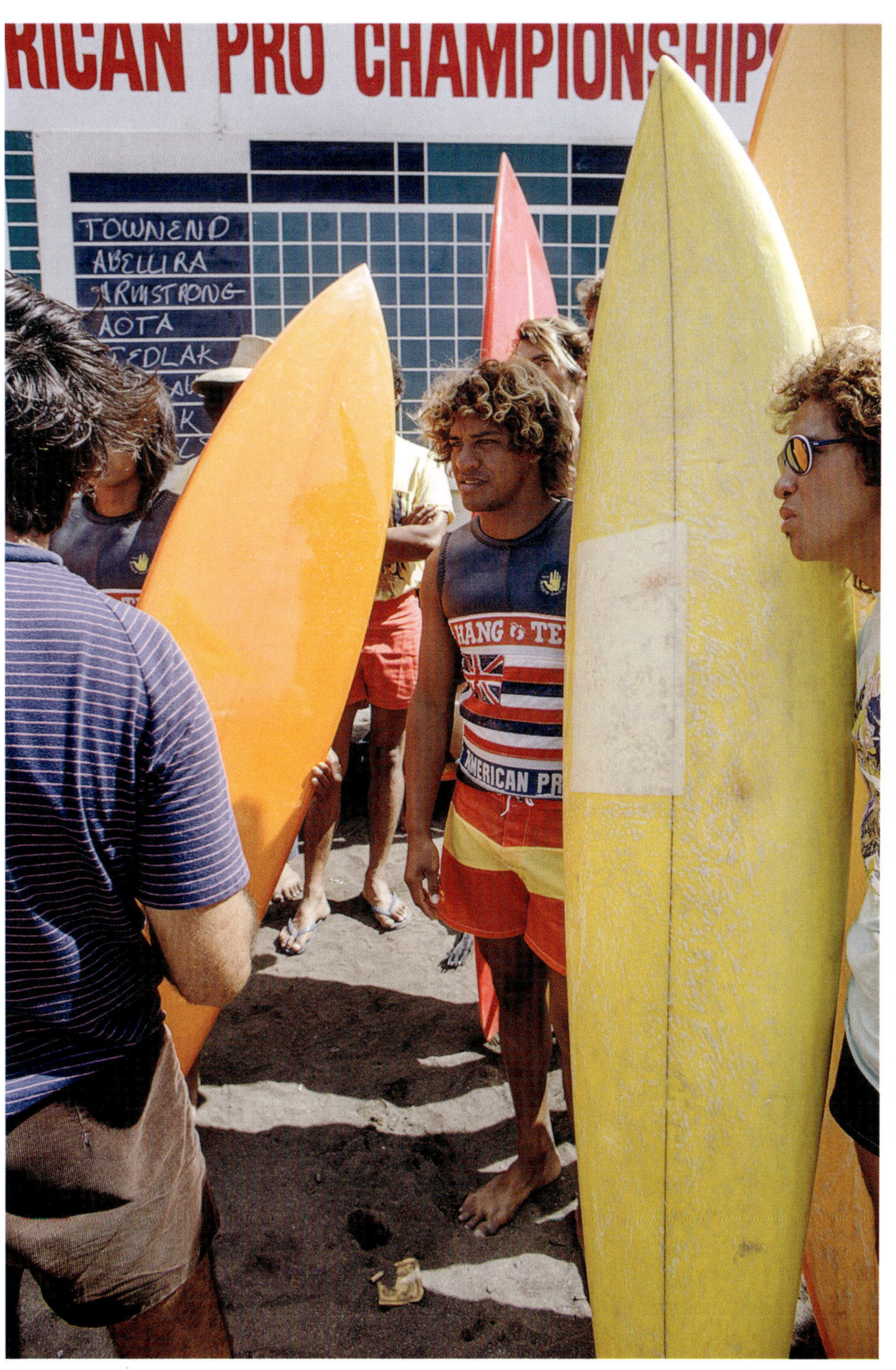

Eddie Aikau, Clyde Aikau, Sunset Beach, Oahu, HI 1974

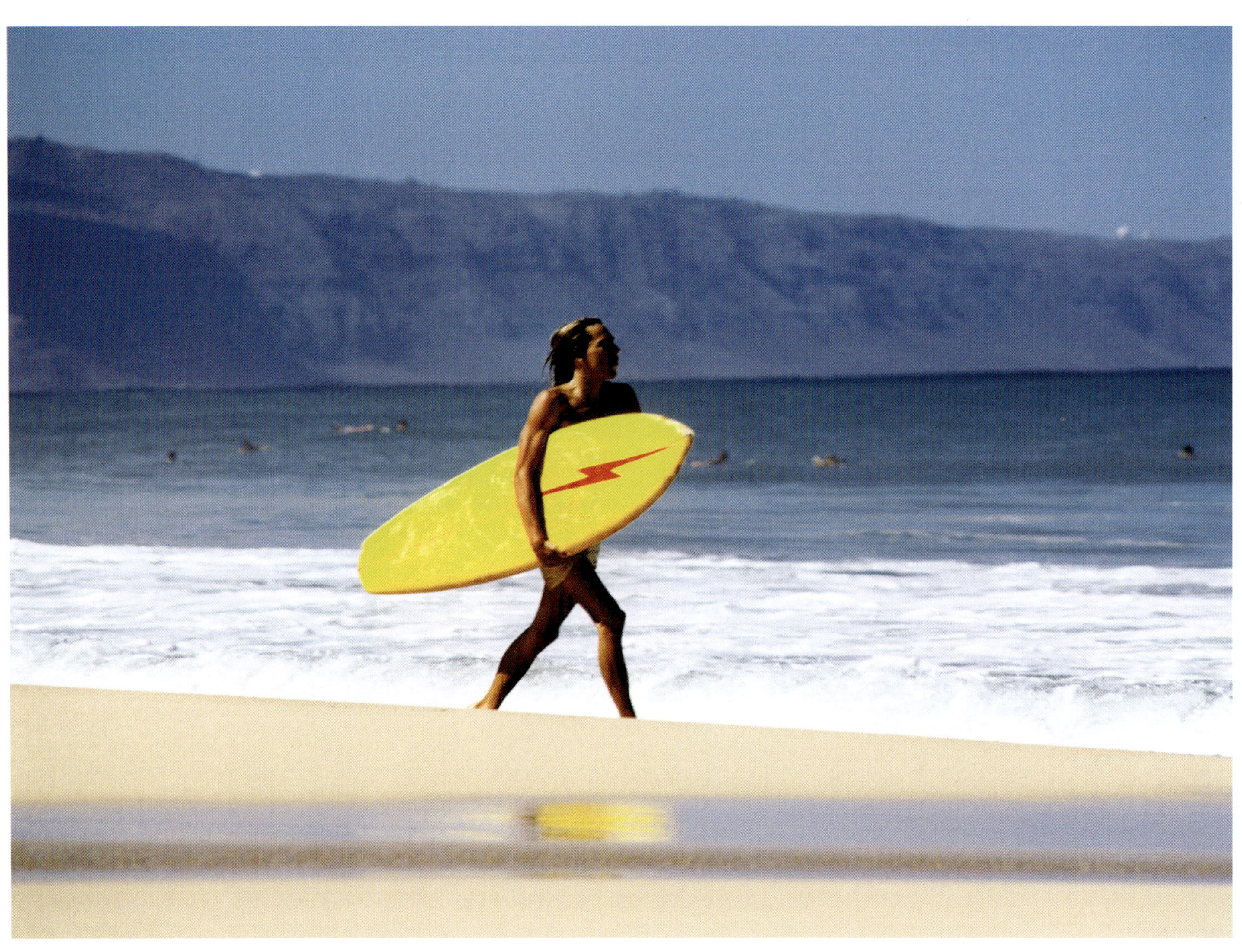

Rory Russell, Rocky Point, Oahu, HI 1973

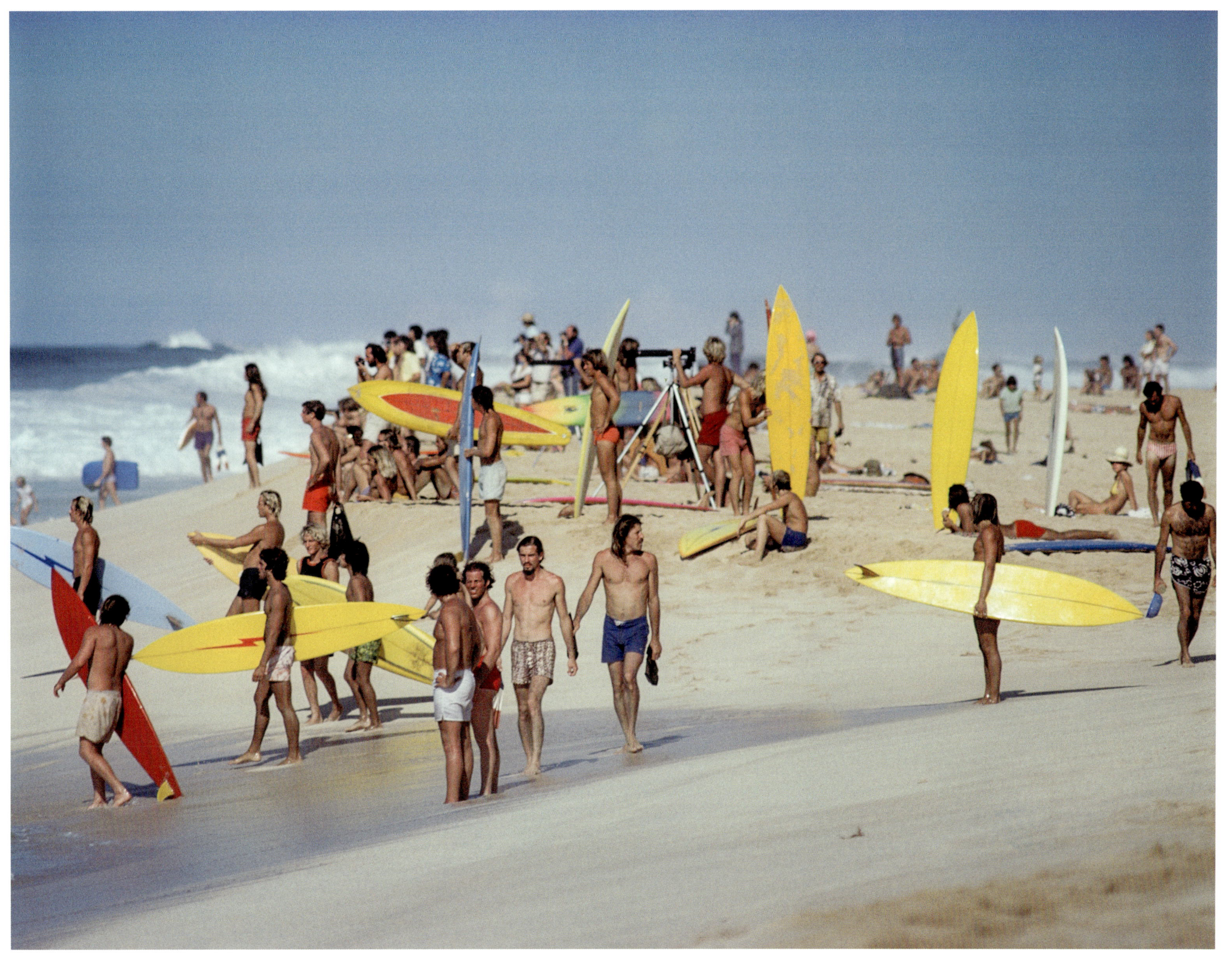

Pipeline, Oahu, HI 1975

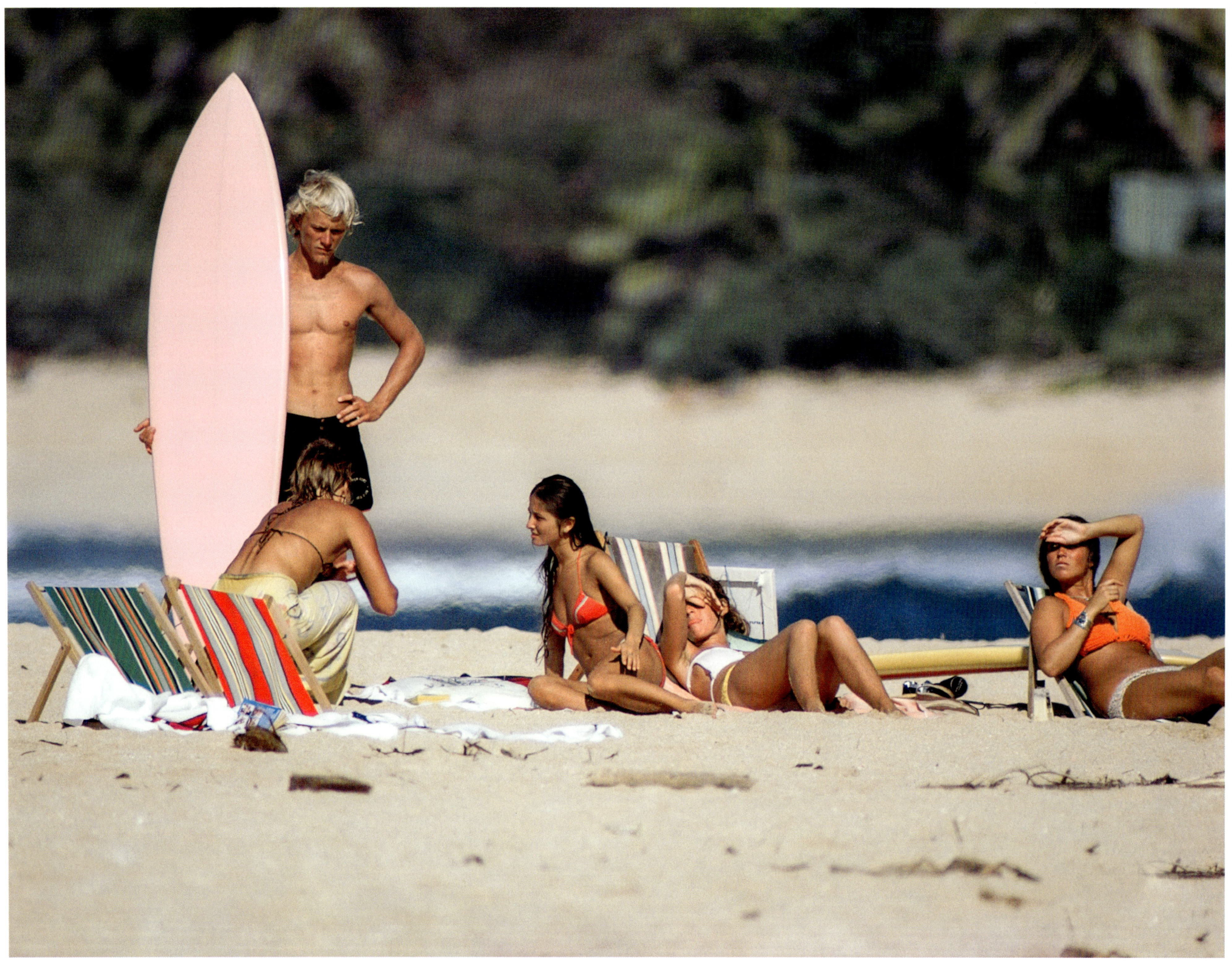

Peter Townend, Rocky Point, Oahu, HI 1974

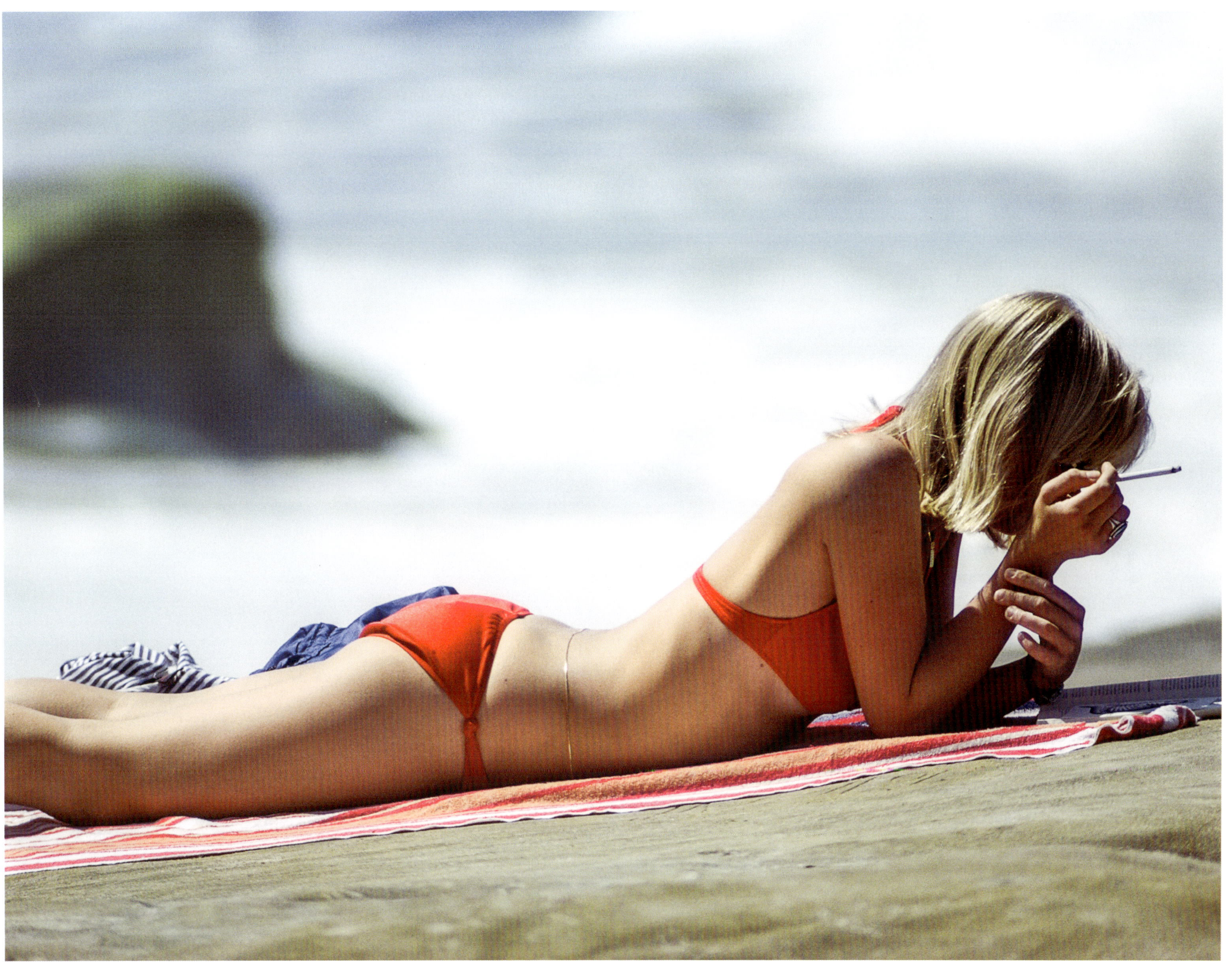

Windansea, La Jolla, CA 1970

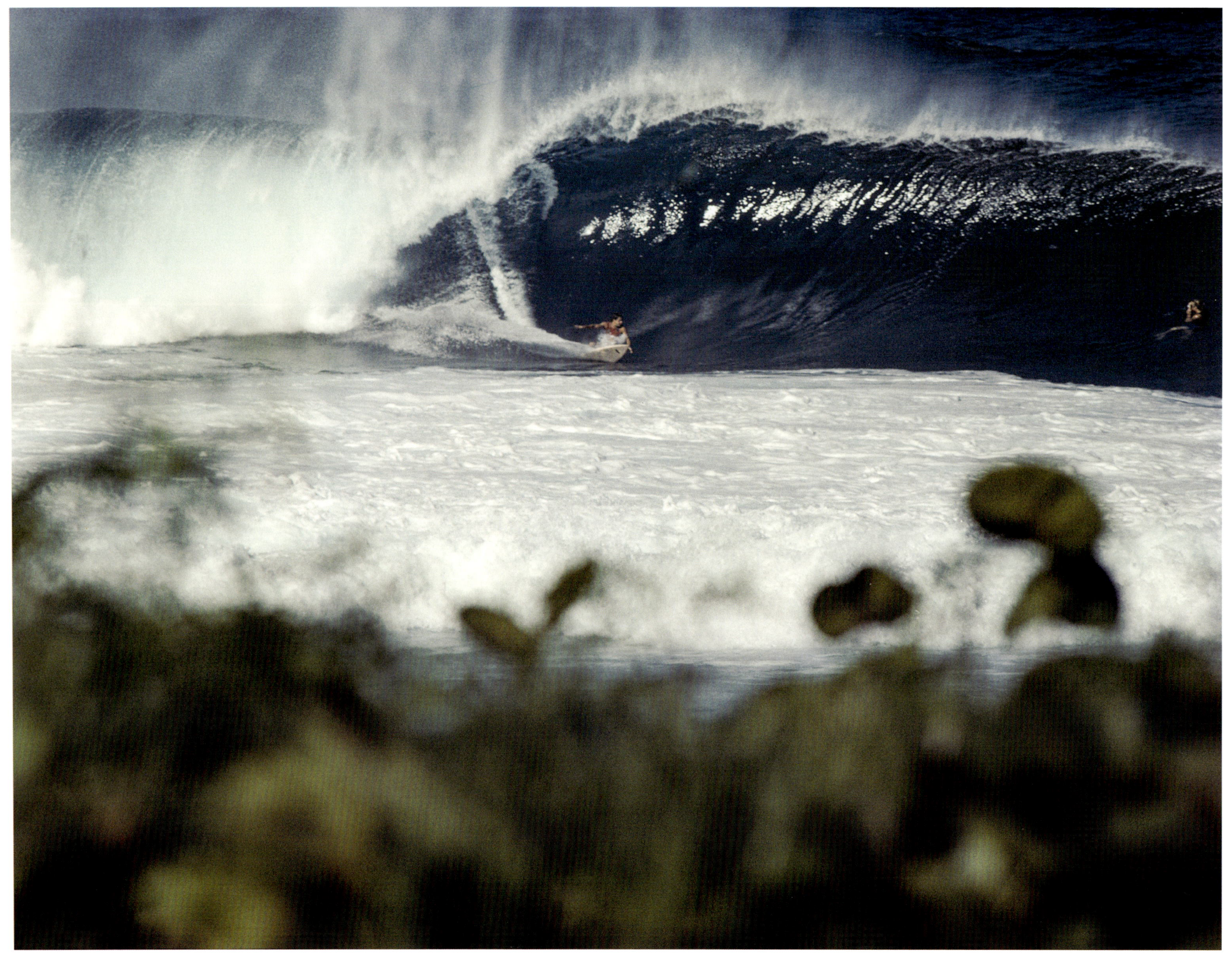

Shaun Tomson, Pipeline, Oahu, HI 1976

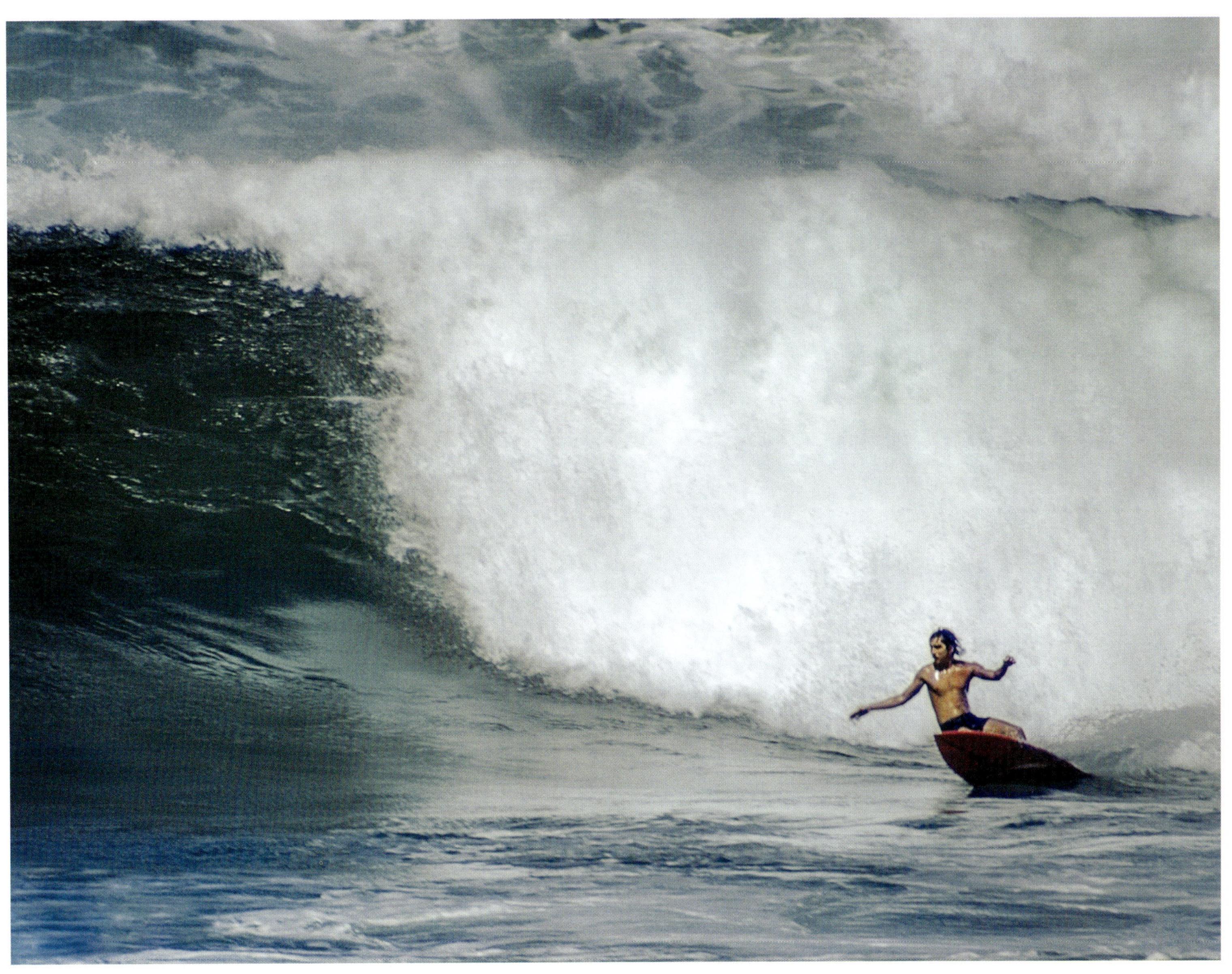

Gerry Lopez, Sunset Beach, Oahu, HI 1971

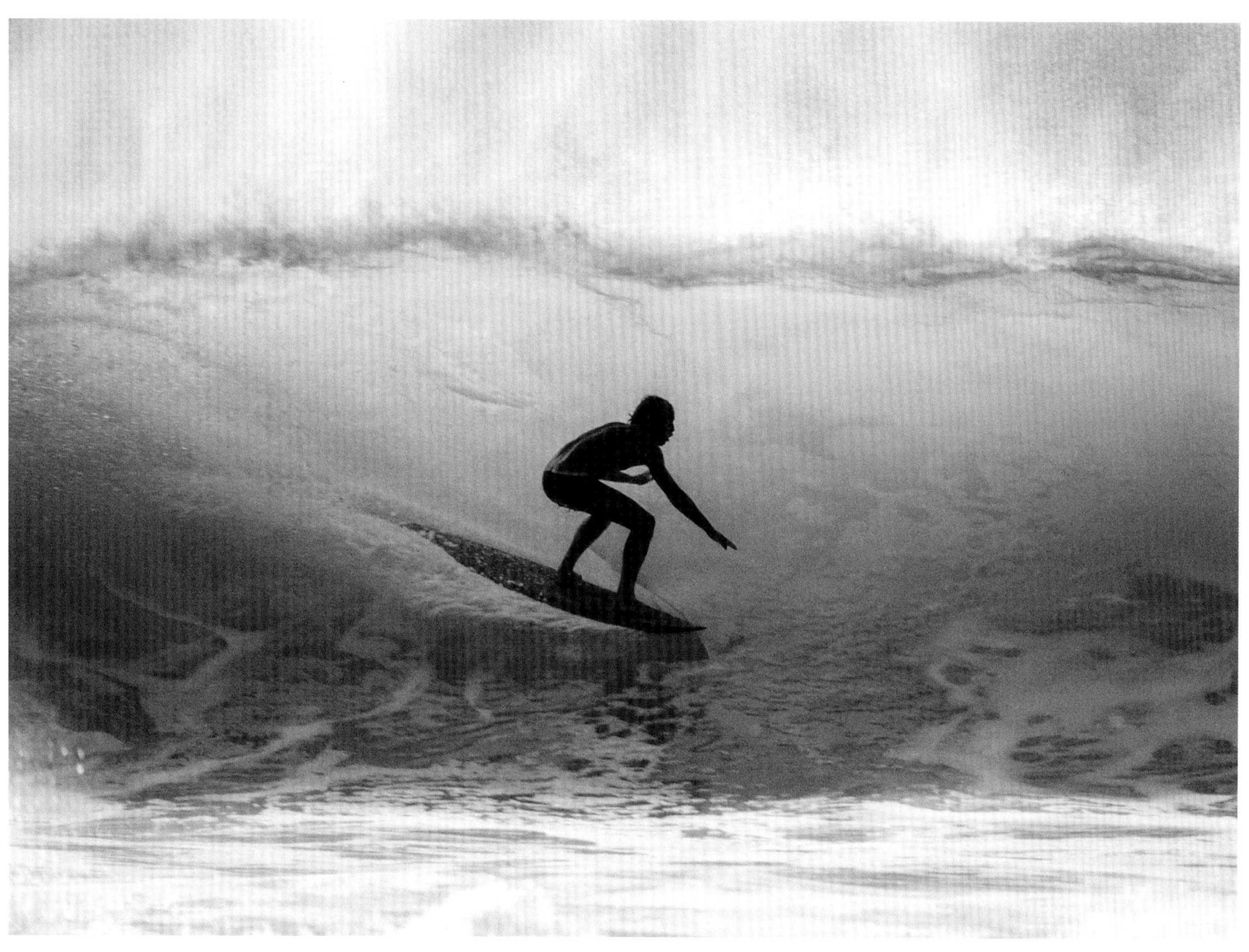

Yuri Farrant, Gas Chamber, Oahu, HI 1974

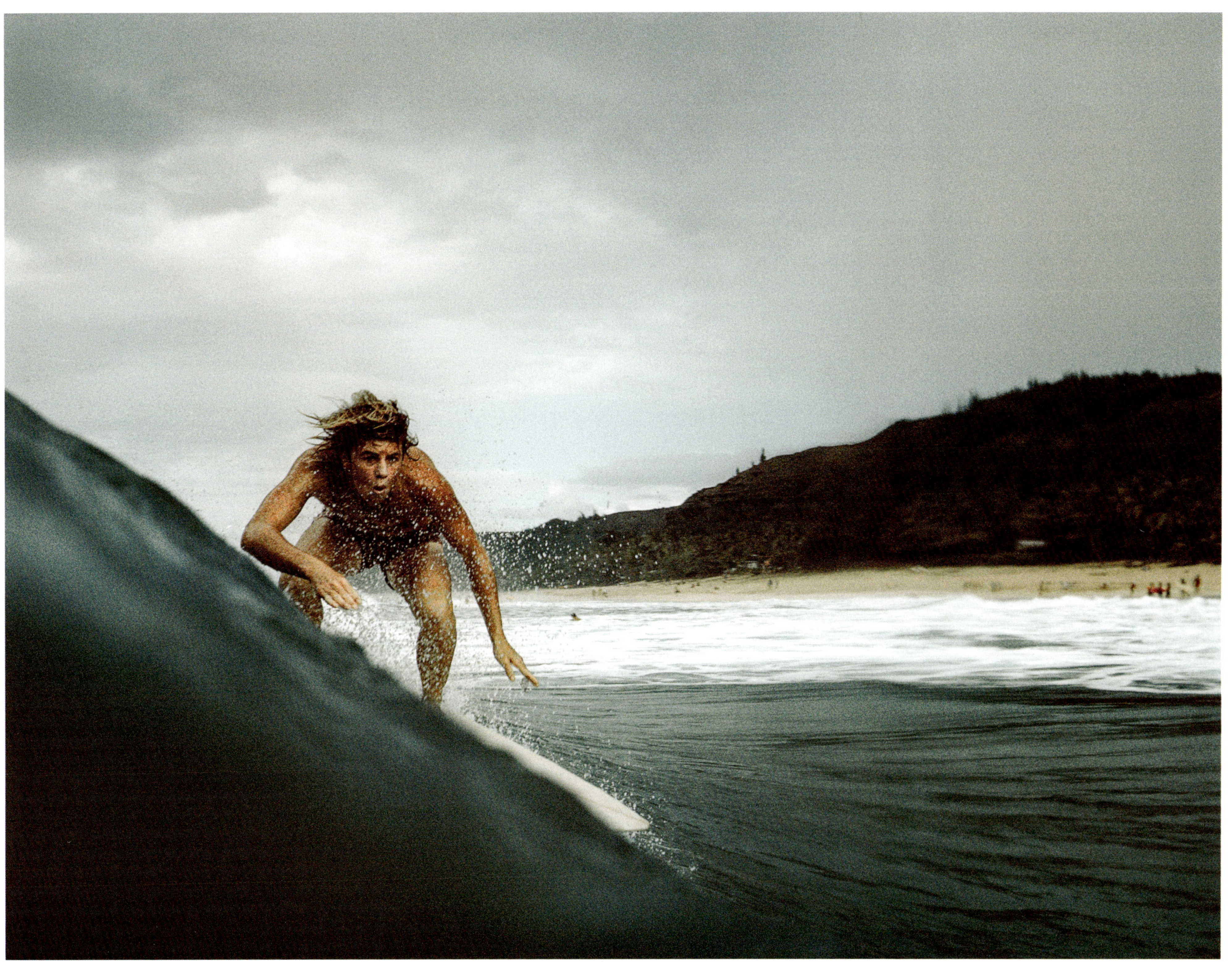

Wayne “Rabbit” Bartholomew, Backdoor, Oahu, HI 1974

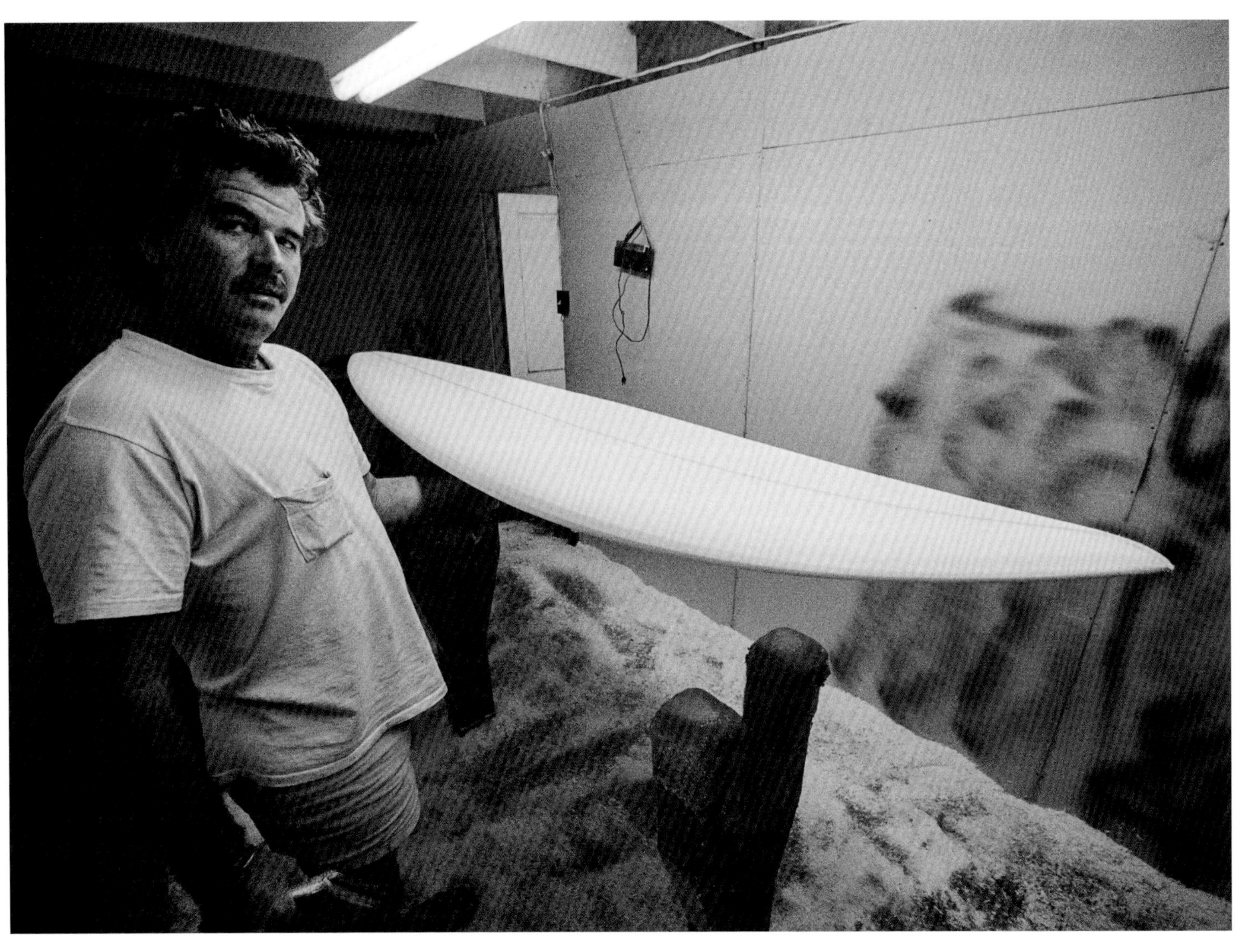

Mike Diffenderfer, Ke Iki Road, Oahu, HI 1976

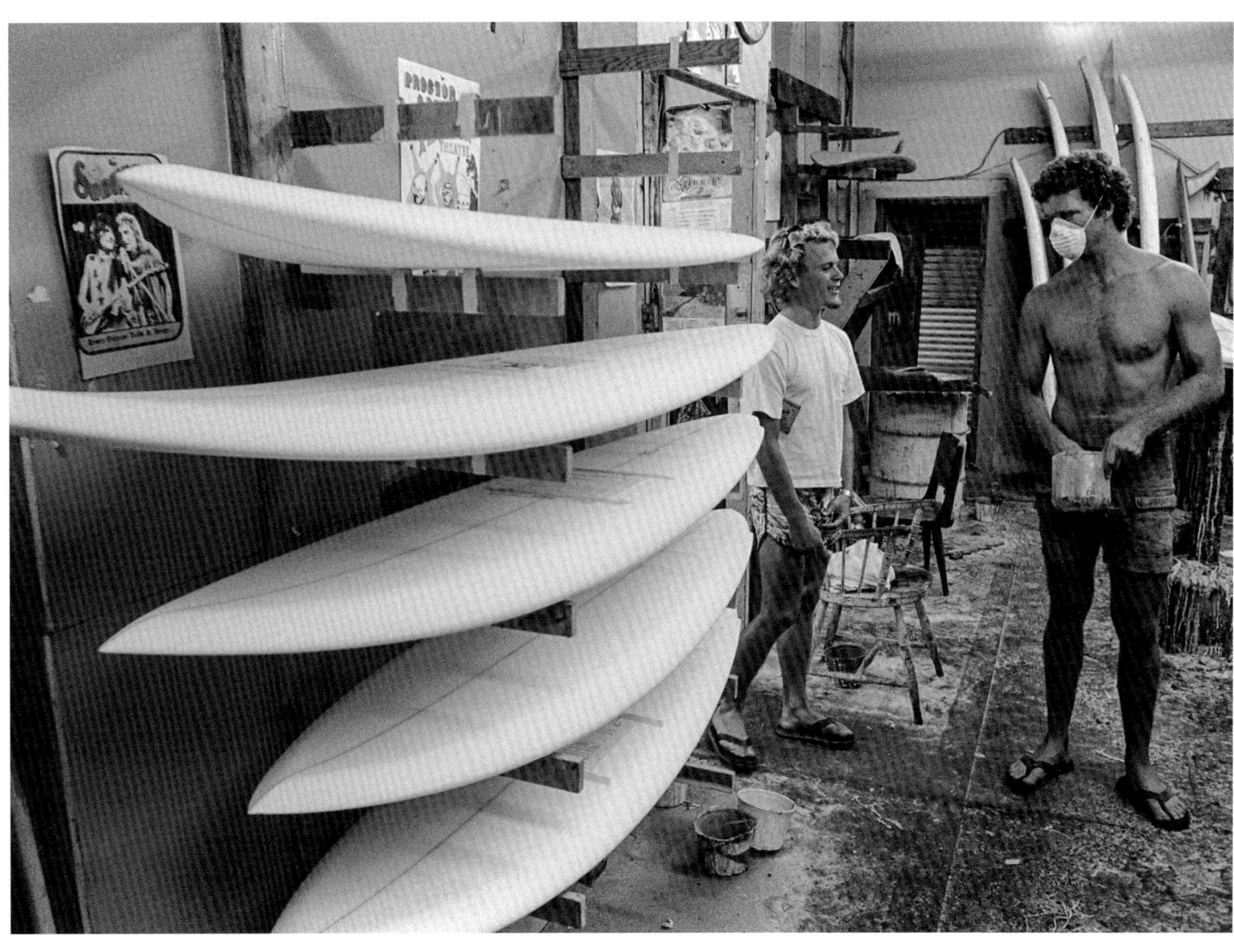

Peter Townend, David Garner, Haleiwa, Oahu, HI 1974

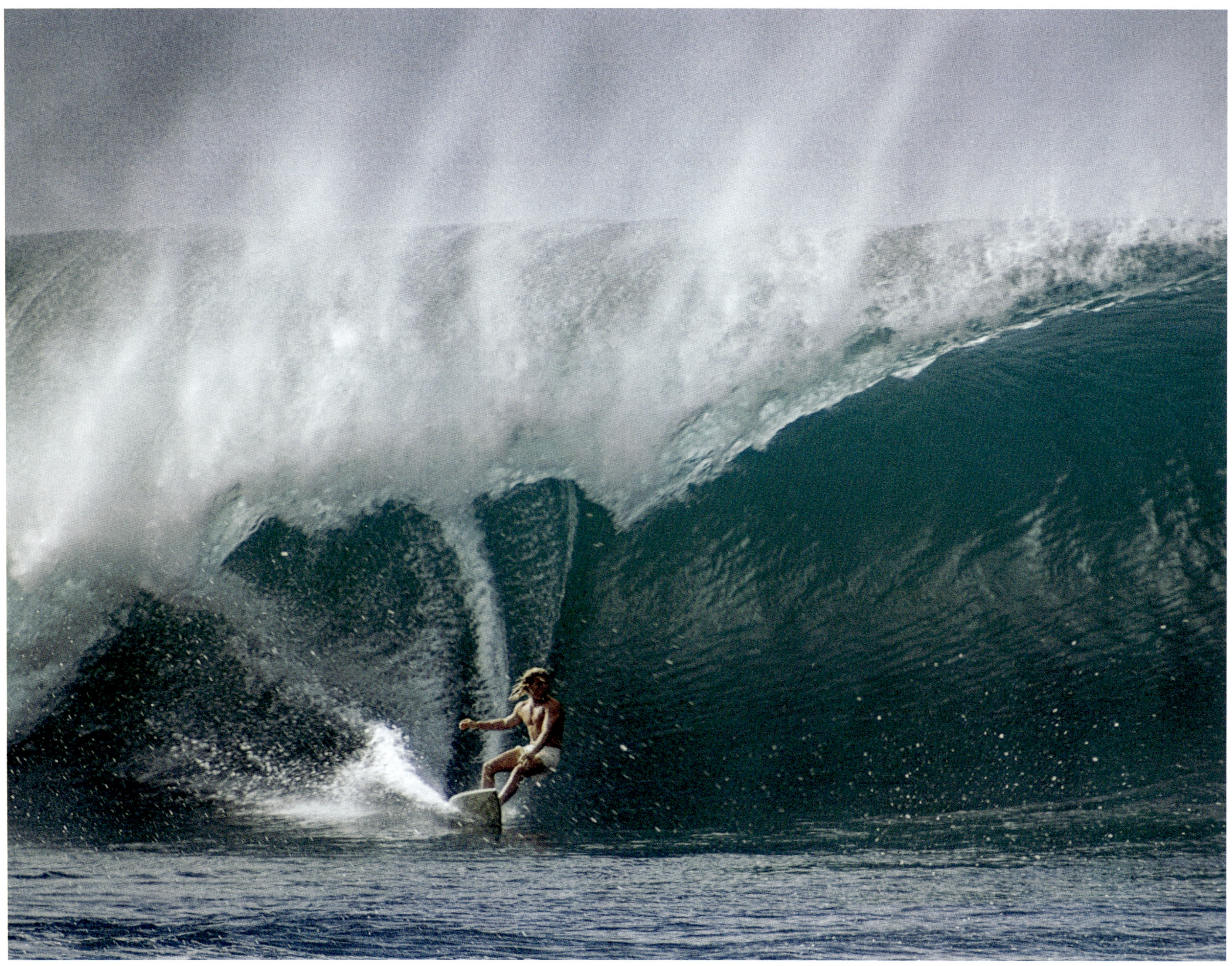

Sam Hawk, Pipeline, Oahu, HI 1971

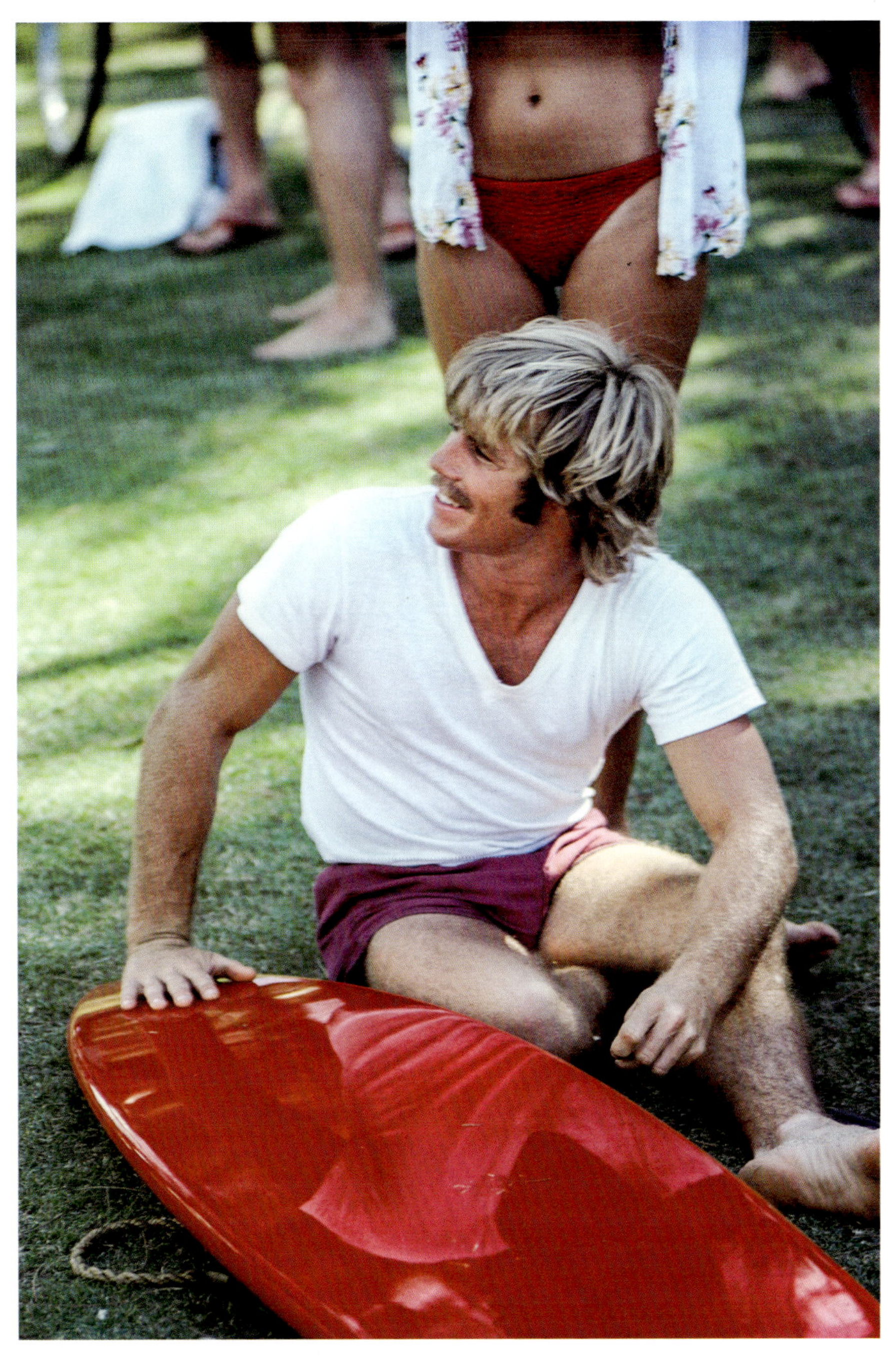

Sam Hawk, Waimea Bay, Oahu, HI 1975

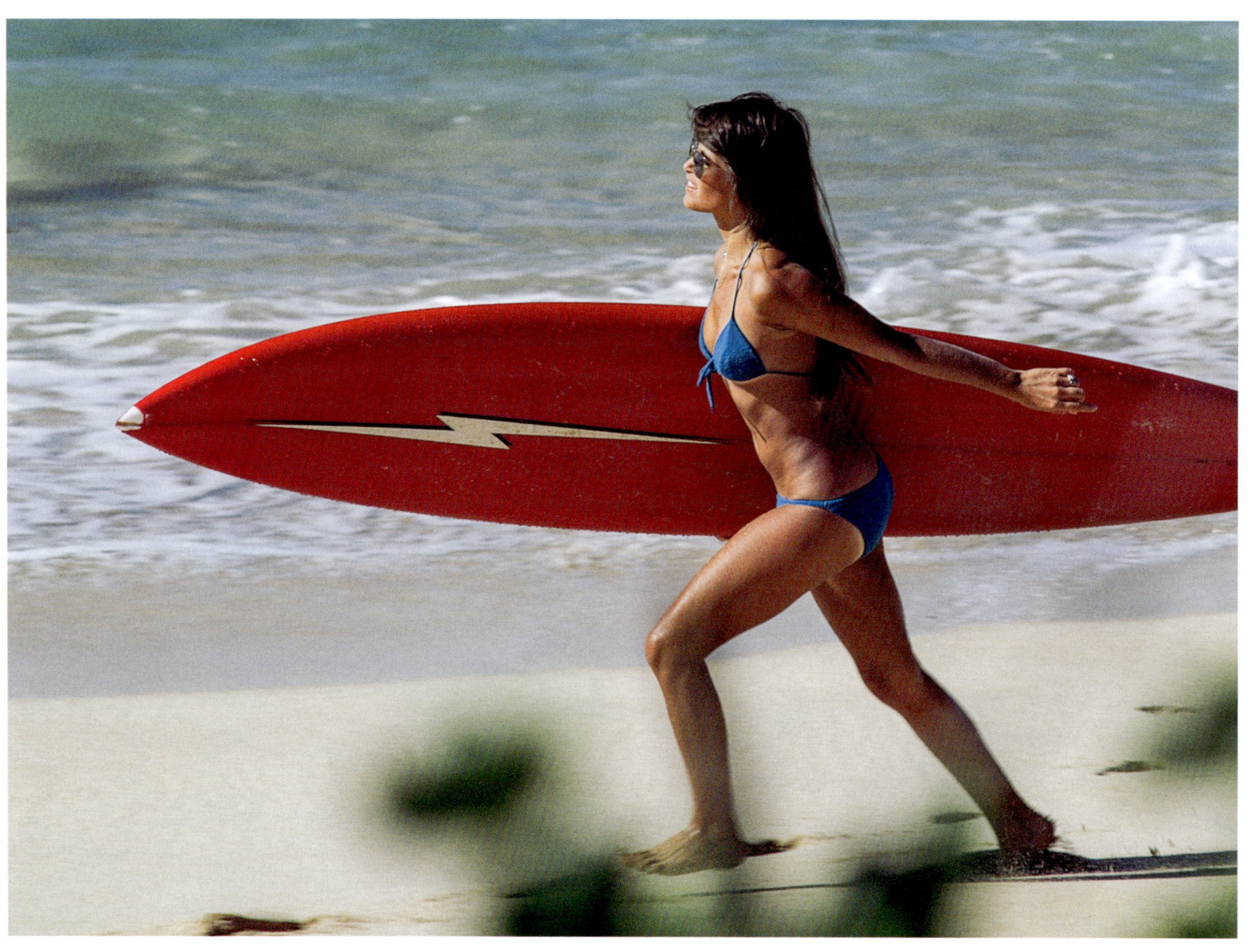

Denice Dixon, Sunset Beach, Oahu, HI 1976

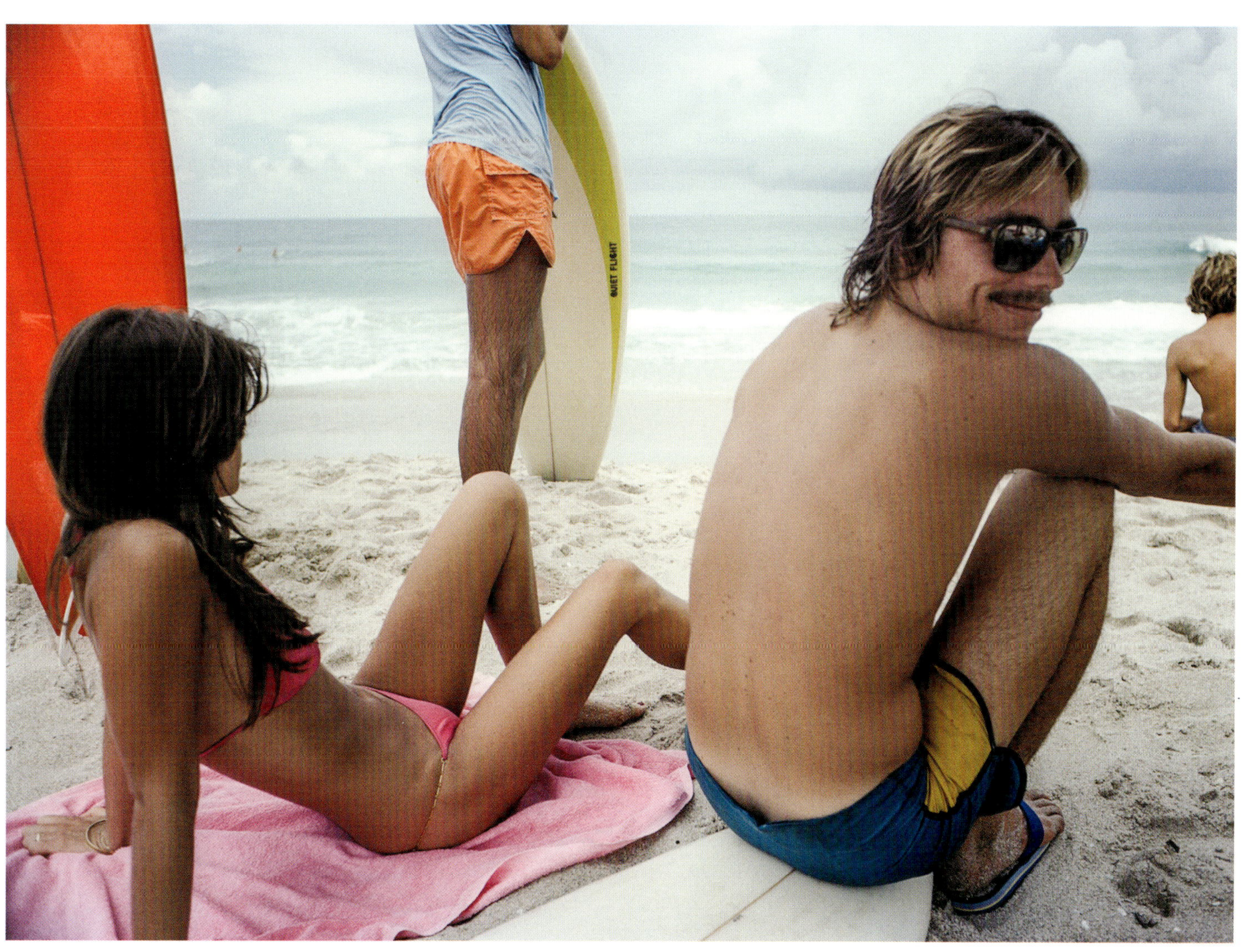

Denice Dixon and Rory Russell, Sebastian Inlet, FL 1977

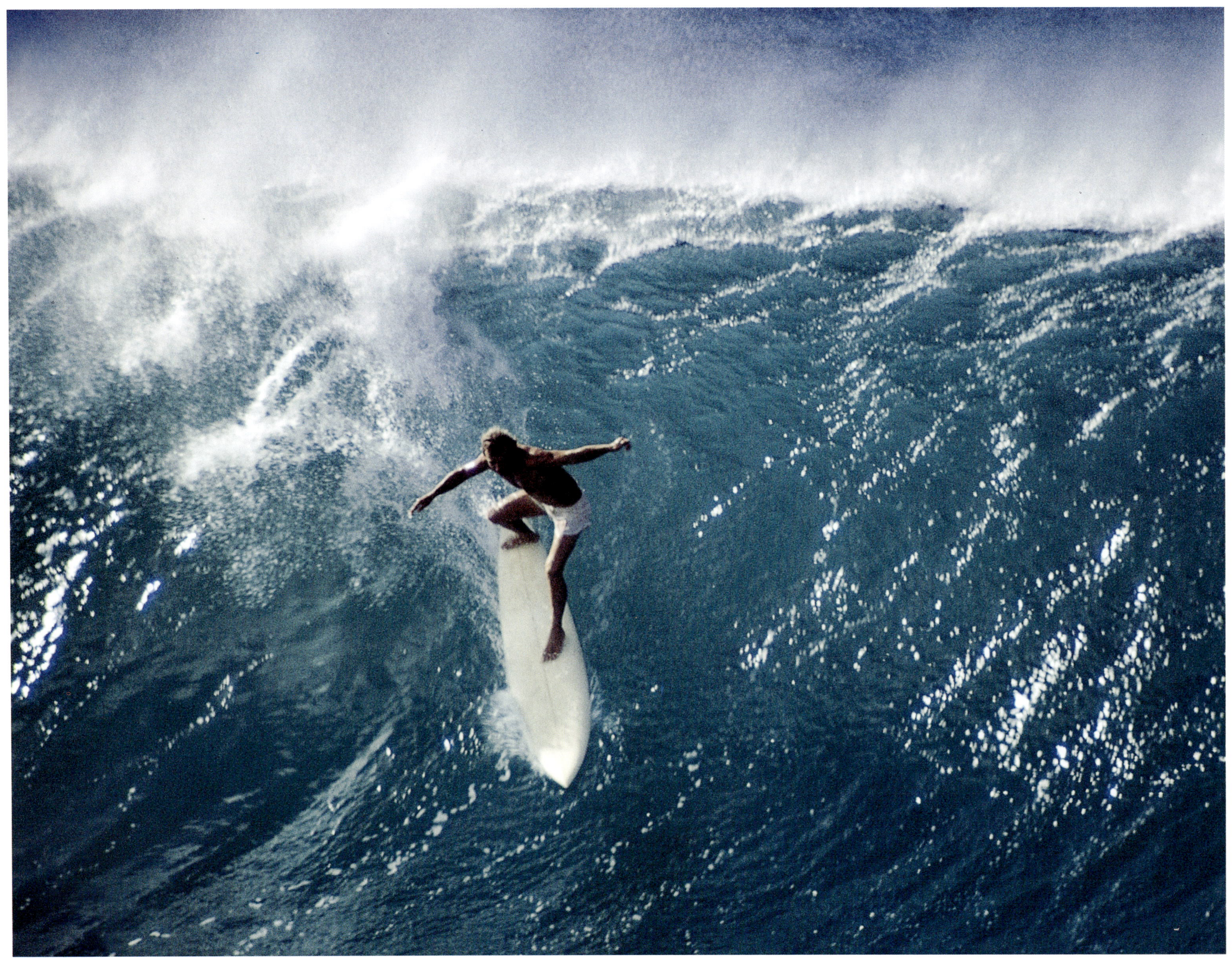

Jackie Baxter, Pipeline "Expression Session" Oahu, HI 1971

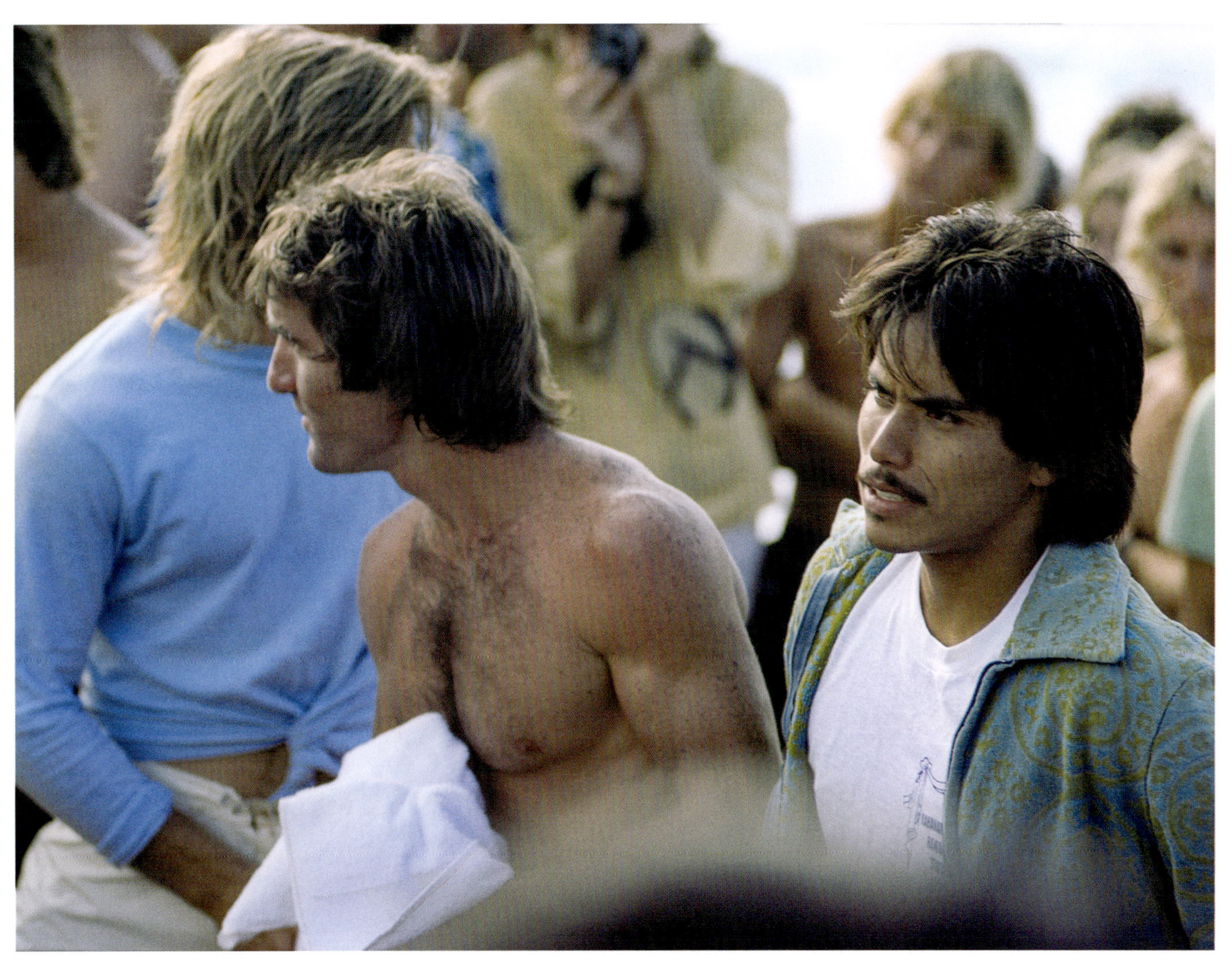

Jeff Hakman, Reno Abellira, Sunset Beach, Oahu, HI 1974

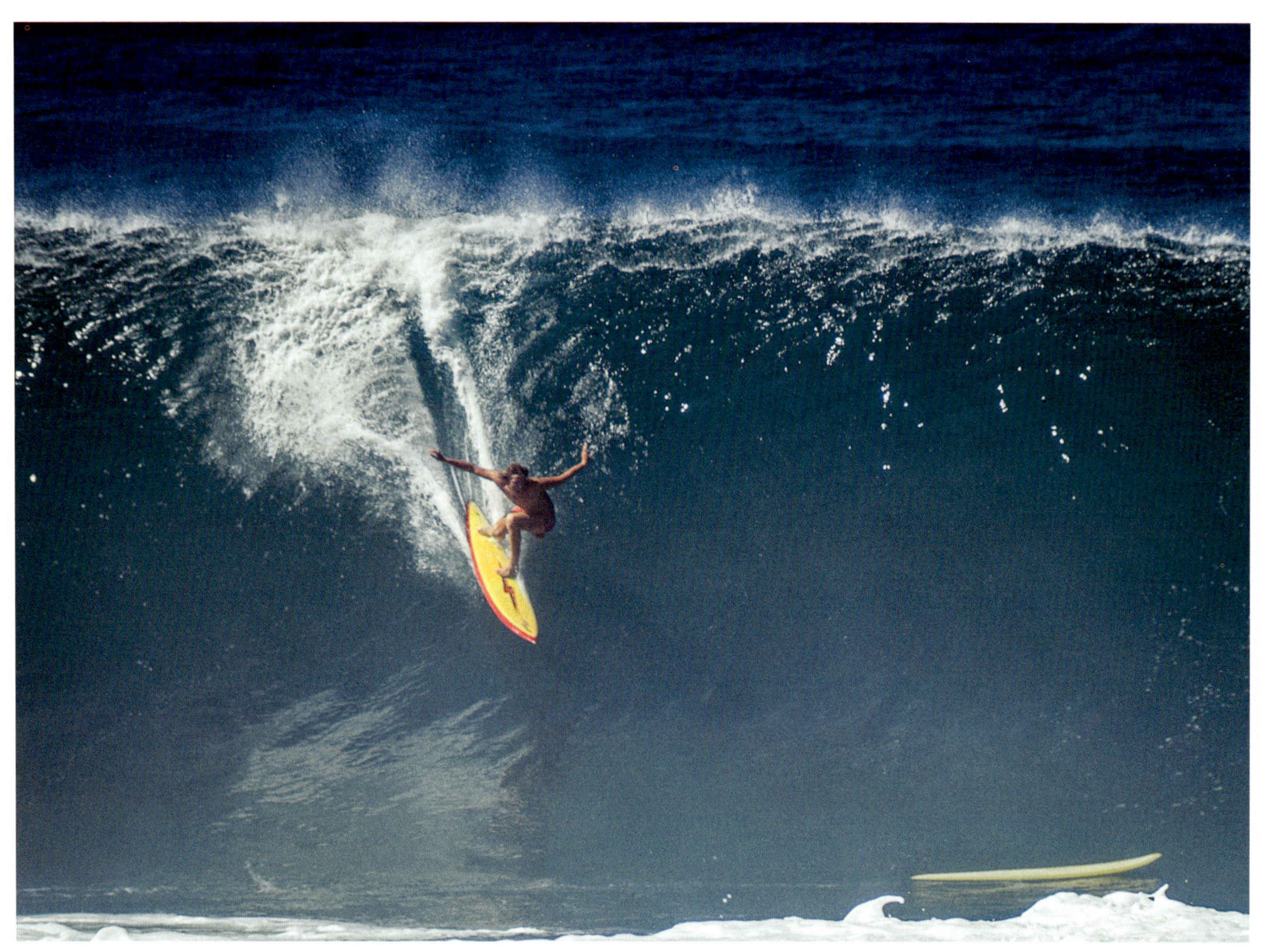

Mark Richards, Pipeline, Oahu, HI 1974

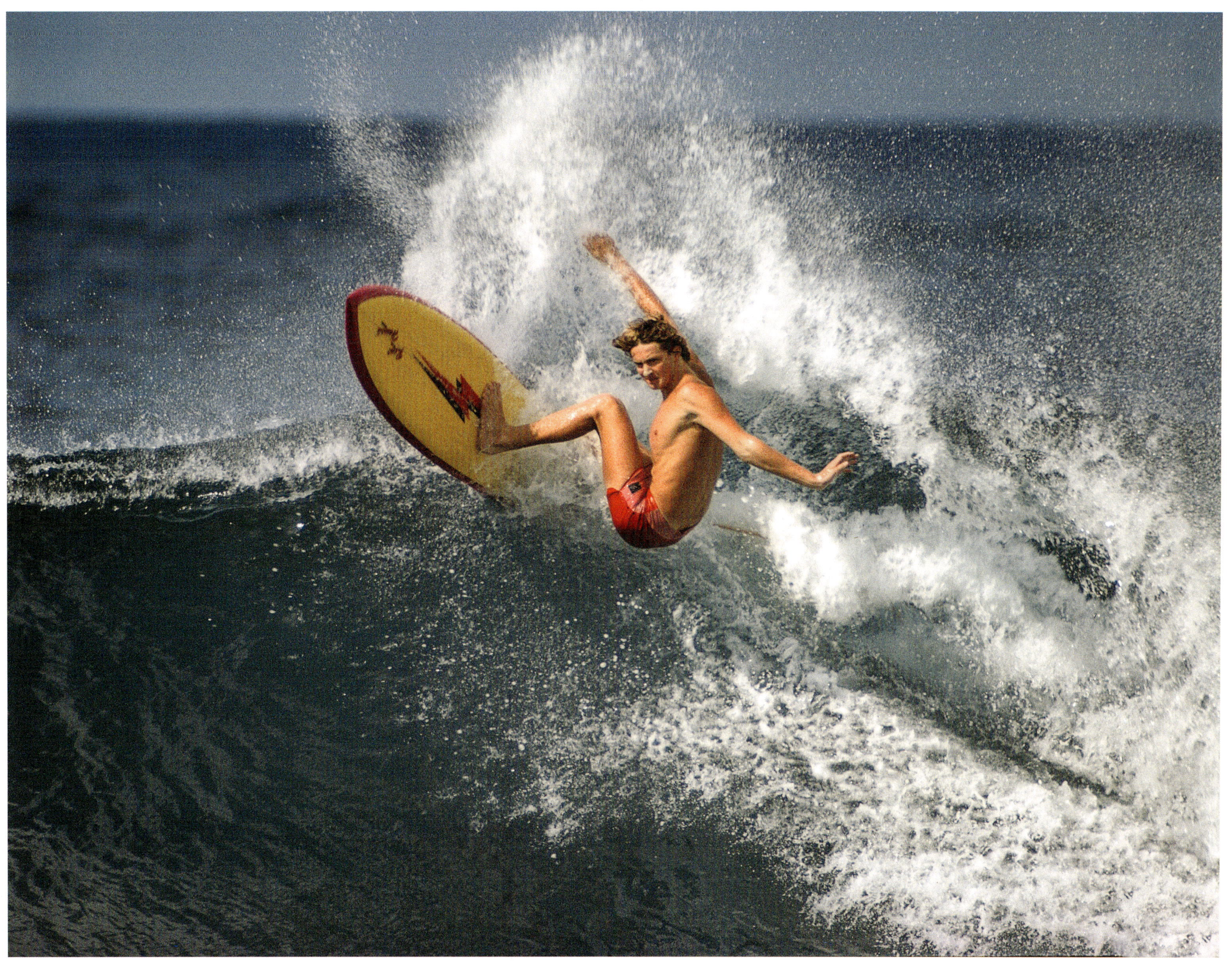

Mark Richards, Off The Wall, Oahu, HI 1974

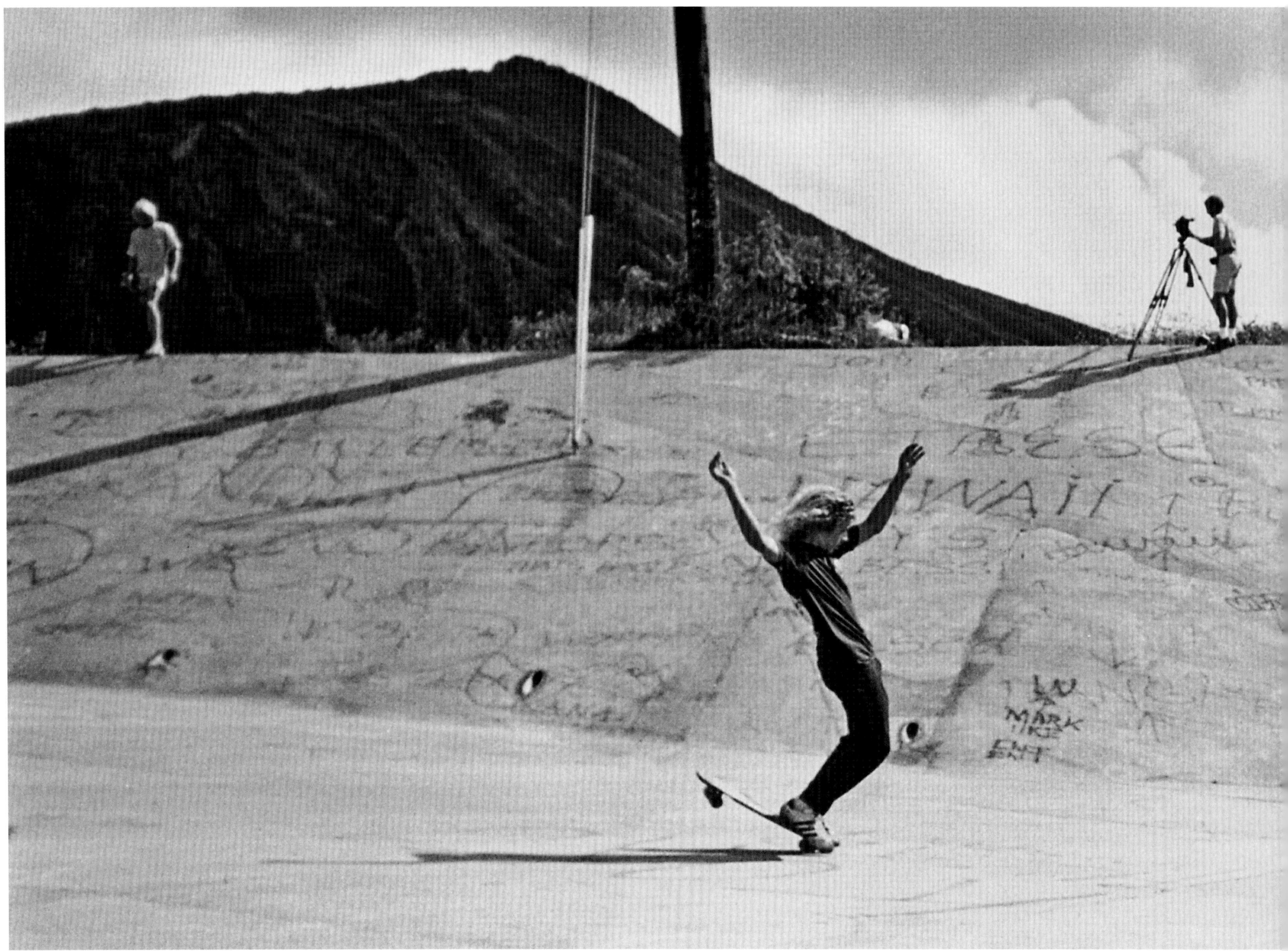
MARK

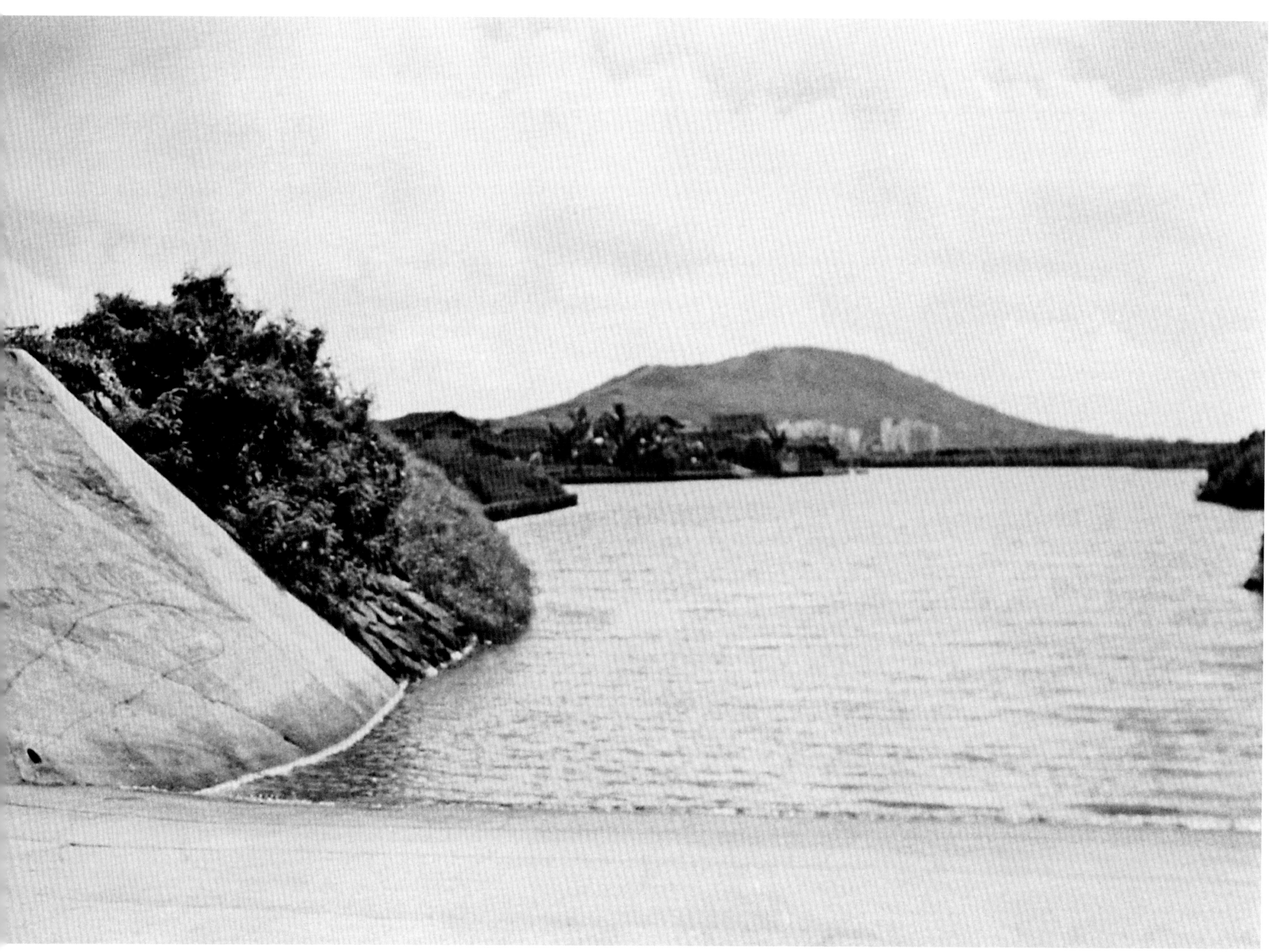

Tony Alva, Hawaii Kai, Oahu, HI 1976

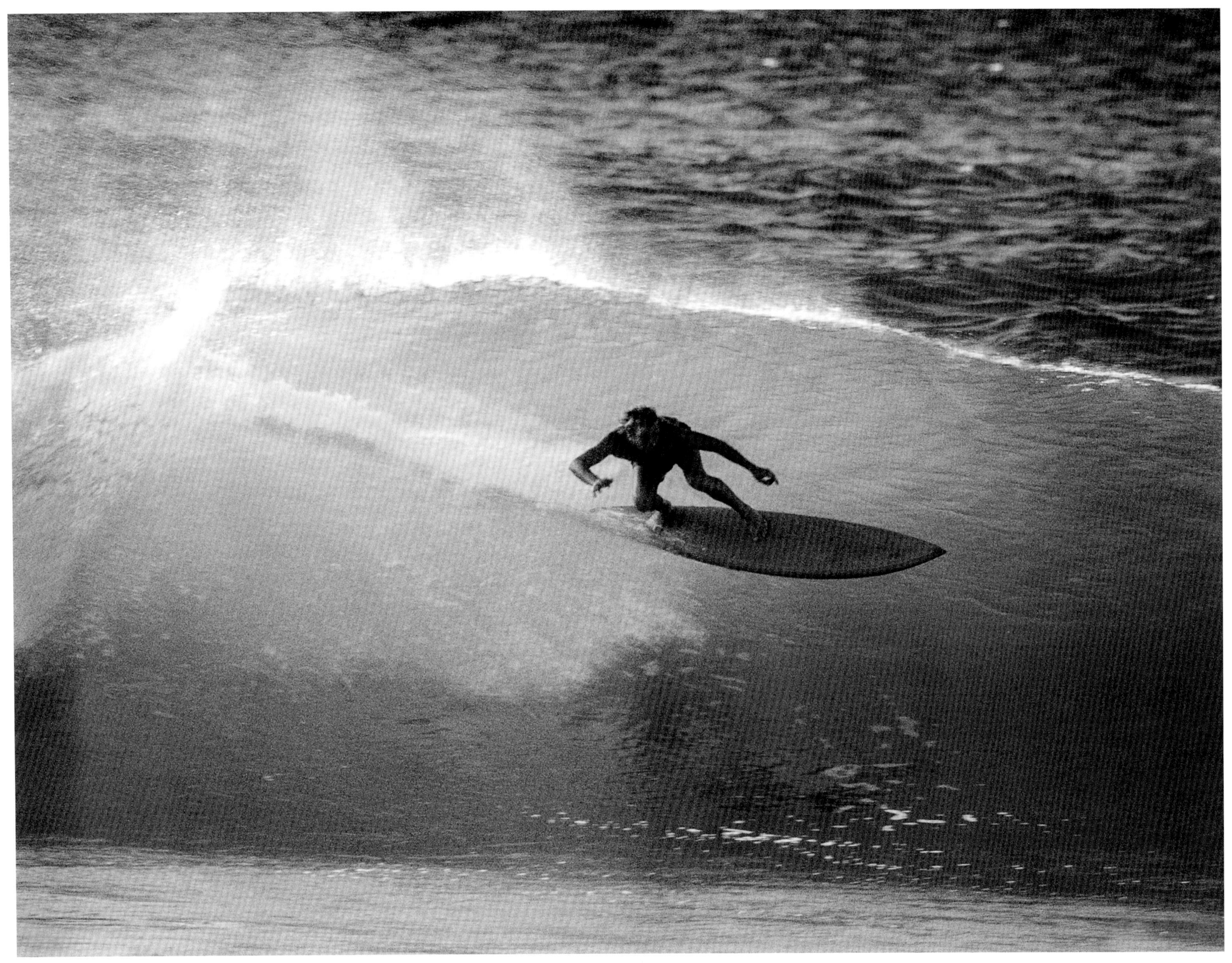

Jim Turner, Rocky Point, Oahu, HI 1971

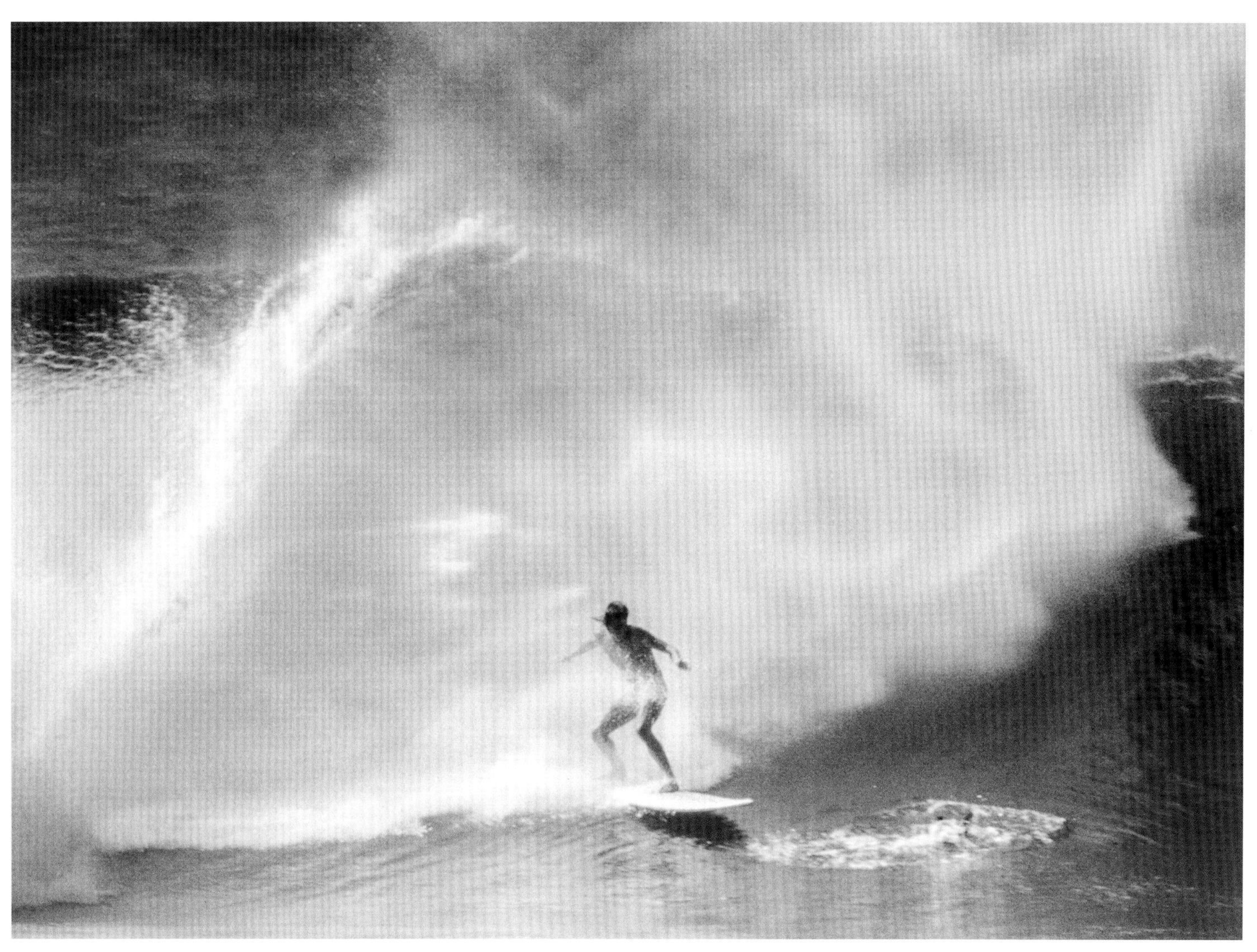

Wayne "Rabbit" Bartholomew, Pipeline, Oahu, HI 1976

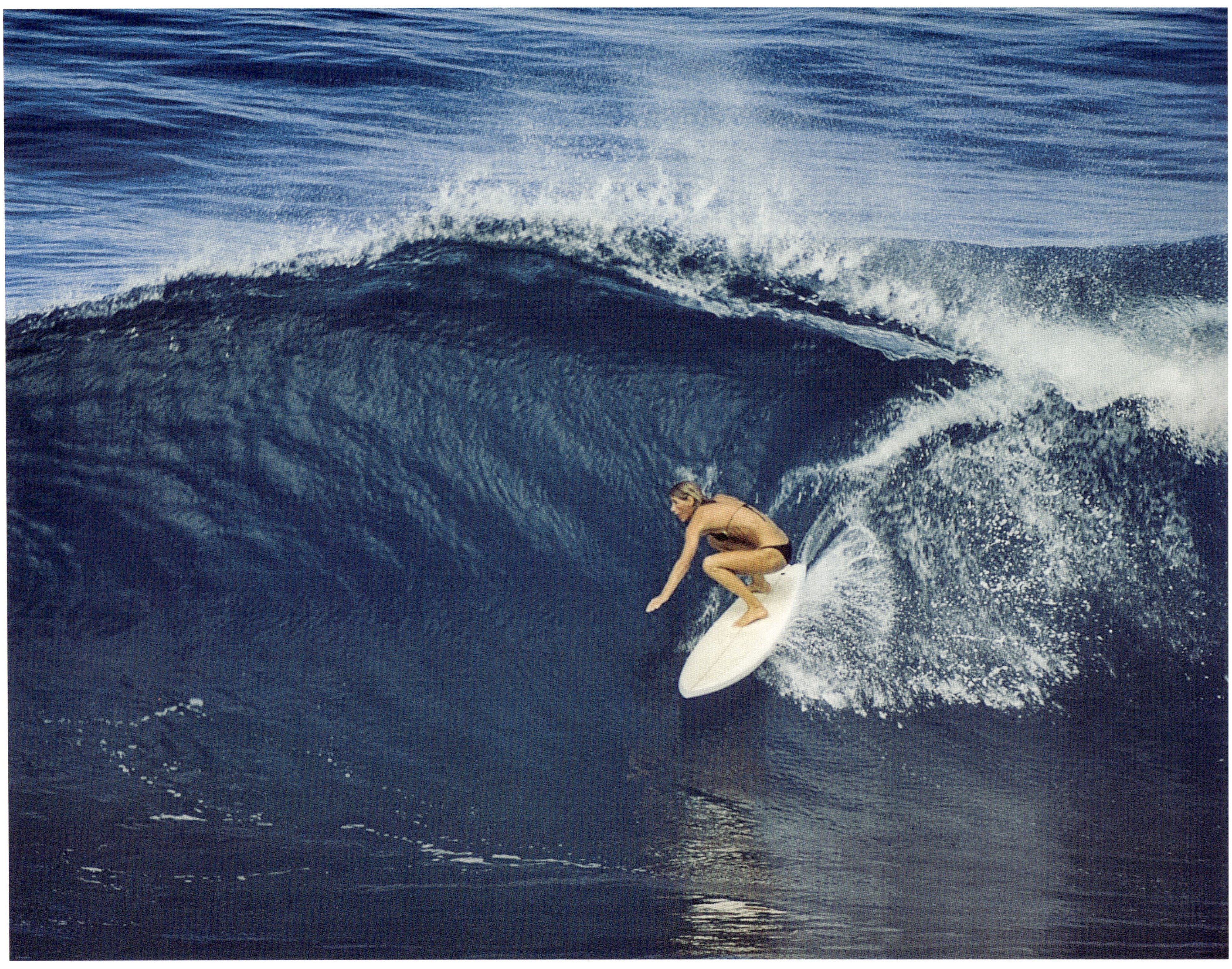

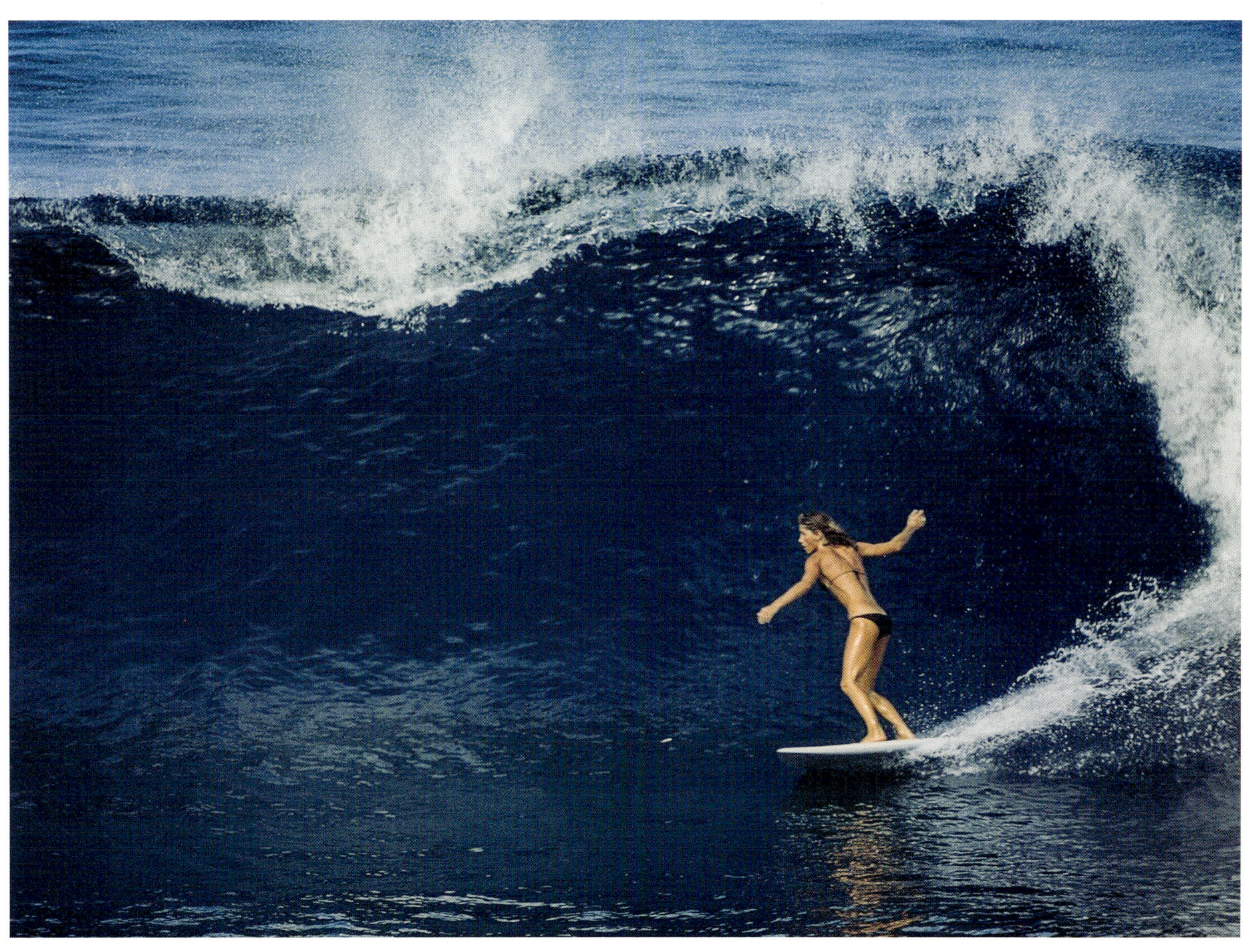

Teri Melanson, Pupukea, Oahu, HI 1976

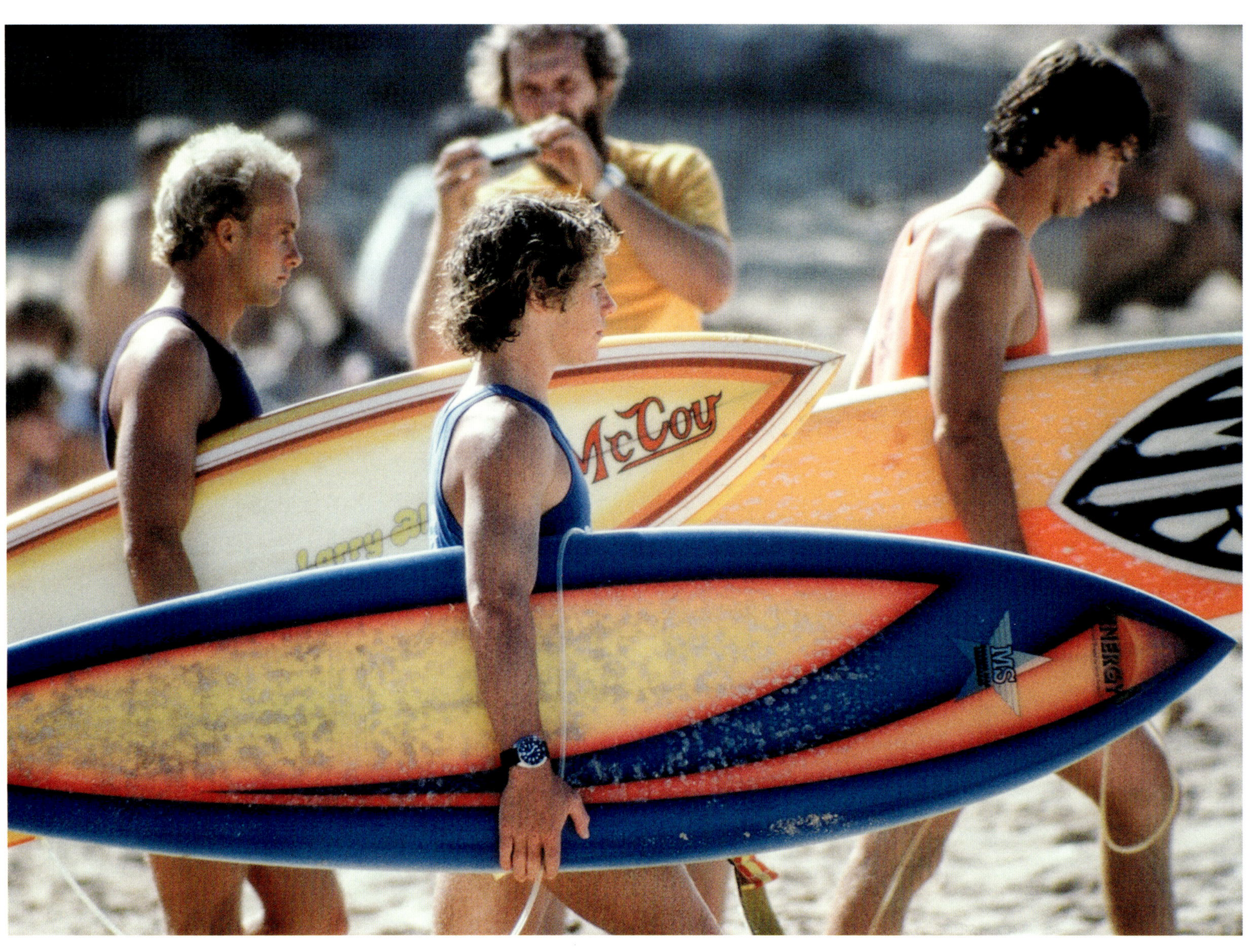

Larry Blair, Tom Carroll, Mark Richards, Pipeline, Oahu, HI 1979

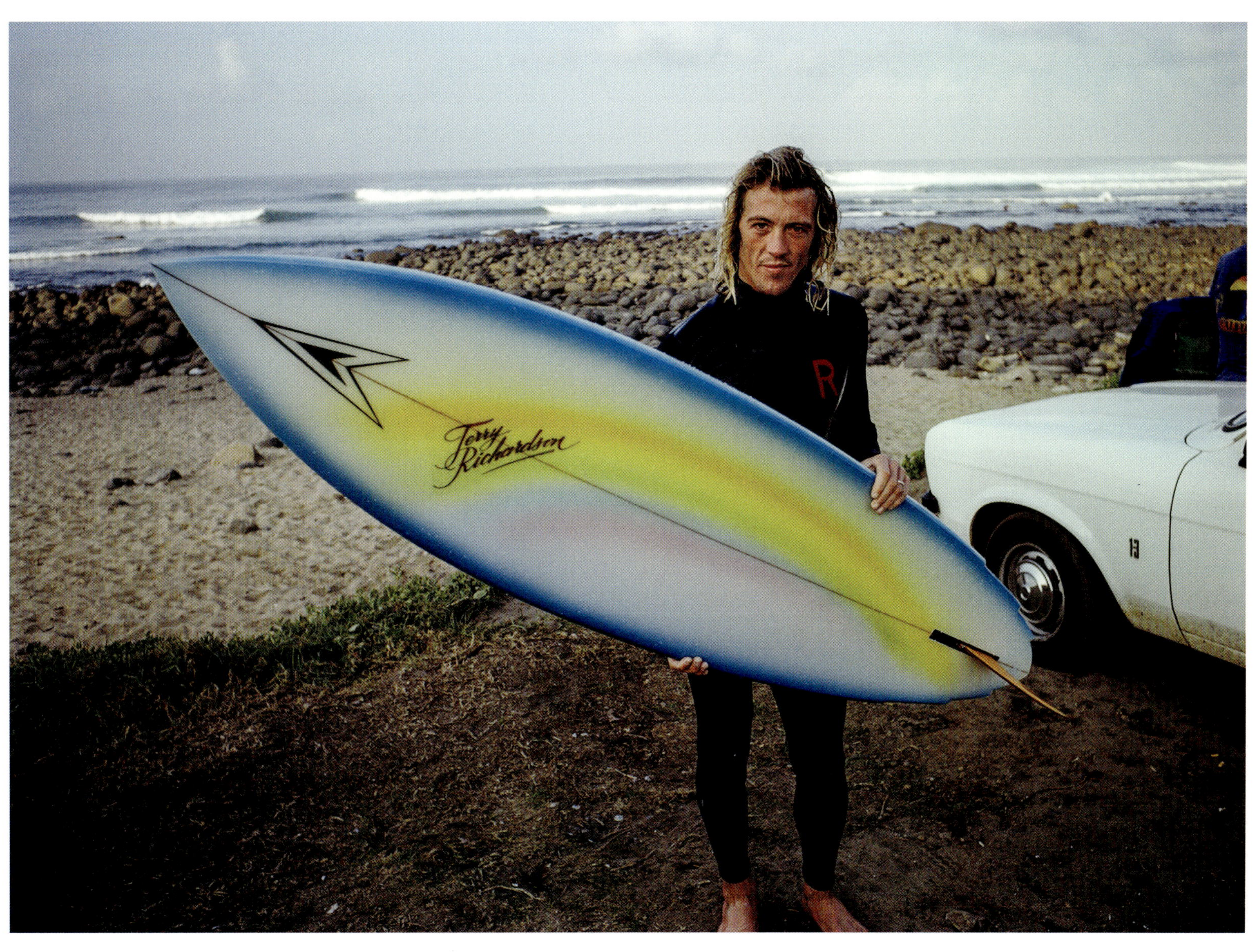

Terry Richardson, Nahoon Reef, South Africa 1978

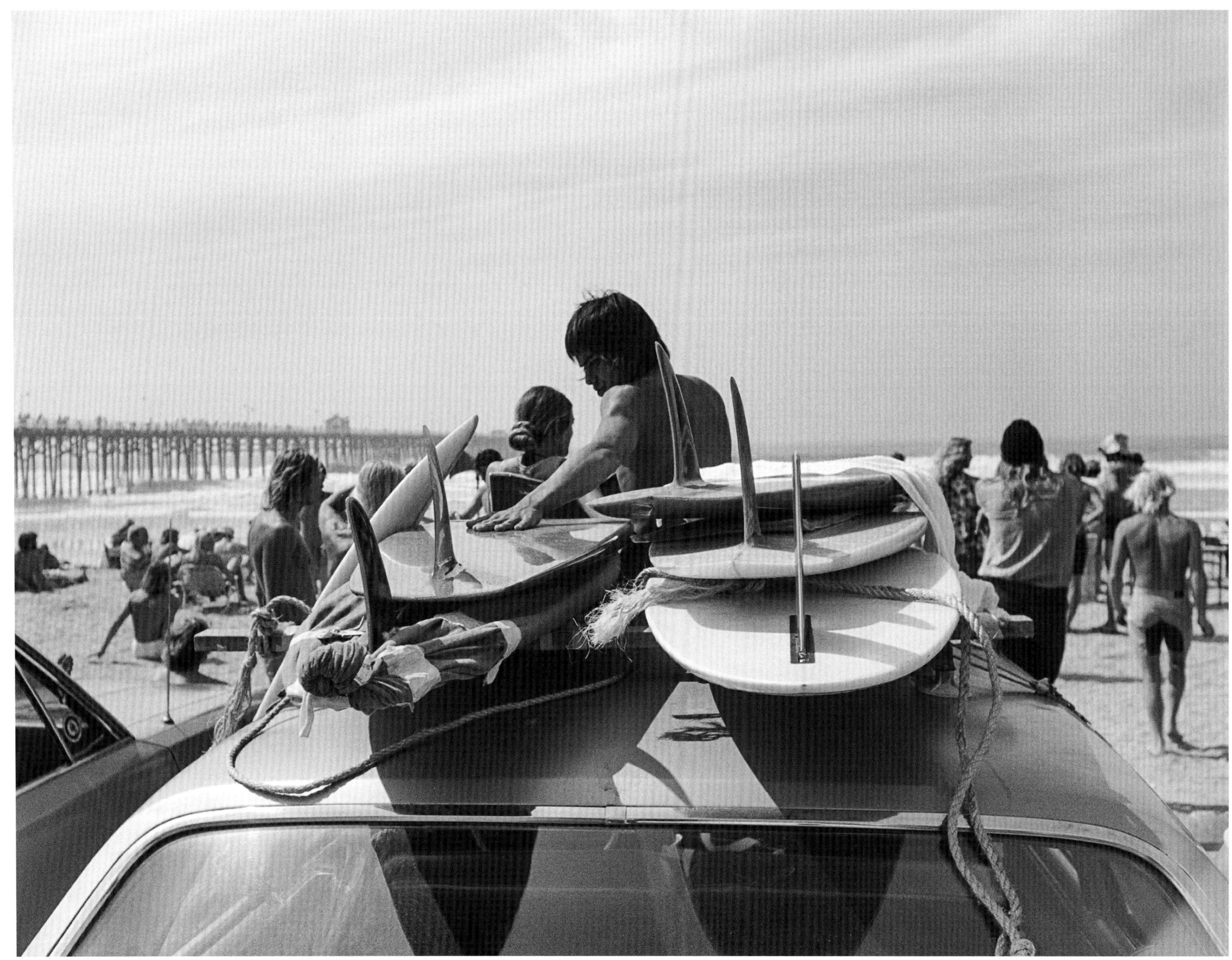

Reno Abellira, Oceanside, CA 1972

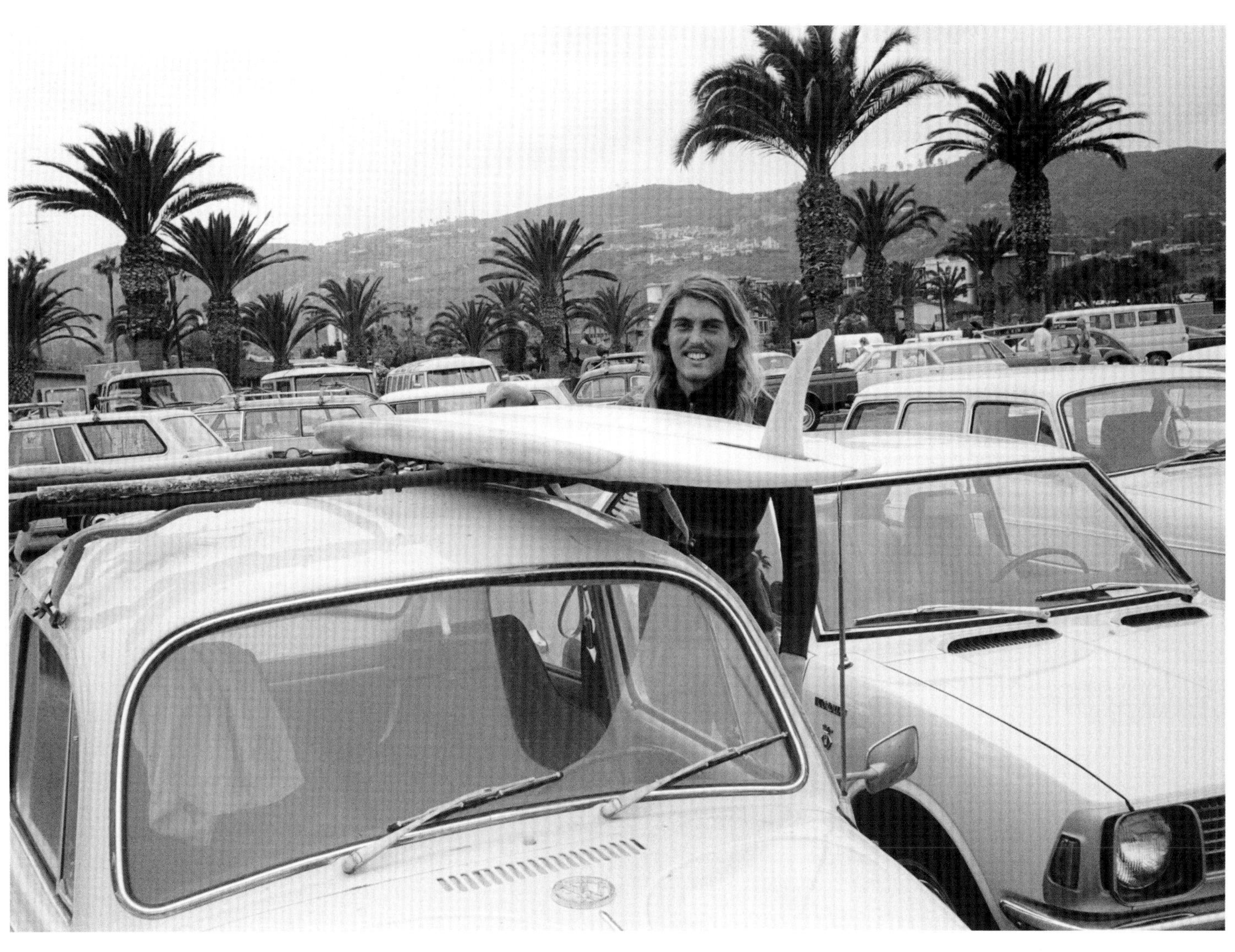

Jeff Divine, La Jolla Shores, CA 1970. Photo by Jon Foster

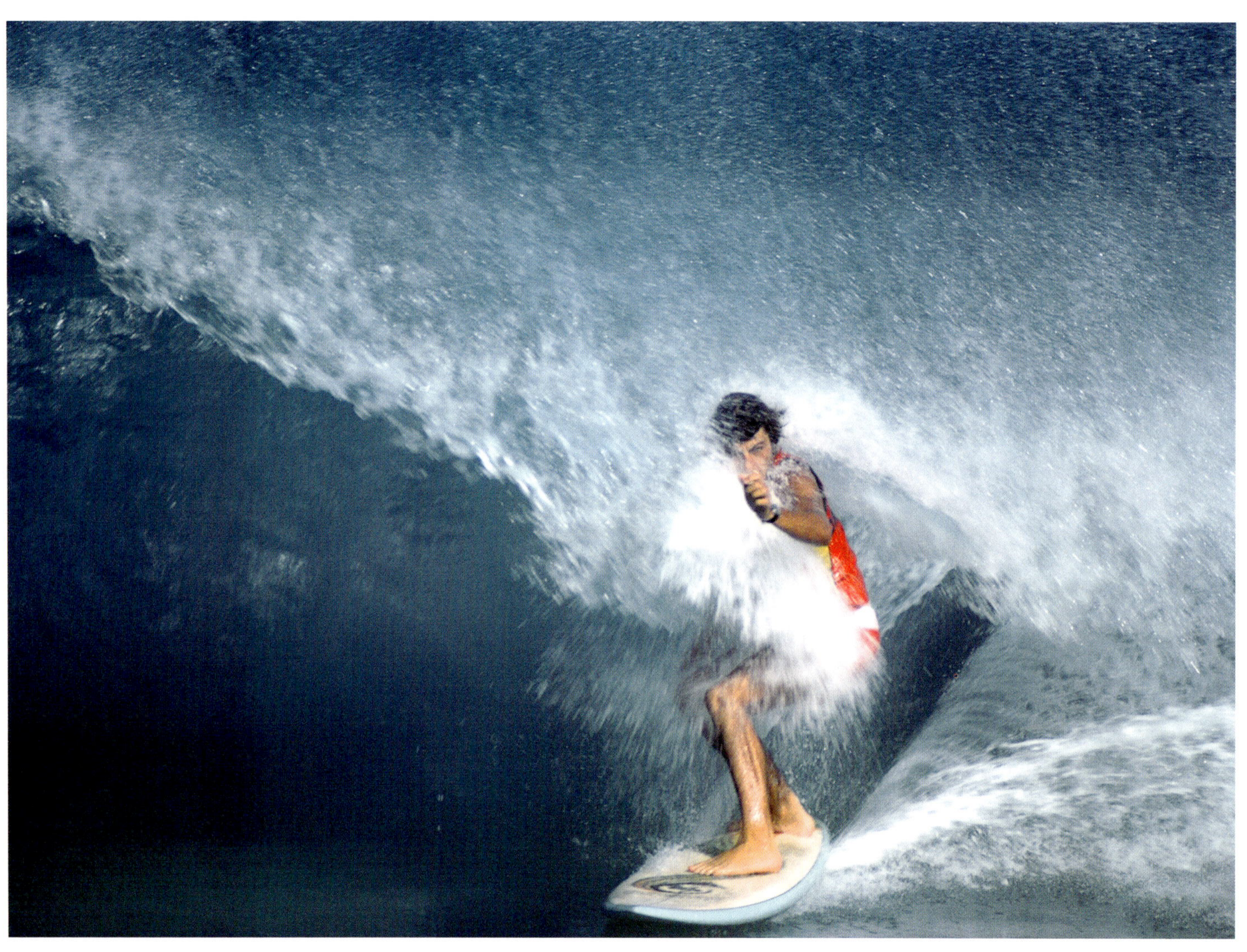

Shaun Tomson, Off The Wall, Oahu, HI 1976

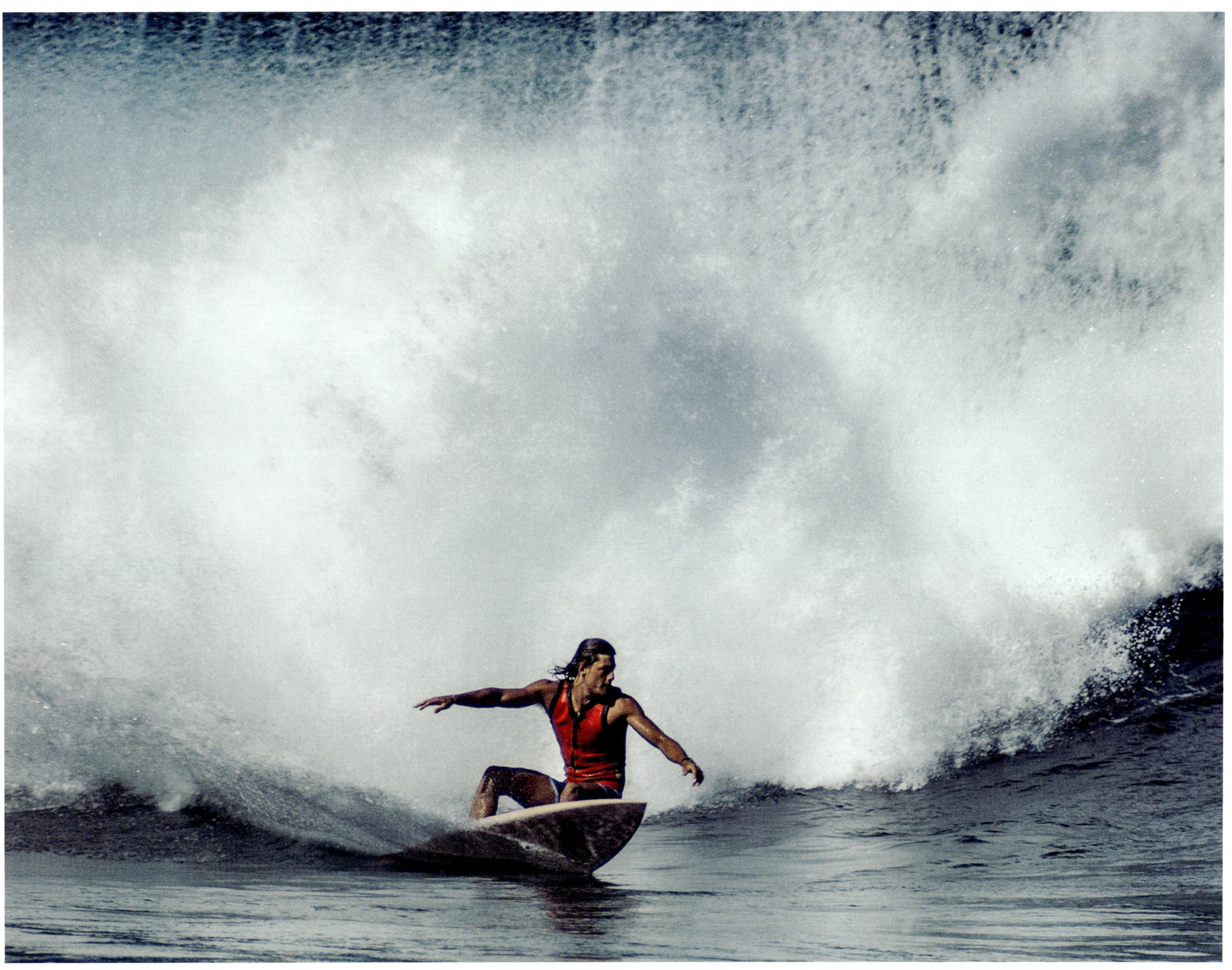

Shaun Tomson, Pipeline, Oahu, HI 1977

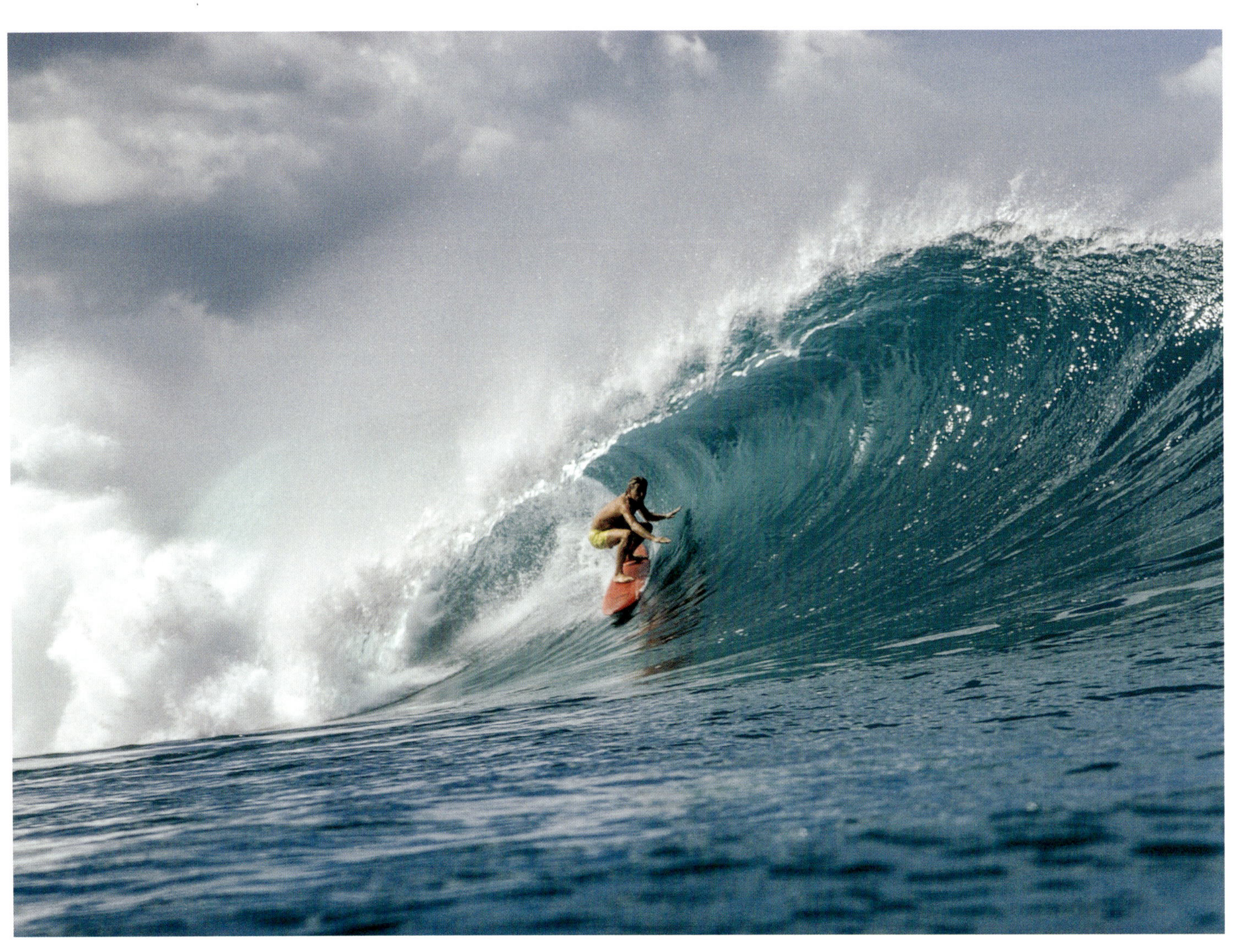

Jeff Crawford, Pipeline, Oahu, HI 1973

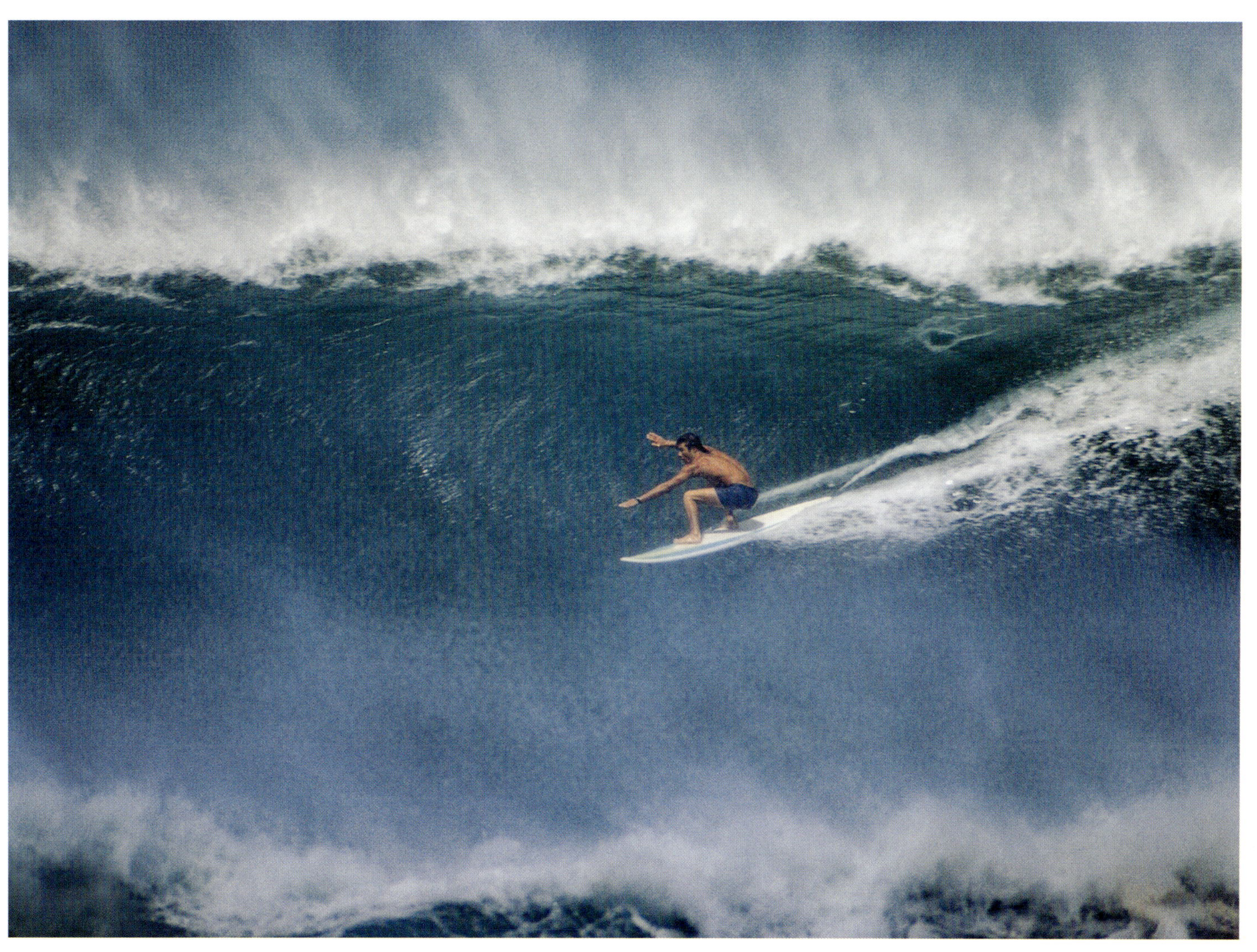

James Jones, Sunset Beach, Oahu, HI 1974

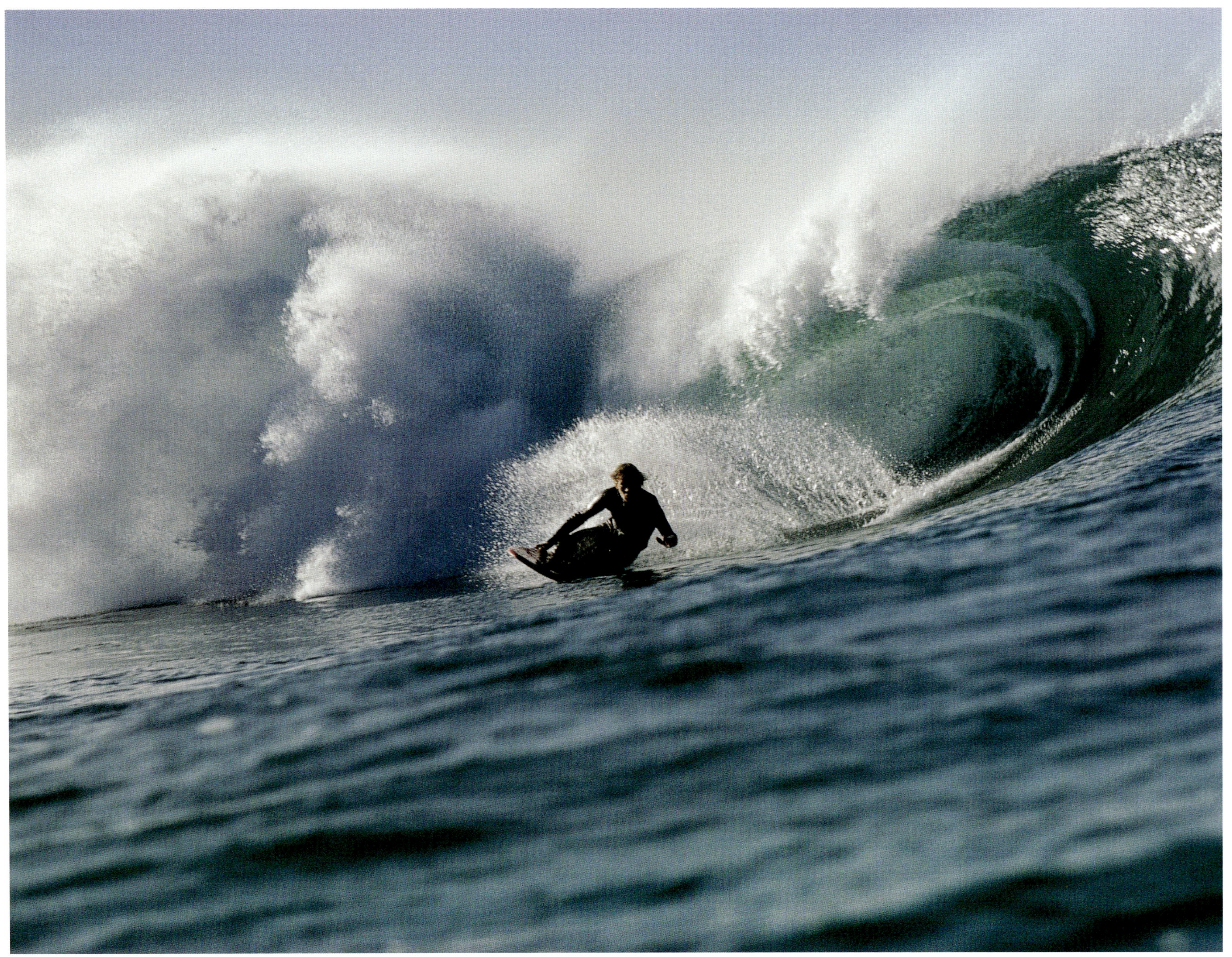

Rex Huffman, Big Rock, La Jolla, CA 1972

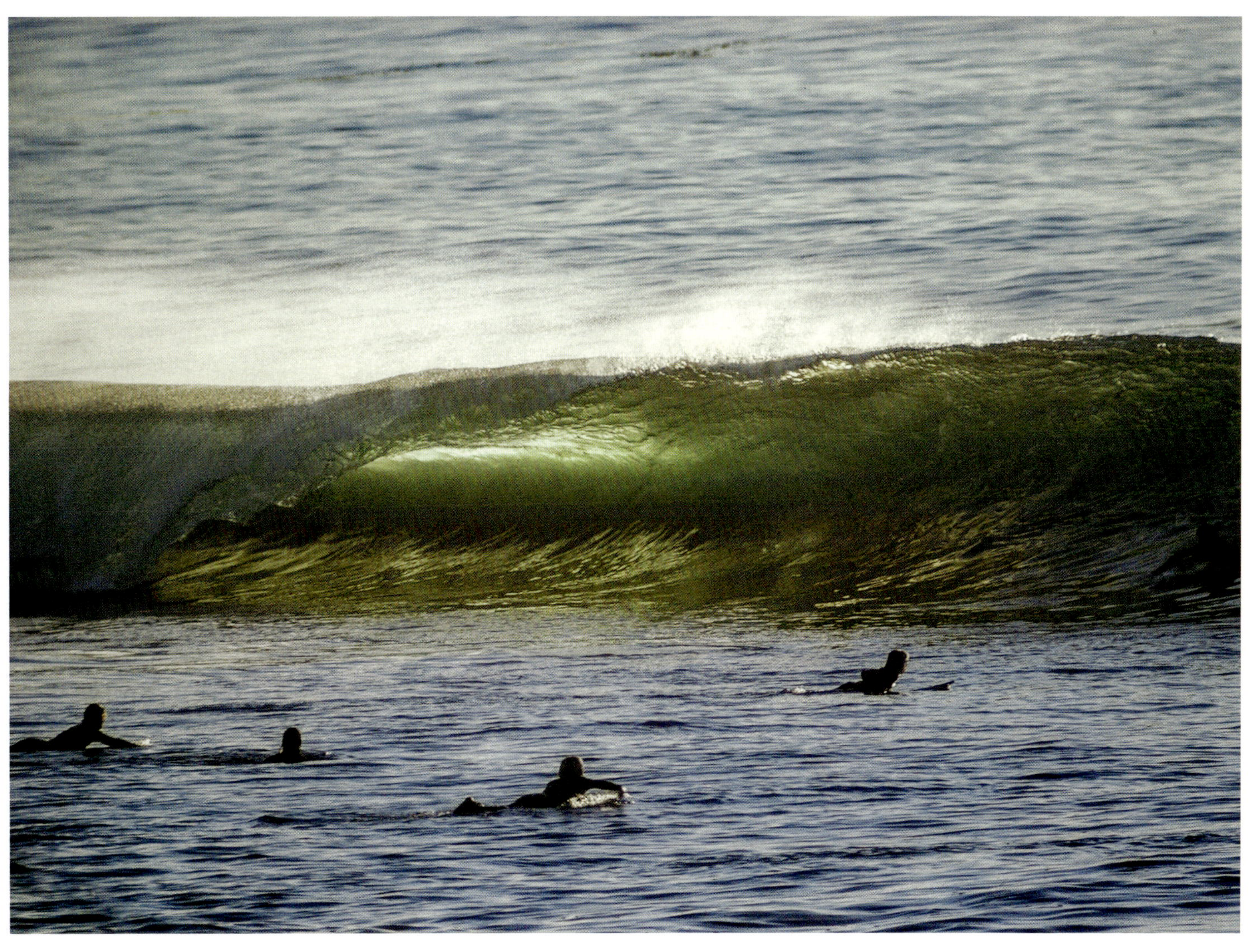

Big Rock, La Jolla, CA 1972

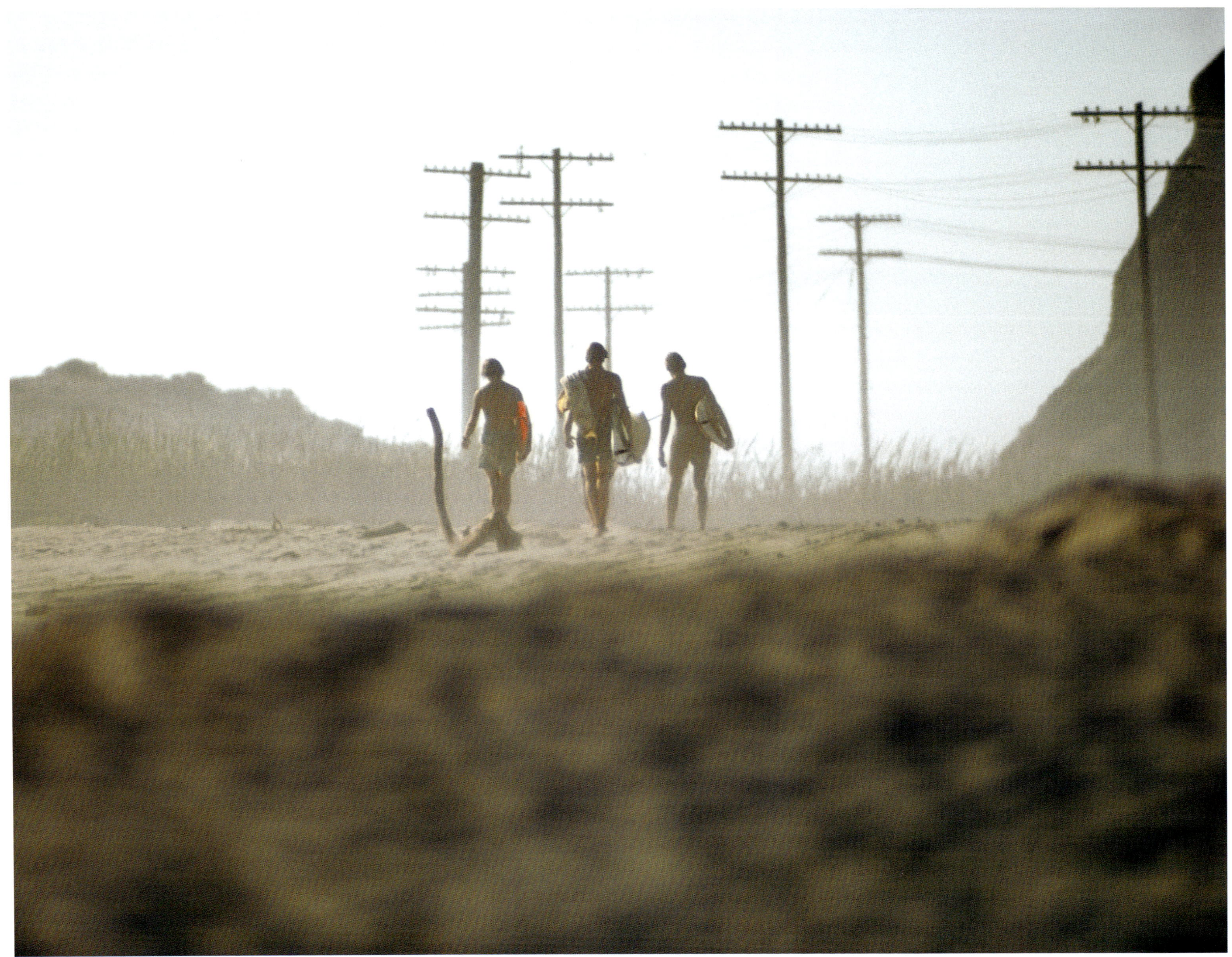

Trestles, San Clemente, CA 1972

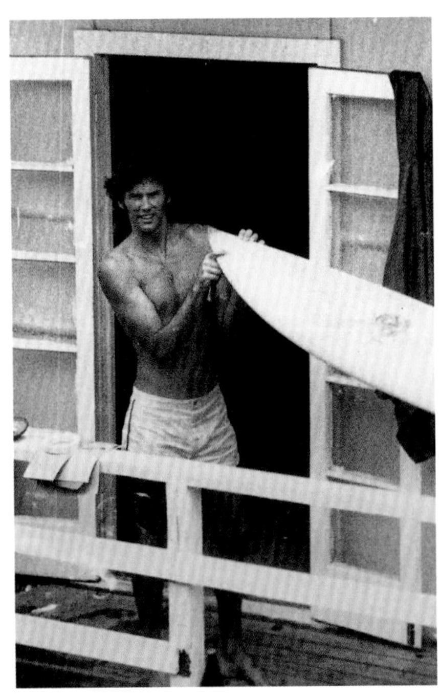

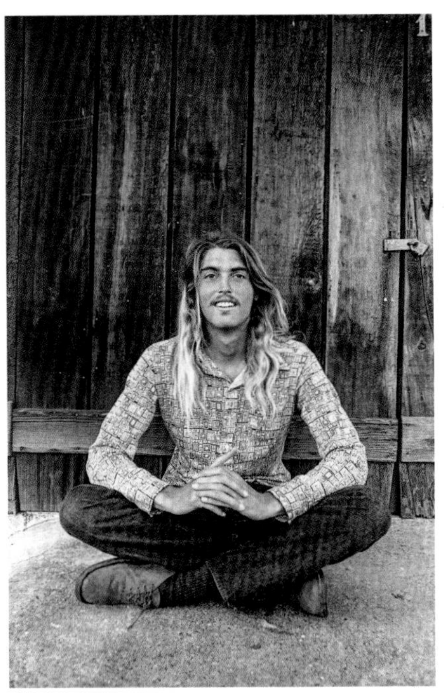

WILLIAM FINNEGAN

William Finnegan is the author of five books, including a memoir, *Barbarian Days*, which won the 2016 Pulitzer Prize for biography. He has been a staff writer at *The New Yorker* since 1987.

JEFF DIVINE

Raised in La Jolla, California, Jeff Divine started photographing the surfing world in 1966. He held jobs as Photo editor for 35 years with *Surfer* magazine and the prestigious *Surfer's Journal*. His works have been displayed worldwide in museums, galleries, books, magazines and media. In 2019 he was inducted into the Huntington Beach Surfing Walk of Fame for his contribution to surf culture in a career lasting 50 years.

William Finnegan, Queensland, Australia 1979 / Jeff Divine, Laguna Beach, CA 1970 – Photo © Art Brewer

T. ADLER BOOKS, SANTA BARBARA (TOM ADLER & EVAN BACKES)

DISTRIBUTED ART PUBLISHERS

PRINTED IN HONG KONG / INTEGRATED COMMUNICATIONS

ISBN 978-1-942884-60-6

SECOND PRINTING 2022

TADLERBOOKS.COM ARTBOOK.COM

EDITION PRINTS: JEFFDIVINESURF.COM / MBART.COM / CLIC.COM / A-GALERIE.FR

FRAMED NON-EDITION PRINTS: ARCHIV-E.COM

We have attempted to provide accurate information throughout this book and apologize for any errors or omissions.

Thanks to the Divines: Julie, Taylor, Jessica, Madeline, Nora, Rosalie.
Steve and Debbee Pezman, John Severson, Jim Kempton, Tom Servais, Steve Wilkings, Art Brewer and Sonny Miller (RIP).
And special thanks to Ben Hoy, Elisa Nadel and Jane Brown.

For Rosalie Isabella Divine, Dash Adler & June Harper

(Cover) Gerry Lopez, Pipeline, HI 1975 (Back Cover) Sunset Beach, HI 1972

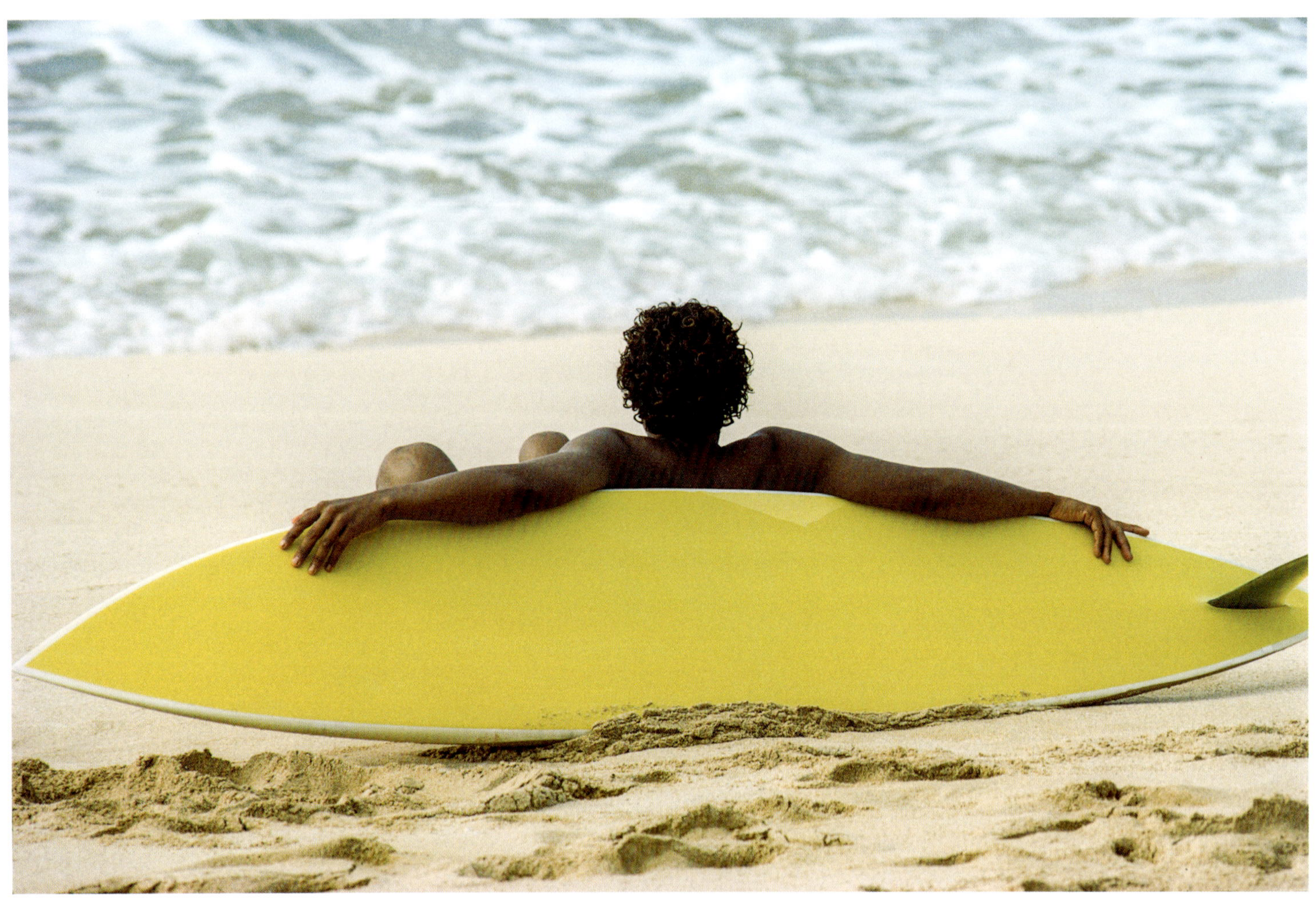

Pipeline, Oahu, HI 1976

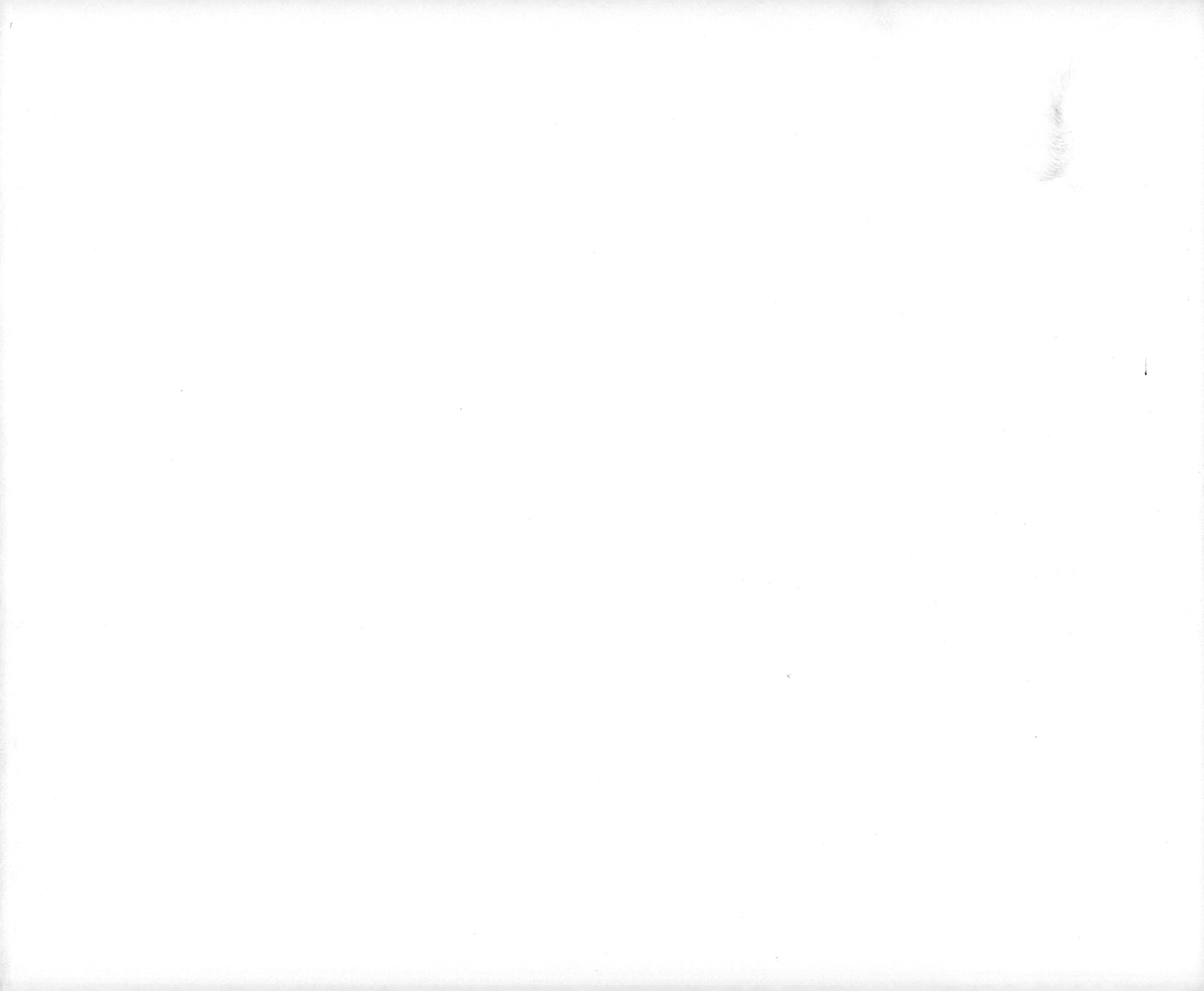